3-79

The Bible Story

Also by William Neil

THE REDISCOVERY OF THE BIBLE

THE EPISTLE TO THE HEBREWS

THE PLAIN MAN LOOKS AT THE BIBLE

ONE VOLUME BIBLE COMMENTARY

THE LIFE AND TEACHING OF JESUS

APOSTLE EXTRAORDINARY
THE LIFE AND LETTERS OF ST PAUL

THE CHRISTIAN FAITH IN ART

with Eric Newton

WILLIAM NEIL

The Bible Story

Drawings by
GYULA HINCZ

ABINGDON PRESS
NASHVILLE & NEW YORK
1971

THE BIBLE STORY

ABINGDON PRESS

ISBN 0-687-03394-2

Printed in Great Britain
Collins Clear-Type Press
London and Glasgow

CONTENTS

ACKNOWLEDGEMENT

The author and publishers would like to acknowledge their indebtedness for permission to reproduce Scripture quotations contained in the book as follows: from the Revised Standard Version of the Bible, copyrighted 1946 and 1952 by the Division of Christian Education of the National Council of the Churches of Christ in the United States of America; used by permission; from the Jerusalem Bible © 1966 Darton, Longman and Todd Limited and Doubleday & Co. Inc., used by permission; from the Moffatt Translation of the Bible, Hodder & Stoughton Ltd.

ILLUSTRATIONS

1. God and Ourselves

EVERY fairy story begins: 'Once upon a time.' The Bible begins in the same way. That does not mean that it is a fairy story, but it *is* a story and it has a beginning. The story that is told in the Bible is not yet finished and all of us are characters in it with our different parts to play. Some people would prefer to call the Bible a drama. Perhaps we may compromise and call it a dramatic story. It claims at all events to be a true story, full of surprises and strange happenings, and we are told that it will all end happily ever after. But before the final chapter, which is not yet written, the Bible tells a gripping tale of courage and adventure, of success and failure, of compassion and cruelty, of despair and hope.

Much that is in the Bible provides the background to the story and we need not concern ourselves overmuch with that. What we shall try to do is to trace the main outlines of the story from Genesis to Revelation, remembering as we do so that the people who wrote it were utterly convinced that what they were writing was the most important story that has ever been told. Were they right or wrong? This is something about which each of us must make up his own mind. For, unlike other stories, the Bible story is not one that we can read for entertainment or amusement and then forget. If we come to the conclusion that it is a true story, then all that we do and say and think will be affected by it. For it is indeed a book about our life, how to make sense of it and how to get the most out of it.

Whatever else the Bible has to say, it makes it quite plain from the outset that life will have neither meaning nor purpose unless we begin with God. The first four words of the story the Bible tells are not 'Once upon a time,' but 'In the beginning *God*'. Everything that the Bible has to say about the world and ourselves is based on the claim that we are not here by chance or accident, that whatever happens is meaningful and not meaningless, and that we are all included in a great creative purpose, the author of which is God.

As the Bible story unfolds it becomes clearer what the writers meant by God, but here at the beginning of the story it would be foolish to pretend that they would be satisfied with any suggestion that God is simply a creation of our own imagination or a useful name to describe everything that exists. God is above, beyond, around and within us, distinct from the universe because he created it, but within the universe as the power that keeps it and us going.

So, right at the start, stands the claim that God existed before there was any universe at all and that it was his act that brought it into being. When we read the first chapter of Genesis we must not expect a scientific account of how he did it. The writer is a poet who looks around at the beauty of earth and sky, the sun, the moon and the stars, at men and women in all their rich variety, at birds in flight and beasts in field and forest, and who says quite simply that this is all the handiwork of God.

It makes no difference to this claim whether we think that the process of evolution took millions or billions of years, or whether we think in terms of untold galaxies, some of them possibly inhabited, stretching out into apparently endless space. This was certainly not the way the biblical writers thought of it, but even if they had known what we know now about biology, astronomy and the rest, they would probably have begun their story in the same way. Their claim is simply that behind all that we see or even dimly guess at is the mind and purpose of God.

And in God's scheme of things man has a major role to play. Amidst all the wonder and beauty of God's created world, man is singled out for a special status. He is an animal, with kinship to the rest of the animal kingdom, but he is different from the rest of creation in that he is made in the 'image' of God. This suggests that there is something god-like in every human being, a spark of the divine, which enables man alone among the animal kingdom to establish a relationship with God. Man is given control of the created world, he is the crown of creation, subject only to the sovereignty and authority of God.

But this ultimate authority of God is just what man has never been willing to accept. He has always tried to run the world his own way. Pride has been our downfall. The story of Adam and Eve and the Serpent puts it all in a nutshell. We are of course not meant to believe that this is the life story of the first man and the first woman, any more than we are expected to believe in a serpent that talks. For the writer of this story Adam and Eve stood for Mr and Mrs Everyman, for man and woman as they have always behaved. The Serpent is the perfect symbol of temptation, subtle, suggestive, and apparently harmless, urging us to disregard the authority of God over the whole of life and promising us rich rewards if we do so.

Thus the Bible in the first few pages paints the grim picture of our human situation. Made in the image of God and with the whole world at our disposal, we abuse our freedom, make the wrong choices, put ourselves in the centre of things instead of God, and make havoc of the good life that has been offered to us.

It is a price the Creator is prepared to pay because he wants us to be the kind of men and women he meant us to be and not puppets. But it is a heavy price, and the grim history of mankind's crimes and follies, his cruelty and aggression, is sketched in the next few chapters of the book of Genesis. Yet right from the outset the Bible makes it plain that, despite everything, God still cares. He is determined to help us to save ourselves from ourselves and to show us the splendour of life as life can be lived. This is indeed what the Bible is all about.

2. The Law of the Jungle

In the story of Adam and Eve the Bible pinpoints the root of the trouble with human nature. It is rebellion against God. In the collection of stories that immediately follow, the point

is further underlined. We should be making a great mistake if we were to dismiss the stories of Cain and Abel, Noah's Ark, the Tower of Babel and the other narratives contained in Genesis chapters 4–11 as being merely primitive folk-tales. They were that originally, of course, but when this part of the Bible came to be compiled, the editors wisely recognised that the best way to teach religious truth was to use ancient and familiar tales. So they took these old stories, which are not historical in our modern sense, and made them serve a religious or moral purpose.

The Bible uses these narratives as a series of little pen-pictures to show what human nature is really like and what happens when we are left to ourselves. It is a realistic and shattering sketch of the world without the gospel. It shows us that when we try to run our affairs without any reference to the law of God, we end up by following the law of the jungle. These chapters are a brutally frank description of the Rake's Progress of humanity bent on its own destruction.

The Bible begins by showing us ourselves as Adam and Eve, with the world at our feet and opportunity knocking at the door. We choose to turn our backs on God, rejecting the way of life he has laid down for us, and deciding to follow the way that seems easiest or pleasantest or best for ourselves. Then in the story of Cain and Abel the Bible takes us a stage further. It shows us that we are all not only rebellious Adams but also murderous Cains.

Cain is as universal a type as Adam. He, too, is Mr Everyman. He begins by resenting his brother Abel's good fortune and broods over the injustice of life, which denies him what he considers to be a fair deal. His resentment grows into hate, and hate, given the opportunity, ends in murder. Confronted with his crime, he utters the plea of the guilty conscience which has been echoed down the ages: 'Am I my brother's keeper?' And when sentence is pronounced on him he whiningly protests: 'My punishment is greater than I can bear.'

It does not need profound self-examination to tell us that this is a true picture of ourselves. Murderers all, without ever necessarily holding a gun or a knife in our hands, we share the guilt of a civilisation which has left behind it a trail of blood. The victims of war, slavery, starvation, gas-chambers and industrial exploitation are our brothers in the common family of mankind and their deaths lie at all our doors. Whether we like it or not we *are* our brothers' keepers. It is not by accident that the Bible follows up the story of Cain and Abel with a list of Cain's descendants, who are supposed to have been the originators of the various arts and crafts and the builders of cities, or that one of them sings a hymn of hate in which he boasts of his power of massive retaliation.

All of this has a singularly modern ring. The Bible is obviously not condemning progress or the march of civilisation. After all, as we have seen, man was put into the world to develop its resources. But we are being warned that the more complex society becomes, the more it offers opportunity for the Cain-like side of human nature – greed, violence and irresponsibility towards those who are our brothers. The war-cry of Cain's descendant, glorying in his programme of even more widespread slaughter, is only too terribly relevant. This is civilisation as we know it.

One of the strangest stories in this part of the Bible is about giants. Here we are indeed in the realm of fairy-tales, the world of Jack the giant-killer and Hercules. We may well wonder what it is all about. It is a story of erring angels who come down to earth, marry earthly women, and produce supermen as their offspring. Later writers tended to think in terms of 'fallen' angels who lost their status as a result of their lapse from grace, were then banished to the demon world and from there instigated all the evils that afflict humankind. This is almost as fanciful as the story itself but it does indicate what the Bible is telling us in this mysterious tale.

When we read in the newspapers of cases of calculated sadistic cruelty, or watch on television the sub-human violence of race riots, or recall the sickening bestiality and butchery practised in Nazi concentration camps, we instinctively feel that behaviour of this kind is something more than human misdemeanour. There is something diabolical about it, something demonic. Our grandfathers would have put it down to the work of Satan, and found no difficulty in laying the evil deeds of men at the door of the Prince of Darkness.

The Bible at this point does no more than suggest that there is this demonic element in the evil of which men are capable. It does not give us a scientific reason for the vileness which sometimes makes us despair of the human race, but a diagnosis of our human situation. The explanations of modern psychologists do not take us very much further. The Bible is saying the problem of evil is more complicated than just our choosing to disobey the laws of God. It is suggesting that there is an all-pervasive corruption in the world which taints everything we do; a poison at work in the human heart and in society which frustrates our best intentions.

St Paul in his letter to the Christians at Ephesus makes the same point as the Genesis story when he says: 'We are up against the unseen power that controls this dark world, and spiritual agents from the very headquarters of evil.' Both are telling us that any hope of society putting itself right by its own efforts is a delusion. It is sheer folly to trust in the onward march of mankind to a better kind of world through scientific advance, higher education or increased social services. Our best-laid schemes and loftiest aspirations founder in face of the perversity of human nature and the gigantic power of evil that confronts us.

No more sombre verdict has ever been pronounced on mankind as a whole than the words which come at the end of this story of the 'fallen angels': 'And the Lord saw that the wickedness of man was great in the earth, and that every imagination of the thoughts of his heart was only evil continually. And it repented the Lord that he had made man on the earth, and it grieved him at his heart. And the Lord said, I will destroy man whom I have created from the face of the ground; both man and beast, and creeping thing, and fowl of the air; for it repenteth me that I have made them.'

If this judgement had been God's last word it would have been the end of the story of the Bible – and of us.

3. Light in our Darkness

So far the picture is black indeed. We have been shown ourselves as we are – self-willed, murderous, diabolical. Having made God's fair world foul, has man any right to exist? The Bible has no hesitation in saying, No! and it pictures the Almighty as being sick at heart as he contemplates the human scene. Gibbon's verdict still stands that 'History is indeed little more than the register of the crimes, follies and misfortunes of mankind.'

This is the human situation and the Bible insists that we treat our predicament with all seriousness. It leaves us no room for shallow optimism but makes us see ourselves as we are. For it is only when we do so that we recognise that if justice were done God would have written us off long ago as an experiment that had failed. But the whole message of the Bible is that this is just what he has not done, because he loves us. And right from the beginning we are told that although God hates sin, he cares for sinners.

In the Adam and Eve story, despite the fact that they had flouted the authority of God and rebelled against his command, 'he made for Adam and for his wife coats of skins, and clothed them.' This is the Bible's picturesque way of saying that God is still concerned about us through all our failures. Then in the story of Cain, the murderer, the compassion of God is stressed again. Banished from society and facing certain death, Cain is marked with God's protective sign. It is not a brand of shame but a token of God's readiness to forgive even murderers.

There is also great significance in the birth of a third son to Adam and Eve. The Bible is so full of symbolism in these early chapters of Genesis that a small point like this might easily escape us. But once we realise that we are dealing not with historical events but with imaginative pointers to the truth about God and ourselves, we begin to look more closely to find out what those old writers are trying to say to us. What then is the point of the third son?

Adam as we have seen is Everyman – made in the image of God but rebellious against his Creator. Cain, the first son of Everyman, develops the worst side of his father's character and rebelliousness ends in murder. Abel, the second son, is the type of the innocent victims of man's inhumanity, who have suffered down the ages at the hands of their brothers. Seth, the third son, takes the place of Abel and acts as a counterpoise to Cain. We are told that he was made in the 'image' of Adam, who was made in the 'image' of God, and that it was in the day of Seth's son that men began to worship the Lord.

Is all this just ancient Jewish folklore or is the Bible saying to us something very profound? We are surely being told: You are all Adam – made in the likeness of God, with a spark of the divine in you, but also earthy, rebellious, and self-willed. You are also all Cain, with the blood of your brothers on your hands and violence in your hearts. But you are also all Seth, who, after the murder of Abel, offers mankind the possibility of a fresh start in a new direction, an opposite direction to that of Cain, not towards hate and brutality but towards worship and obedience to God.

In a sense, then, Seth is the foundation member of a new kind of community within the world. This is an idea which we shall shortly see more fully developed, the creation of a People of God who, in a world dominated by the spirit of Cain, stand for something different. It is as if the Bible is saying that right from the beginning of history there have been two ways open to man, the way of life and the way of death. Adam has both elements in him. His eldest son Cain chooses the way of death, his youngest son Seth chooses the way of life. This choice has always been open to men, long before the days of the Old Testament faith, to say nothing of Christianity.

Primitive man was not without his moral standards and pagans had their own virtues. It is to this that the Bible next draws our attention, in the story of Noah's Ark. Noah stands in the line of Seth. Although he is neither a Jew nor a Christian,

he sets his face against all that is represented by the descendants of Cain. We may think of him as an enlightened pagan or as a devout and worthy man who follows the light of conscience. In bringing him into the picture the Bible is saying that God has never left himself without a witness and that even in the dim beginnings of civilisation men have always had some kind of knowledge of God and some sense of the difference between right and wrong.

The story of the Ark is a splendid fantasy. It is the biblical version of a Mesopotamian folk-tale. The only historical element in the narrative is the fact that there was a severe inundation at the top of the Persian Gulf, possibly about 4000 BC, which wiped out the city states that lay there. Traces of it were found by Sir Leonard Woolley while he was engaged in archaeological work in the area in 1929. Racial memory of the disaster and imaginative embellishments have produced the dramatic story as we now know it.

The details are unimportant. The Bible is simply using the folk-tale to teach theology. The Flood stands for the judgement of God on a world that turns its back on him, in the twentieth century as much as any other century. This is what we deserve and but for the goodness of God, says the Bible, this is what we would get. But for the sake of the small minority, represented by Noah, who live up to the best standards that they know, the life of the world is allowed to continue. For the sake of even one good man, the human race is given another chance.

But this kind of 'natural' goodness is not enough. The kind of society that is based on Noah's policy of 'doing no harm to anybody' is not the kind of world that God intended. It is too shaky a foundation on which to build. God means man to live in harmony with his neighbour because he regards him as his brother, not because he is afraid of what will happen to him if he does him an injury. The world of Noah is one under the rule of law; it is dominated by fear, a world of second-bests.

In the story of the Tower of Babel, the Bible suggests that the world of Noah is little different from the world of Cain. It pictures civilisation advancing, learning new techniques, establishing cities. Yet once again the twist in human nature wrecks man's progress. He wants to be God or, as the Bible puts it, to build a tower whose top would reach to heaven. It is the old root sin of rebellion and defiance, not: 'Glory to God in the highest,' but: 'Glory to man in the highest.' Man would be the master of all things; man, he says, not God, is supreme. The end of the story is, of course, disaster for man's enterprise – confusion, disharmony and misunderstanding.

It is at this point that the story of the Bible takes a new turn.

4. The Plan and the Man

SOME people like to think of the Bible not so much as a dramatic story but as a proper drama – a drama of the acts of God. If we look at the Bible in this way, we can divide it up quite easily into three acts with a prologue and an epilogue. What we have so far been thinking about is the prologue to the drama (Genesis 1–11). As we have seen, it is not historical in anything but the most general sense. There *is* after all a universe which has somehow or other come into existence and there *was* a flood in Mesopotamia a long time ago, but that is about as much as we can say.

Whether any of the characters in the prologue ever existed and bore the names which are attached to them is really of no importance. The Bible uses myth, legend, poetry and symbolism as readily as it uses the facts of history to convey its message. But it is quite clear that when we reach the twelfth chapter of Genesis, which begins the story of Abraham, we are in quite a different atmosphere. We start now to deal with real people.

So far we have been given, in the prologue to the drama, a picture of ourselves and the world we live in. It has been presented largely in the form of brief stories but the message is unmistakable. On the one hand, the Bible has hammered home the point that the twist in human nature cannot be straightened out by ourselves. Whether we call it original sin, or rebellion against God, or just plain selfishness, there is something in us all that shatters our dreams of Utopia, makes a mockery of our good intentions and wrecks every well-meant enterprise. On the other hand, we have been shown that this is not how God intended our life to be. He meant us to be free and it is not his fault that we abuse our freedom. Yet because he created us he wants to save us from ourselves, since we are our own worst enemies. Time after time in the prologue we have been given hints of his intention, pointers to the divine compassion which will not leave us in our plight.

But now the drama proper begins. Act I, which starts at the twelfth chapter of Genesis, discloses God's plan of action. Towards the end of the prologue, in the story of the Tower of Babel, we are left with a picture of mankind at loggerheads with itself and estranged from God. Before the prologue ends, in the last few verses of Chapter 11, attention is focused on a particular group which is to be the instrument of God's purpose. Out of the whole human race the choice is narrowed down until it rests upon one tribal group of Hebrews, and in the last resort upon one man, Abraham, who is to be the founding father of a new kind of community within the world, the People of God.

The mythological figures of Seth and Noah have already pointed in this direction, but now we are in touch with a man of flesh and blood who is selected for this high vocation. The divine plan is to build out of this man and his descendants a people who will be taught the truth about God and themselves, and who will be charged with the task of communicating this knowledge to the rest of the world. They are to be the nucleus of a new community, bound to God in obedience and service, setting an example which will attract the remainder of mankind and turn them in the end into the sons and daughters of God that all of us were meant to be.

Why, out of all the peoples of the world, it should have been the Jews, and not the Egyptians, Babylonians or Assyrians – to say nothing of Greeks or Romans – was as much a mystery to the Jews then as it is to us today. As far as numbers, power, culture and skill are concerned any one of these others would have been a better candidate. Nor was it that the Jews had

any greater natural flair or aptitude for religion than the rest. Yet the fact remains that it was the Jews who were chosen. 'How odd of God to choose the Jews!' No one was more puzzled about this than the Jews themselves.

Yet, as far as Abraham was concerned, nobody could deny that he was a worthy choice. Where he and his people came from originally is uncertain. They formed part of the bedouin peoples who from time immemorial had drifted out of the sparse scrubland of the desert into the rich lands of Mesopotamia and Egypt, well watered by their rivers and irrigation systems, and known as the Fertile Crescent. Abraham first appears in the biblical record at Ur of the Chaldees, an ancient city of Babylonia a hundred miles or so from the top of the Persian Gulf in present-day Iraq. Being nomads, pasturing flocks of sheep and goats, it is unlikely that Abraham's family lived in the city itself, though guides confidently point out Abraham's house among the ruins of Ur which the archaeologists have excavated. It is much more likely that they lived in tents nearby and made use of the city markets.

In the stories that are told of Abraham and his descendants in these early days, we have to make allowances for the growth of legends connected with them over the years. Abraham probably lived about 1750 BC and none of the Bible was written before about the tenth century BC. Before that time stories were handed down by word of mouth from father to son, told by story-tellers around camp fires, sung by minstrels in the form of ballads, or recounted by priests at shrines and sanctuaries.

Yet we should remember that oriental memories were better trained than our own, especially in an age when most people could not read or write, and when there were no distractions such as television. We also know how reluctant children are to accept a different version of a story from the one with which they are familiar. If someone telling the story of Red Riding Hood were to suggest that grandmamma swallowed the wolf there would be an outcry. Similarly we can imagine simple tribesmen protesting if a story-teller departed from the well-known details of a particular tale. This would be especially true in the case of venerated figures such as Abraham and his descendants, who were regarded with ever-growing respect as time went on.

Nevertheless we have to allow for exaggeration, occasional confusion and the inevitable pious legendary elements that grow up around saintly characters. Yet legends can tell us quite a lot about the people who figure in them, and the Old Testament has many which help us to form a clearer picture of the men concerned than we should get from a prosaic history book. Archaeologists tell us that the stories of the patriarchs – Abraham and his successors – are full of background detail which is confirmed by excavations. But of course we cannot expect particular incidents or dialogues to have been accurately remembered over so long a period of time. These are shaped by the story-teller's imagination.

5. Abraham: The Friend of God

I F the Bible were an ordinary history book, it might say that Abraham was a landless nomad who left Mesopotamia for political or economic reasons, who spent most of his life in true bedouin fashion on the uplands of Palestine and who cherished the dream of a day when the land where he was a stranger would belong to his people. That, however, is not what the Bible says at all, because it is not an ordinary history book but the story of the People of God. We have to accept the fact that in this story nothing is thought of as happening by chance or accident. People do not do things because a bright idea strikes them, but because they are being directed and guided by God.

We know of course that nowadays – or indeed later in the Bible – God is not given to holding long conversations with people as he did for example with Abraham. We tend to think rather that if we keep our minds and hearts open, God speaks to us in a variety of ways, through things that happen to us, through the voice of conscience, through intuition. No doubt it happened the same way with Abraham and the other Old Testament characters, but as the stories have been handed down in the Bible God is represented as speaking much more vividly and directly so that there is no doubt about what he is saying.

This makes the narrative much more dramatic and no less true. By the time the Bible came to be written down, Abraham's descendants had grown into a nation – the nation of Israel – and occupied the whole of the territory that Abraham had wandered through as an immigrant without rights or property, apart from the freedom of the hills and the possessions he carried with him. It is not surprising that on looking back the prophets and priests of Israel who wrote the Bible saw the hand of God in everything, and thought of Abraham as a man who, by his readiness to respond to what he believed God was calling him to do, was the ideal pattern for every Israelite and the perfect foundation stone on which to build the People of God.

So Abraham is pictured setting out with his family from his Mesopotamian homeland in response to God's summons. He believes implicitly that he is embarking on a momentous enterprise. He is to go to the land of Canaan which he is told will one day belong to his descendants. They are to grow into a great nation and through them in some way as yet unknown the blessing of God will be extended to the whole world. The Old Testament writers look upon this moment as the beginning of Israel's story; the New Testament writers think of it as the beginning of the Church.

This man, then, with God's promise locked in his heart, went out into the unknown, unaware of what might lie ahead, but trusting in the God who had laid his hand on him and ready to do whatever he told him to do. In Canaan he found himself in a land that was thickly populated on the plains but where it was always possible for bedouin tribesmen like himself to find pasture for their flocks among the highlands. Apart from an

occasional warlike encounter and the periodic incidence of famine, Abraham seems to have prospered. As he moved from place to place (later to become sanctuaries associated with his name), stories that are told of him are concerned mainly with the problem of an heir.

We are told that Abraham was seventy-five years old when he started out for Canaan and that he lived for a century after that. The ages of the patriarchs are of course exaggerated, though they were mere children compared with Methuselah who is said to have lived to be almost a thousand! It was a common supposition that the ancients lived far longer than ordinary mortals and their ages as given in the Bible are quite unreliable. But if we say that Abraham and his wife Sarah were both well on in years and still childless we can well understand their anxiety. Without an heir the promise of a host of descendants made nonsense.

According to the custom of the time Sarah suggests that Hagar, her Egyptian maid, should provide the heir that she herself is apparently unable to produce, and Ishmael is born. Sarah's impatience is rebuked, however, when to the incredulous astonishment of both Abraham and herself she finds that she herself is going to have a child. When the son of their old age, Isaac, is born, Hagar and Ishmael are banished from the scene but are preserved under divine protection to serve their own purpose. From now on the spotlight falls on Isaac, who, according to God's promise to Abraham, held the future of the People of God in his hands.

It must have seemed the end of everything when God suddenly appeared to be demanding that Abraham should now kill his only son and offer his body to be burnt as a sacrifice on a rough and ready hill-top altar. To us the whole thing seems unbelievable and barbarous in the extreme. But Abraham lived at a time when shepherds and farmers thought that God wanted them to show their gratitude for good crops, healthy sheep and cattle, and heavily laden fruit trees by offering the best of them on the altar as a token of their thanksgiving. We still partly follow their example at Harvest Thanksgiving services in our churches.

But in those days it was not just fruit and flowers but lambs and calves and goats. The animals were slaughtered and their carcasses were burnt on log fires on top of stone altars. In ancient times, though not in Israel, human beings were also sacrificed in this way as an offering to the gods. So even the idea of human sacrifice was not altogether strange to Abraham. Isaac had been a special gift from God, loved beyond anything else by his parents, and it may well have seemed to Abraham that he must offer what he treasured most to God who had given it. So he set off on a three-day journey into the mountains, with a donkey loaded with food and bedding, two of his shepherd-lads, and Isaac. When they came near to the place where the sacrifice was to be made, Abraham left the lads with the donkey, and father and son went on together. No one knew what was in Abraham's mind, least of all Isaac. The boy carried kindling wood on his back, the old man carried a brazier and a knife.

When they got to the top of the hill Isaac said in all innocence, 'Father, we have the wood and the fire but where is the lamb for the burnt offering?' The broken-hearted father could only answer, 'God will provide the lamb.' So Abraham gathered stones and made an altar, put the kindling wood and some logs on top to make a flat surface, tied the boy up and laid him on the altar. Just as he was drawing his knife his hand was stopped in mid-air. God spoke to him again, and this time he knew what it was all about.

Abraham was being tested. Was he ready to give up what he loved most, if need be, as an offering to God? Yes, he was. Somehow or other he believed that God could in the last resort bring his son back to life, because he had promised that Isaac would be the father of a great people. Abraham believed that God could not lie. And sure enough, when he looked round, there was a ram caught by its horns in nearby bushes. God had provided an offering instead of Isaac. So Isaac was set free, the ram was sacrificed, and Abraham knew that what God wanted was that we should be ready to give up our dearest treasures rather than disobey his commands.

When we read this story we cannot help seeing in it something that makes us think of Jesus. Just as the ram offered itself for sacrifice, instead of Isaac, so Christ offered himself to God instead of us.

6. Jacob: Father of the Israelites

IN the early part of the Bible story, Abraham stands out as the supreme example of a man of faith who trusted God implicitly.

He spent his days as a wanderer in the land that had been promised to him, and at his death the only part of it he owned was the cave where he buried Sarah his wife and where he himself was later buried. Yet his faith did not waver, and when we add to that his warm-hearted plea that the Lord should spare the corrupt cities of Sodom and Gomorrah if there should be even ten good men found in them, we can see why in the New Testament he is acclaimed as 'the friend of God'.

The Bible has little to say about Isaac. He does not seem to have been as noteworthy as his father Abraham or as his son Jacob. There is a lovely description of how Isaac got his wife Rebekah, but almost at once we are confronted with the chequered career of their son.

Jacob was a born twister. Indeed he did not even wait till he was born before he started. The Bible tells us that he tried to come into this world before his twin brother by catching his heel and trying to slip past him. This is an amusing way of putting it but it shows what the Bible thought of him. He got a nickname as a result of that, 'the heel-catcher', which is one meaning of the word Jacob. Such was the beginning of the story of this cunning rascal. Yet when we turn to the New Testament we find Jesus bracketing him with Abraham as one of the great and godly men of faith of Old Testament times.

Now anybody would say that of Jacob's grandfather Abraham – the friend of God, the great-hearted and courageous pioneer who became the founder of his people. But Jacob – why, almost everything about the man suggests that he was a

smart Alec or, worse still, a plain crook. How on earth did a man like this ever come to be regarded as a shining light and an example to the rest of us? Let us look at his story.

Jacob was the younger of the twins who were born to Isaac and Rebekah. Two of the tales told about him in his early days show him up as being as crafty a character as you would ever be likely to meet. His brother Esau, an open-air type, came in one day from hunting, ravenously hungry. Jacob was sitting down to an appetising-looking plate of stew. Esau asked for some but Jacob, with his eye always on the main chance, traded the stew for the right of inheritance which belonged to the eldest son. At that moment Esau could not have cared less about his future prospects. All he knew was that he was famished. So the deal was made. Esau got his stew and Jacob became his father's legal heir.

The other tale is even worse. In the old days a father's blessing on his son was something of the highest importance. It was particularly important in the family of Isaac. The old man was almost blind and very frail. But he still liked his food, so he sent Esau out to kill a stag and make him a venison pie. Then he was to bring it in and get the old man's blessing.

The mother, Rebekah, was much fonder of her younger boy Jacob, so she herself made the kind of pie that the old man liked and put Jacob up to the idea of dressing himself in his brother's clothes, taking in the dish to the old man, and passing himself off as Esau. All that worried Jacob was the risk of being found out. The old man was pretty suspicious – he thought it sounded like Jacob's voice – but the trick was successful. Jacob got the blessing and with it the right to be head of the family, before his brother came back. By the time Esau returned, it was too late. The blessing had been given and could not be recalled.

Jacob was terrified at what he had done. His brother was furious and swore he would be revenged. Jacob had to run for his life. He knew that if ever he returned home his brother would murder him and he had the guilty conscience of a man who had tricked his own brother twice out of his rights. And then something happened to him. He was on his way to his

uncle in Syria to keep out of his brother's reach, when he had
a dream. It was an extraordinary dream. He seemed to hear the
voice of God speaking to him, promising to protect him and
never to leave him, to bring him back home in safety because
he had a great purpose for him.

Nobody could have been more surprised than Jacob. But
little did he know what lay ahead. God certainly did not leave
him but it was not in the way Jacob expected or wanted. He
got to Syria to his uncle's farm and found his uncle as big a
crook as himself. He fell in love with his cousin Rachel and
wanted to marry her. His uncle said he would have to work
seven years on the farm without pay before he got his bride.
Then when his seven years were up his uncle said he could
not have her. The elder sister Leah had to be married first – the
uncle had accidentally forgotten to mention that this was an
old Syrian custom. So he said, anyway. Poor Jacob had to
work for nothing for another seven years to get his Rachel.
Uncle Laban had been too clever for him.

At last, after another six years' gruelling grind on the farm,
he had made enough to keep his family and wanted to go back
home. There was no future for him in Syria. As he crossed
the frontier of his own country, he heard that his brother was
coming to meet him with a crowd of supporters. He did not
know whether this meant a friendly welcome or the finish of
life's journey. Was this to be how it would end for him? He
saw to the safety of his family and then for a whole night he
wrestled with his guilty conscience.

These twenty years of slavery had been his penance. He had
paid the price for his trickery with the sweat of his body and
the misery of his soul. But now he would not go back to his
own country, whatever the future held, without having it out
with God. He must be sure that God had forgiven him so
that he could be at peace with himself. Prosperity had come at
last but not peace of mind. So that night at Jabbok he knew
all the agony of a tormented soul, he lived his past life again
and hated himself for what he had done. He saw himself as the
cheat and rogue that he had been, admitted it before God and
asked God to forgive him.

At daybreak it was a new Jacob that saw the dawn. The old Jacob, the twister, was dead and buried and a new Jacob was born. As a sign of it he got the new name Israel, which means God's warrior, and he became the father of the people whose story is told in the whole of the Old Testament. In the event, he found that his brother Esau was there to welcome him and not to kill him, that he too had forgiven the past. Jacob tried to atone for his old treachery by giving him half of all he had. The rest of the story of Jacob is really part of the story of his favourite son, Joseph. He had certainly no easy time for the remainder of his days and in the end he died in a foreign land but he left a memory as one of the great figures of the Bible.

Well, what does all this add up to? Surely this. The Bible is saying to us in the story of Jacob that some people are what we might call naturally good – like Abraham – and some like Jacob are what we might call naturally bad. But God can use bad types for his purpose for the other qualities that are in them. Jacob, for all his craft and cunning, had in him under the surface the stuff that saints are made of. He had been a schemer and a twister, but behind it all was this tremendous fixed purpose by hook or by crook to be his father's heir, to carry on where his father had left off, to shoulder responsibilities which his brother shirked, because he knew at the back of his mind that this was what he had to do. He felt he was earmarked for God's service, but he had to be shown that he was going the wrong way about it. So because God knew him better than he knew himself he made him a different man. He laid his hand on him in his dream at Bethel, tested his patience and determination in the long twenty years, and at last brought him to the point where he was ready to turn his back on the past, humble himself before his Maker, acknowledge his faults and face the future as a new man ready to do the job that God had destined him for. He did not become a saint overnight. He had a long way to go, but in that momentous night at Jabbok Jacob the twister became Jacob the fighter for God.

7. Joseph: From Shepherd-boy to Prime Minister

JACOB had a large family and his twelve sons were always regarded as the founders of the twelve tribes of Israel. The Bible, however, spotlights one of them, Joseph, who was almost the youngest, and devotes far more space to him than to all the rest put together. The story of Joseph reads like a modern success story of the local boy who makes good, on the lines of 'From log-cabin to White House'. Joseph began as a shepherd-boy in Canaan and ended as prime minister of Egypt. But of course the Bible sees far more in his story than that.

He was obviously his father's favourite, which did not endear him to the rest of the family, especially when Jacob bought him most expensive clothes including the famous 'coat of many colours'. More annoying, however, was his habit of not only telling tales about his brothers but also telling them of dreams in which he always played the leading role, while they did him homage. This was too much even for his doting father, especially when he was told that in one of Joseph's dreams he too was bowing and scraping in front of his big-headed son.

The brothers plotted a terrible revenge. They planned to kill Joseph and throw his body into a well. He was saved from death by his eldest brother who managed to persuade the rest merely to throw him down an empty well, hoping to pull him out later. In the eldest brother's absence, however, the others sold Joseph as a slave to a passing caravan and he was carried off to Egypt. The brothers dipped his famous coat in goat's blood and pretended to his old father that the boy had been devoured by wild animals.

Meanwhile Joseph had been sold again to Potiphar, an important official in the royal court of Egypt. He soon became this man's personal servant and was so good at his job that he rose to be manager of the whole estate. Unfortunately Potiphar's wife took a fancy to him and tried to make love to him.

When he refused, she spread the story that Joseph had molested her and the poor young man found himself in the palace dungeon.

But even here his luck did not desert him. He was promoted charge-hand over the rest of the prisoners and his gift for telling the meaning of other people's dreams stood him in good stead when it came to the ears of the king. Joseph was able to interpret the king's dreams successfully. They meant, said Joseph, seven years of plentiful harvests followed by seven years of famine. He advised Pharaoh to build great granaries to store the corn in the good years in preparation for the lean years to come. The king was so impressed that he made Joseph his grand vizier, in charge of the country's food supply and of everything else in Egypt. So by the age of thirty Joseph, the Hebrew slave, had become second-in-command of a kingdom.

He managed affairs with his usual skill so that, when the famine came, Egypt alone in all the Near East had plenty to eat. Canaan like everywhere else was hard hit and among the hungry mouths were those of old Jacob and his family. The brothers were sent down to Egypt to buy grain, all except Benjamin who had become his father's favourite after the loss of Joseph. When they arrived they had to do homage to the man who was in charge of all the sale of corn. Little did they think it was their own brother Joseph, dressed like an Egyptian, talking through an interpreter and surrounded by servants. Joseph knew them at once but decided to play cat-and-mouse with them for a while and kept his identity secret.

He accused them of being spies, but gave them the corn they wanted and let them go back to Canaan on condition that they returned with their youngest brother. Old Jacob at first would not hear of it but he had a starving family to think of and the Egyptian corn soon ran out. At last he agreed to let Benjamin go. This time Joseph treated his brothers royally, but when he sent them off he arranged that his own silver cup should be put in Benjamin's sack and sent his steward after them to search their belongings. The cup was found, the brothers were brought back, and Joseph demanded that the thief should pay for his crime by becoming his slave.

The brothers pleaded so pitifully that if Benjamin was not returned safe to his father the old man would die of a broken heart that Joseph could not keep up the pretence any longer. He sent all the Egyptians out of the room and told his brothers who he really was. Then he told them to go back and fetch their father and all their wives and families and he would give them enough land in Goshen, east of the Nile delta, to feed all their cattle and keep them alive during the remaining years of the famine. Pharaoh was in full agreement and added a lavish present for Jacob.

Jacob could hardly believe that his long lost Joseph was still alive, far less that he was head of state in Egypt. However, as much to see Joseph again as anything else, and to save the family from the danger of slow starvation, the old man decided to move with all his children and grandchildren, his sheep and cattle, from the land of Canaan to the land of Goshen in Egypt where they all settled down happily. Joseph meantime, as the famine continued, emptied his granaries of the corn he had stored and sold it to the Egyptians in return for their land which then became the property of Pharaoh; when they had no more land they sold themselves as Pharaoh's slaves. When they were all in the king's power, Joseph released the grain for sowing the fields and demanded a fifth of the harvest for Pharaoh.

Before old Jacob died he insisted that his body should be taken back from Egypt to Canaan and buried in the same tomb as his grandfather Abraham and his father Isaac. Pharaoh gave him an elaborate funeral, and his sons carried out his wishes. When it was Joseph's turn to die he made his family promise that one day his bones should rest in the same tomb. It was the only bit of land in Canaan that belonged to them but Joseph believed that Canaan was their real home and that his descendants would in God's good time return to it.

This splendid story must have been one of the favourite tales told by story-tellers round the fire when in later days the Israelites were masters of the land of Canaan. Archaeologists tell us that the background details which the Bible gives of Egyptian customs in those days are quite accurate, and suggest that what made it possible for a Hebrew to become prime minister of Egypt was the fact that for a time between about 1700 and 1550 BC, Egypt was ruled by a dynasty of pharaohs who were not Egyptian but of the same racial stock as the Hebrews themselves.

No doubt some features of the tale are fanciful, but there is no real reason why success-stories of this kind should not have happened long ago as well as today. But of course the Bible does not include the story of Joseph as an example of how to become a tycoon. Behind Joseph is the patriarchal figure of Jacob, and behind both of them is the purpose of God. Joseph's affairs prospered not through good luck but because he was a link in the chain which binds Abraham and his descendants with Christ and the Church in God's great design for the salvation of men.

We are not expected to admire Joseph particularly. He had bad points in his character as well as good ones. On the whole the good side of his nature is more impressive. If he had chosen to do so, he could have wreaked vengeance on his brothers when he had them in his power. Instead of that he was content to give them some anxious moments, but nevertheless in the end he treated them handsomely. His love for his father Jacob and for his favourite brother Benjamin is also a mark in his favour. But what the Bible is really emphasising in this, as in all the other stories of the patriarchs, is the invincible power of God to achieve his ends. Disaster after disaster threatened to bring Joseph's life-story to a sudden end. Yet he survived them all because he was a necessary agent of God's purpose.

It was through Joseph that the family of God's choice which began with Abraham was preserved from the famine, and it was through Joseph that the people of Egypt were also saved from death by starvation. The story illustrates the role of the People of God in the world. They are to be a blessing to all the nations, and the story of Joseph reflects this theme which is to run through the whole Bible. Both the Old Testament and the New Testament make it plain that God constantly brings good out of evil and chooses for this purpose those who are best fitted to serve him.

We have seen how the Bible insists that God sometimes lays his hand on most unlikely characters. Crafty Jacob was preferred to Esau, his more attractive older brother, and now Joseph, another rather dubious choice, turns out to be the man who is thought fittest by God to carry out his plan. There is an interesting example of this at the tail-end of the Joseph story. When old Jacob was on his death-bed, Joseph brought his two sons to receive the old man's blessing. To his surprise the old man crossed his hands and put his right hand on the younger boy's head, indicating that he would have a bigger role in the future than his older brother. Joseph thought the old man was getting blind but Jacob knew very well what he was doing. He was illustrating the great biblical truth that God does not pick the people of his choice in the same way as we do – by seniority, by social status, or any other human standards. As we are told later on in the Bible: 'Man looks at appearances but the Lord looks at the heart.'

8. Moses and the Exodus

So far the story of the Bible which has been told throughout the book of Genesis has centred on four leading figures, Abraham, Isaac, Jacob and Joseph, the patriarchs of Israel. They have been shown to us as very human characters, with a mixture of good and bad qualities, yet still the kind of people whom God chooses for his purpose. They are all presented as men with a sense of destiny, unaware of the outcome but believing that God is using them to further some great design.

If we try to see them in the context of world history, we should have to say that they were mostly insignificant bedouin sheikhs: Abraham, who drifted into Palestine from the desert in quest of better pastures for his cattle; Isaac, who seems to have been so ordinary that little or nothing is remembered of him; Jacob, a wily character who eventually became a re-spectable and prosperous sheep-farmer; and Joseph, the only real success-story, who became first minister of Egypt. The Bible, however, sees them as the founding fathers of Israel, the nation which God had chosen to be the means of bringing the light of truth into the darkness which mankind's folly had created.

The period of the patriarchs is, historically speaking, very shadowy indeed. We do not know very much about it apart from the vivid stories that the Bible tells and the assurance of the archaeologists that the background details are generally confirmed by their discoveries. Scholars are agreed, however, that when we come to Moses and his times we are on much more solid ground. We cannot say that all that we are told about him is a reliable account of what actually happened. As with the stories of the patriarchs, pious imagination has added its quota of legends to the record, but what is quite indisputable is that Moses stands head and shoulders above all other Old Testament figures, and indeed on any showing was one of the outstanding men in world history.

He was long credited as having been the author of the first five books of the Old Testament and, although this is obviously not the case, his life and work inspired those who compiled them. More than anyone else he moulded the future of Israel. Moslems and Christians as well as Jews revere his memory. It is perhaps too much to say that he made the Hebrews into a nation, gave them a distinctive faith and moral code, but at least he shaped the beginnings of all three.

When his story opens, the days of the patriarchs were past. Their descendants had long been settled in Goshen and had become a sizable colony. But alas, they were no longer welcome guests in Egypt. As the Bible puts it: 'A new king arose over Egypt who had no knowledge of Joseph.' It was not just that Joseph's great service to his adopted country had been forgotten. The Egyptians had thrown out the foreign rulers who had been in power in Joseph's day and who had made the migration of Jacob and his family possible.

The Israelites were now, in about 1300 BC, a minority problem, disliked because they were of a different race, feared because their numbers were increasing. The pharaoh of the time, Rameses II, took swift and drastic measures to cut their numbers and break their spirit. The able-bodied men were torn from the fields and press-ganged into slave labour on the building projects in the great cities which Pharaoh had decided to develop. Worse than that, an edict went out that all male infants were to be drowned at birth in the Nile. It was a policy of extermination which Hitler with more scientific techniques was to apply to the same race three thousand years later. Both attempts failed.

Hitler failed to wipe out the Jews because in the providence of God he lost the war. Rameses II failed because also in the providence of God one boy escaped and grew up to be the saviour of his people. The romantic story is told of how Moses' birth was concealed from the Egyptian authorities, and how his mother hid him on the banks of the Nile where he was discovered by an Egyptian princess and brought up in the royal court.

Josephus, the Jewish historian, tells a tale of Moses as a child in the Egyptian royal palace throwing the crown of Egypt on the floor as a sign that, for all his Egyptian up-bringing and his Egyptian-sounding name, his destiny lay with his own afflicted and enslaved people. Whatever truth there is in the tale, events settled his future for him. The first act that the Bible records of him when he has grown to manhood shows where his heart lay. It shows him also to have been a passionate and violent man. Hot with anger at the sight of the brutal treatment of one of his Hebrew countrymen by an Egyptian guard, he killed him on the spot.

So for Moses the die was cast. Distrusted by his countrymen as a quisling, outlawed for murder by Egyptian law, he fled for his life. In Midian, well outside Egyptian territory, he found safety, a job and a wife. Living quietly as a shepherd with his young family he might have seemed to be at the end of his particular road. But God had work for him to do. He laid his hand on him and spoke to him and called him into his service.

This was an experience that Moses shared with Amos and Isaiah, with St Paul and St Francis, with Martin Luther and John Wesley. Each of them was singled out for some gigantic task which was far beyond his own power to accomplish, but God chose them to be the instruments of his purpose and gave them the strength to carry it out. What was Moses' particular task to be? It was so vast and formidable that his mind boggled. He was to go back to Egypt and lead his people from bondage to freedom. It meant winning their confidence, it meant confronting the new pharaoh face to face with the demand that he should give the Israelites their freedom and it meant persuading his countrymen to dare to take that freedom and go with him into an unknown future.

The idea which Moses had to sell to these downtrodden dispirited serfs was that they had been singled out from all the nations of mankind; they, the most unlikely conglomeration of life's rejects – stateless, landless men of no standing, power or privilege in the world – were to be the nucleus of the People of God, the foundation members of the Almighty's pilot scheme for the renewal of the life of the world.

God had selected this unlikely group of slaves. He would mould them, instruct them, inspire them with the words of psalmist and prophet, bring them to the knowledge that through them the world would learn the truth about itself, about the meaning and purpose of life, about the beginning and the end of the mystery that surrounds us. Moses felt that his own particular role was far beyond his powers. The only thing that made him attempt it was the conviction that God was behind the enterprise.

So back he went to Egypt with his wife and his two little boys on this forlorn hope. Meantime the plight of his countrymen had become more acute. Something in them bridled at the thought of having no roots, no rights, no hope, no future. In a sense their plight was not unlike our own. We too are in the grip of forces beyond our control – economic forces, political forces. Automation is here to stay. Machines count for more and more. Men and women count for less and less. We feel that we do not matter any more, that we are drifting aimlessly without an anchor and that there is nothing very much that anybody can do about it. That is why this story matters to us still.

These Hebrew slaves in Egypt looked into the future and saw nothing ahead but darkness. The one certainty for each of them was that he was chained to his labour until, broken in body and broken in spirit, he was thrown like refuse into a common grave. Pharaoh's latest edict seemed to spell the end of all hope. His orders were that they were to make the same quantity of bricks each day but that they would have to find for themselves the straw that was necessary to hold the clay together.

Bricks without straw – the command was to do the impossible – a political excuse to wipe out the whole people. What had become of the God who in all their wanderings had inspired and encouraged Abraham, Isaac and Jacob, who had richly blessed Joseph, who had led his people in fairer days into an Egypt that welcomed them and offered them shelter? Where was he now, this God who had deserted them?

It was then in their darkest hour that God sent them a leader. A leader who used a succession of plagues to persuade Pharaoh to let the Israelites go free. No doubt some of the stories about all this have grown in the telling. Some scholars make a plausible case for attributing the plagues to volcanic action somewhere around the upper reaches of the Nile – volcanic ash would turn the river the colour of blood and the poisoned waters would give rise to most of the other disasters. Others see the plagues as an unusually intensive occurrence of natural phenomena which are common in that part of the world.

What certainly happened was that in the general confusion and commotion caused by a rapid succession of national crises, Moses seized the opportunity to rally the slaves to revolt and escape. But what is more important is that it was the personality of this one man that persuaded them to take any action at all: and almost immediately they regretted it. No sooner did they realise that the Egyptian charioteers were hot on their heels than they began to accuse Moses of having led them out of the frying pan into the fire.

The moment of truth came when, on their only possible escape route, they came face to face with the sea. The Hebrew words make it clear that this was not the Red Sea but what was then called the Sea of Reeds, probably the Bitter Lakes which lay between Egypt and Palestine and have now been absorbed by the Suez Canal. The oldest account says that a strong east wind blew all night and drove the waters back. If this was near the top of a lake or a fordable passage across it, it is easy to see how the fugitives could cross in safety on foot while the heavy Egyptian chariots got bogged down in the sand and were caught in the returning tide. Some people think that the crossing of the sea was made possible by the bed of the lake rising and subsiding, followed by a tidal wave, due to volcanic action. The same thing happened at Naples in 1538.

It is very difficult to tell precisely what happened. What is abundantly clear, however, is that the memory of the Exodus is indelibly written on the minds of the people of the Old Testament, and indeed of the Jewish people to this day. The commemoration of the Passover keeps the event alive in twentieth-century New York as much as in Old Jerusalem.

No proud and independent people could possibly have invented such a story, since it reflects no credit on their war-like skill or resolute determination. It spotlights the fact that if it had not been for Moses nothing was surer than that Israel would have perished. It would have been one of the countless tribal groups that emerged and disappeared in the ancient world of what we call the Near East.

But this was just what did not happen. What did happen was that what appeared to be certain death and the end of everything was transformed into a new beginning. That motley horde of runaway slaves became the nucleus of a fighting force. Under Joshua and the Judges it established itself as the military aristocracy of the Levant. It built the kingdom of David and Solomon, and left the world the priceless legacy of the faith of Israel which Jesus carried over into Christianity.

With one accord the prophets and psalmists of Israel look back on the Exodus not as a national triumph but as the signal act of God. For the first time he made it plain that he is a God who rescues us from death and sets us on the path to new life. The keynote of the Exodus was deliverance. God showed his hand as Saviour then, and time and again the people who came after have returned to this theme. It is no accident that St Luke describes the death of Jesus as his exodus, his deliverance of his people, not from their mortal enemies like the Egyptians, but from the greater enemies of sin and death.

When St Paul says Christ has made us free he strikes the same note. God sets us free, frees us from the sense of aimlessness and futility which so often overwhelms us, frees us from the feeling we so often have that life has no meaning or purpose, frees us from anxiety about the future and a guilty conscience about the past. So when these Hebrew slaves sang their hymn of thanksgiving to God for deliverance from bondage, there was more to it than just a song of triumph at their escape from Egypt. It was the beginning of their understanding under the guidance of Moses that it is in the very nature and purpose of God that people should be free.

Many of us can remember the sense of liberation that lifted the hearts of most of the world in 1945 when Nazi tyranny was finally crushed. We could breathe again and look forward to spacious days ahead – a time of rebuilding and renewal, of peace and stability, of a world united for the common good, of atomic energy and all the other benefits of a scientific age being harnessed to the enrichment of human life. Once again we were free and the future was bright ahead.

There is no need to dwell on our increasing disillusionment – on the failure of the United Nations, on the abuse of nuclear power, on a world divided into two hostile camps, on the attitude of 'I'm all right Jack' and 'You've never had it so good' when two thirds of the world's peoples do not have enough to eat, on restrictive practices and the exploitation of the Welfare State. All of this we know too well and it is bitter to the taste.

And this was Moses' problem too. No sooner was the Israelites' first flush of enthusiasm over their new-found freedom past than the rot set in. The brave adventure was going adrift. As the straggling column of Israelites made its way through the scrubland of the Sinai peninsula, with scarcely enough food and water to keep body and soul together, the

Hebrews looked back on slavery as preferable to this. They yearned for the flesh-pots of Egypt.

If we think of the Exodus as a procession of starry-eyed high-souled idealists marching to the Promised Land we had better take another look at the record. It was a disorderly and rebellious mob held together by the will-power of one dedicated man who knew what God had called him to do and that somehow he would make it possible. So, unexpectedly, bread fell from heaven – a kind of honey-like substance which dropped from tamarisk trees. The Hebrews called it manna, meaning: 'What is this?' They had never seen it before. In the same way, Moses, having lived in the area when he was a fugitive from Egyptian justice, knew how to break through the thin crust of limestone rock to the water underneath, when desert oases were few and far between.

But the climax came when the people rejected both Moses and God – Moses who had led them and God who had delivered them. In the chaos that followed, Moses realised that he could never knit together his unruly self-willed followers into any kind of worthwhile community unless they recognised the overruling sovereign authority of God. So the whole story of the Exodus finds its crux and meaning in the giving of the Law. We cannot hope to put into plain prose the majestic and powerful scene when Moses in solitude upon the mountain top carved on tablets of stone the words which God put into his mind as the rule of life for his people:

I am the Eternal, your God, who brought you from the land
   of Egypt, that slave-pen.
You shall have no gods but me.
You shall not carve any idols for yourselves.
You shall not use the name of the Eternal, your God, profanely.
Remember to hold the sabbath sacred.
Honour your father and your mother.
You shall not murder.
You shall not commit adultery.
You shall not steal.
You shall not give false evidence.
You shall not covet.

Exodus 20 : 1–17

These words of the Ten Commandments are as relevant in the twentieth century as they were three thousand years ago. They proclaim the supremacy of the Creator and show us to be bound by laws which are not of our making. They make us realise the need for worship, for a healthy family life, for respect for our neighbours' rights, for integrity and self-discipline. They keep us on the right lines in times of uncertainty such as our own.

On any showing, Moses was a giant among men, one of the great figures in the history of mankind. But it is foolish to try to wrest him out of his times or to tear him from his ancient background. He spoke and behaved like a Hebrew of a bygone age. In knowledge of facts about the age of the universe, the secrets of outer space, the miracles of modern science, any schoolboy is his master. But in strength of character, resolution, and insight into the meaning and purpose of life he towers above the ordinary run of men.

And, of course, in the last resort, the whole sum of Moses' achievement goes back to the fact that he was a man of God, a man whose heart God had touched. He saw himself not as a political leader or a national hero but as a humble and inadequate man whom God had called to a gigantic task and who had somehow been given the strength from day to day to carry it out.

He himself was not destined to reach the Promised Land to which he had led his followers. But before his death he went to the top of a mountain from which he could see the whole land stretching in front of him, the land which was to become Israel, the holy land for Christians as well as for Jews. He had had the vision: he had played his part. God had called him, he had responded magnificently. Other men would take over where he left off.

9.　The Promised Land

THE Bible indicates that it took about a generation for Moses to consolidate his rabble of runaway slaves into something

like a coherent body. They could not have numbered more
than a few thousands, since they had to exist on the sparse
nourishment afforded by the Sinai peninsula. After Moses'
death the leadership passed to Joshua, whose whirlwind conquest of the land of Canaan is described in the book that bears
his name. When we look a little more closely at the record, and
particularly when we compare it with the book of Judges which
covers the same period, it is clear that what actually happened
was much less spectacular, although the net result was the
same.

The land of Canaan was at this time, about 1250 BC, inhabited as it had been in the time of Abraham by people of
the same racial stock as the Hebrews. These people too had
made their way into that part of the world by migration,
though at an earlier date, and they had been long enough
settled there to make it impossible for a relatively small body
like the escaped Israelites to dislodge them. Although Egypt
was the nominal overlord, Canaan was left pretty much in the
hands of its petty chieftains who from their walled strong-
holds in the plain controlled the country with well-armed
troops and chariots. They were more than a match for the
Israelites, armed at best with clubs and slings.

Under the leadership of Joshua, the Hebrew tribesmen
secured a foothold in the hill country of Judah, and other
spearheads of invasion in the north and south met with some
success. But it was far from a wholesale occupation of the
land flowing with milk and honey, as Canaan must indeed have
seemed to these landless half-starved bedouins. Yet it was for
them the Promised Land, the land where the patriarchs had
sojourned as strangers but which they believed to be their
destined home.

By the time the story of these early beginnings came to be
written down, the whole of Canaan was in Israelite hands and
it is not surprising that the book of Joshua makes it appear
that it all happened much faster than it did. The book of
Judges tells a much more sober story of a long process of
infiltration, intermarriage, trade and settlement. In fact, it was
more than a couple of centuries before the Israelites could call

the land their own, and it was less by conquest than by peaceful pressure that this came about.

It seems that many of the descendants of the patriarchs had never left Canaan, and that when the fugitives from Egypt reached the Promised Land they quickly settled down with their kinsmen who were already there. The tough tribesmen who had come through the testing-time of the Exodus brought a new spirit to the Hebrews in Canaan, and became their leaders. It was this new martial mood of the Exodus element that resulted in the Hebrew tribes becoming the military backbone of the country. They did not fight against the Canaanites so much as they fought for them, and for themselves, against desert raiders bent on plundering the good farmlands.

The book of Judges gives some vivid scenes from these times. 'Judges' in this sense mean something quite different from bewigged dispensers of justice in our law courts. The Judges of Israel were her champions, men who, when the occasion demanded, took over the leadership of their own tribe and its neighbours to resist foreign invaders. They succeeded more by ingenuity and clever tactics than by force of numbers. Once the danger was past, the 'judge' returned to his ordinary job. There was no question of a monarchy. The tribes were free and independent, ruled by their councils of elders, a loose federation with a common ancestry which went back to Abraham, but now, since the Exodus, also with a common religious loyalty to the God who had so marvellously delivered his people from certain extinction.

This religious bond was all-important and from the point of view of the Bible it was the only thing which distinguished the Hebrew tribes from the miscellaneous racial groups which surrounded them. Under the leadership of Moses the Hebrews had pledged themselves to the service of the God of their fathers. As a token of the dramatic turn in their fortunes, it was under the new name which Moses had taught them that they now worshipped God as Yahweh. It was a name which suggested the sovereignty and power of the Being who had called them to a unique vocation, which became clearer to them only as they saw his purpose being worked out for them and through them.

To begin with, of course, they thought of Yahweh as the god of Sinai, the god of the mountain and of the desert, who had led them to the Promised Land, who had enabled them to defeat their enemies and who was more powerful than the gods of the nations that surrounded them. It took them many centuries to realise that Yahweh was the only God and that none of the other so-called gods existed.

But when they arrived in Canaan, their loyalty to Yahweh was severely tested. They were simple desert tribesmen with an austere faith and a high standard of behaviour based on the Ten Commandments. The tablets of stone with the words of the Commandments inscribed on them had been brought from Sinai in the box which they called the Ark of the Covenant, and which they regarded with superstitious veneration. It was their sacred talisman and while it was housed in its tent or Tabernacle in their religious centre it served as a constant reminder of the greatest moment in their history.

The religion of Canaan was, however, very different from this. It was closer to the religions of Greece and Rome, with their large collections of gods and goddesses, each with his own temple, who were thought of as one big family and usually an unhappy one, with rivalries, quarrels, and generally bloodthirsty behaviour. This was how the town-dwellers regarded them. The villagers on the other hand had their own local gods, each with his little shrine where the people offered sacrifices to ensure good harvests and general prosperity. All this was quite foreign to the Israelite immigrants fresh from the desert. There was nothing like the Ten Commandments to give a simple but strict rule of life, and there were so many gods and goddesses that it was impossible to know how to please them all. And since the religion of the Canaanites was based on the idea that the fruitfulness of the soil sprang from the sexual union of gods and goddesses, it was the practice to have sacred prostitutes at the temples and shrines with whom the worshipper had intercourse. This was supposed to guarantee the blessing of the particular deity on a man's land and possessions.

When the Israelites came into the Promised Land they had

to learn to become farmers, to grow grain, vines and olives; a totally new way of life to a people who had been mainly wandering shepherds, moving from place to place to pasture their flocks. And since they had to learn so much from their new neighbours, it is not surprising that they took over many of their customs and also much of their religion as well. Yahweh was not replaced by the Canaanite gods, but was worshipped alongside them and soon became indistinguishable from them. The Israelites still called themselves the People of Yahweh but it was a different Yahweh from the God whom Moses had once taught them to serve.

The religion of the ordinary Israelite tended to become very similar to that of his Canaanite neighbours. Nevertheless, there were always some Israelites who protested against the rot that had set in, and who tried to maintain the high standards of faith and behaviour which Moses had commended. Fanatically devoted to Yahweh and the distinctive role of his people, they chose to avoid the towns and lived, as their forefathers had lived, on the fringe of civilisation, where there were no temptations to fall in with Canaanite ways. In many respects they were narrow and reactionary, standing out against all forms of progress; yet these were the people who carried on the legacy of Moses and the austere standards of the desert and prevented them from becoming submerged in the paganism that surrounded them.

The stories that are told in the book of Judges of how one champion after another rescued his people from the danger of marauding tribes make good reading but have little religious value. The reason why they are included is that each champion is in one way or another a rallying point for the old Yahweh tradition. When there was peace, the Israelites were quite happy to drift into Canaanite ways. When danger threatened, they relied on Yahweh to deliver them. It seems that they needed to feel that their very existence was in peril before they remembered the God of their fathers. In this sense they were not much different from ourselves.

10. Saul: First King of Israel

THE story of the Old Testament is from a Christian point of view the story of the education of the People of God. This makes it sound a much duller story than it really is! But education comes through the experience of living, and Israel learned through the things that happened to her as they were explained by her long line of teachers beginning with Moses. One stage in her education was, as we have seen, when she learned that the faith and moral standards which she had been given and which marked her out from all her neighbours centred on the insight into her peculiar role in the world which had been given to her through Moses. She had pledged herself by solemn covenant in Sinai to the service of Yahweh and there were always some more sensitive spirits in the community who kept reminding her of it.

She had come through a testing-time when she reached Canaan and discovered that it was only by holding fast to this tradition that she could save herself from being swallowed up in the hotch-potch of pagan beliefs and moral standards which she encountered in the Promised Land. The next stage in her education taught her a different lesson. It was that it was not the role of the People of God to be a nation like other nations. She had to learn that power-politics, empire-building, nationalism and commercial expansion, things which are good enough in themselves, have no part in the distinctive contribution which God expected from the people of his choice. But all this could only be learned by bitter experience of trial and error.

One of the most cherished possessions of these democrats of the desert was their independence. The tribes of Israel wanted no king to rule over them. They had no happy memories of their treatment under the pharaohs of Egypt. But as time went on and their numbers grew, through intermarriage and trade but especially by their tough resistance to invaders from beyond the river Jordan, they had become the most powerful element in Canaan. Indeed Canaanites and Israelites had to all intents merged into one people. Now, however, a new threat to their existence appeared in the shape of the Philistines.

These sea-rovers from the Aegean had landed in Palestine and settled on the coastal plain soon after Joshua had staked Israel's claims to the highlands of Canaan. At first the Philistines were content to live at peace with their new neighbours. But they were an ambitious and warlike race and soon set their hearts on conquering the whole country. About the year 1050 BC they swept into the hills, sacked Israel's towns including Shiloh, the religious centre of the tribes, and captured their most sacred possession, the Ark of the Covenant. It needed a catastrophe of this magnitude to make the tribes sink their differences and, for the first time, agree to have a king to rule over them.

The man who dominates the scene at this point in the story of the Bible is the prophet Samuel. It is difficult, however, to glean from the narrative just what part he played. At one moment he is described as the man who reluctantly agreed to popular demand for a king and warned the people that they were preparing a rod for their own backs. The next moment we find him secretly selecting the man who in his view was the one whom the tribes needed at this point to pull them together and to rouse them against the Philistines.

It is not impossible that there is a measure of truth in both stories. Samuel emerges in either case as the most significant religious leader since the days of Moses. He was involved in the election of Saul as first king of Israel and later in rejecting Saul in favour of his successor David. But for all this he may well have had misgivings, as many others did, about the whole idea of a monarchy among a people whose supreme loyalty and responsibility should be to Yahweh as their only liege lord.

At all events, Saul makes his first impact on the tribes through his dramatic reaction to an appeal from an outlying Israelite settlement for help against marauders from the desert.

The Ammonites had laid siege to the town of Jabesh-Gilead beyond the river Jordan and had announced that the whole settlement would be spared if the men of the place agreed to have their right eyes put out as a lesson to the rest of the Israelite tribes. The men asked for a week's grace and sent messengers to their kinsmen begging for help. Gibeah, where Saul was a farmer, was one of the Israelite townships to which they appealed. Saul heard the story as he came in from ploughing his fields. He belonged to a class of men who feature in the narrative quite a lot about this time, for whom the Hebrew word is *nabi*, which is translated in the English Bible as 'prophet'. The word is the same as that which was used of Isaiah, Jeremiah, Amos and other great spokesmen of Israel, whose influence on the faith of Israel and on the whole of the Old Testament was, as we shall see, quite incalculable.

The early type of *nabi* was, however, as different from the later moulders of Israel's fortunes as night is from day. He was more like the dancing dervish of modern times, a weird-looking holy man, usually wandering around the country, and rather looked down on by more solid citizens. He was normally a member of a group and could work himself into a kind of contagious hysteria or frenzy. When these people were caught up in one of their mass ecstasies they were indifferent to pain and could slash themselves with knives without apparently feeling it.

Saul had at one time been in contact with these people and, while remaining a respectable farmer, to some extent shared their odd behaviour, and was occasionally seized with the characteristic frenzy which later in his case turned to madness. But the main importance of the early type of *nabi* lay in their fanatical devotion to Yahweh and their intense nationalism, and in this respect Saul was wholeheartedly one of them. A frenzy again came over him when he learned of the affront to his countrymen in Jabesh-Gilead, and there and then he slew his oxen as he walked behind them from the field, cut them in pieces and sent them like a fiery cross through the tribes of Israel with the threat that whoever did not now rally to the cause of Yahweh and Israel would suffer a like fate.

The effect was electric. Not so much by reason of the threat, which was no more than a form of words, but by the sense that here at last was a leader, a new champion, a man whom all

Israel would be prepared to serve. The clans rallied to his summons, Jabesh-Gilead was relieved and the remnants of the Ammonite army were sent fleeing back to the desert. But the heart of the whole people lifted at the thought that now the Philistine yoke could be broken. Saul's great opportunity came largely through his daredevil son Jonathan.

The Philistines had a garrison in Saul's own town of Gibeah, and Saul had gone up into the hills with a tiny force of six hundred men. Jonathan, taunted by the garrison, took them by surprise. Saul rushed to his aid, scattered tribesmen joined his tiny force and the Philistines were driven from the hills into the plain. This was a notable victory for Israel, and the battle of Michmash meant that she was for a time free from Philistine rule. It is perhaps worth mentioning that during the Palestine campaign against the Turks in World War I, a British commander who knew his Bible followed Saul's tactics and relying on the geographical details given in the story routed the Turks as Saul and Jonathan had routed the Philistines.

The result of the battle was that Saul was elected the first king of Israel. In Saul's lifetime the Israelite kingdom was small enough, a narrow strip of territory among the hills, but it was a beginning. For the rest of his days, Saul had to fight for it against the Philistines and it was in battle against them that he died. From now on, however, his career was affected by two quite different things. One was the increasing deterioration of his mind. The nervous frenzy which had given him such a hold over the tribesmen now turned into brooding melancholia which burst into mad fits. At such times he was capable of murder, and it was doubtless this instability that lost him the support of Samuel. The other factor that changed his fortunes was the emergence of a rival to his throne in the person of a young and dashing general, David.

11. David and the Golden Age

IT had been a great day for Israel. Her army had won a decisive victory over the Philistines at the battle of Elah and now the victorious King Saul was marching back at the head of his troops. From every town and village on the way the women of Israel came out with cymbals and tambourines, dancing and singing and crying with joy as they welcomed the warriors home. But the real hero of the day was not the king but his brilliant young general David, handsome, brave, successful, the most popular man in the kingdom. The words of the women's song were, 'Saul has killed his thousands, and David his tens of thousands', which must have been galling for the king to listen to.

What was the secret of David's success? How had this farmer's son, this one-time shepherd boy from Bethlehem, reached the top so quickly? Nature seems to have endowed him with all the gifts – good looks, a quick brain, a warm heart, an attractive manner and a flair for leadership. But what first put his foot on the ladder of fame was his skill as a musician. King Saul suffered, as we have seen, from fits of depression which later on turned into spells of dangerous madness. His advisers prescribed the soothing effects of music to charm away his melancholy. In a land of music-lovers David's early skill, which later earned him his reputation as 'the sweet singer of Israel' as he accompanied himself on the harp, was enough to gain him a place in the king's service and the royal court.

His charm won the king's heart and he made him one of his squires. This was David's opportunity and led to the occasion which made him the hero of the whole people. The immortal story of David and Goliath tells how the Israelite and the Philistine armies faced each other on the hillsides overlooking the vale of Elah. This giant of a man Goliath, armed to the teeth, used to shout a daily challenge across the valley to any Israelite to take him on in single combat. David took up the challenge.

'And Saul dressed David in his own clothing, put a bronze helmet on his head, and clad him in a coat of mail. David buckled his sword over his coat, and tried to walk, but in vain, for he was not used to such armour. So David said to Saul, "I cannot move with these; I am not used to them." And David put them off; he grasped his club, picked five smooth stones from the stream and put them in the shepherd's bag that served him for a knapsack, took his sling in his hand, and went to meet the Philistine. But when the Philistine looked and saw David, he despised him for his youth. "Am I a dog," said the Philistine to David, "that you attack me with a club?" And the Philistine cursed David by his gods. "Come here," said the Philistine to David, "and I will give your flesh to the birds of the air and the beasts of the field." Then David answered the Philistine, "You attack me with sword and spear and javelin, but I attack you in the name of the Lord of hosts, the God of the armies of Israel, which you have insulted this day. The Eternal will deliver you into my hands, and I will cut off your head and give your corpse and the corpses of the Philistine host to the birds of the air and the wild beasts of the earth, so that all the world may learn that Israel has a God, then all here present learn that the Eternal does not save by sword and spear – the fight is in the Eternal's hands, and he will put you in our power.

'As the Philistine then started to approach and attack David, David hurried forward to meet the Philistine. Putting his hand into the bag, David took out a stone and slung it, striking the Philistine on the forehead; the stone sank into his forehead, and he dropped on his face to the ground. Then David ran and stood over the Philistine, drew his sword from the sheath and killed him, cutting his head off. When the Philistines saw their champion was dead, they ran away, and the men of Israel and of Judah rose with a shout and chased the Philistines as far as the entrance to Gath and the gates of Ekron.'

David was now the people's darling. Promotion in the army quickly followed. The king's daughter fell in love with him and it was not long before she became his bride. The king's son Jonathan had become his closest friend. As the record says:

'Jonathan's soul was knit to David's – Jonathan loved him as himself.' The shepherd boy from Bethlehem had come a long way in a very short time.

But trouble lay ahead. The king's mind was becoming more and more unhinged. Jealousy of his popular young son-in-law began to eat into his soul. When the mad fits came over him he grew homicidal and on several occasions David missed death by inches from a throw of the king's spear while he was playing or singing to calm Saul's troubled spirit. When the madness had passed, all was well and David was back in favour. But it was a precarious existence and bit by bit Saul's obsessive jealousy darkened David's whole future. For a time Jonathan managed to placate his father.

But Saul's jealous hatred could not be mastered. He saw in David a rival claimant for the throne and told Jonathan he was a fool to defend the man who would one day rob him of his inheritance. When Saul tried to kill his son as well as David, the two friends knew that this was the turning point. David must leave the court and become an outlaw. So he fled the king's anger and lived the life of a Robin Hood in the forest of Hereth. For some time he had his headquarters in a cave at Adullam and there he gathered round him not only his own brothers and the men of his own clan but mercenaries, desperadoes, men with a price on their heads and all who were 'agin the government'. Their numbers grew to about four hundred, bold and reckless men with a lust for adventure, willing to throw in their lot with this daring young outlaw chief.

So with his band of hunted men David embarked on a hand-to-mouth existence in the Judaean hills, living off the land, raiding the surrounding territories, often on the run when Saul and his pursuing troops got too close. Many tales are told of those days; for example, how on two occasions David spared Saul's life when he was close enough to have killed him. But none is more revealing than the story of how three of his bodyguards crept through the enemy's lines to bring their beloved captain a drink of water from the well at Bethlehem, his boyhood home. In a thoughtless moment he had uttered this nostalgic wish and his men had risked their lives to gratify his whim. David was so moved that he refused to drink the water but poured it on the ground as an offering to God with these words: 'Be it far from me, O Lord, that I should do this: is not this the blood of the men that went in jeopardy of their lives?'

But King Saul had soon a greater problem on his hands than chasing David and his outlaw band. The Philistine armies marched against Israel and at the battle of Gilboa the flower of the nation's manhood died. Jonathan and his brothers were slain; the king took his own life in despair; the kingdom of Saul was no more; the land of Israel was now a Philistine province.

Meantime David was in exile in enemy territory. When he heard the news his grief knew no bounds. His lament for the death of Saul and Jonathan came from the heart:

> The beauty of Israel is slain upon thy high places:
> How are the mighty fallen! . . .
> Saul and Jonathan were lovely and pleasant in their lives,
> And in their death they were not divided:
> They were swifter than eagles,
> They were stronger than lions.
> Ye daughters of Israel, weep over Saul,
> Who clothed you in scarlet, with other delights,
> Who put on ornaments of gold upon your apparel.
> How are the mighty fallen in the midst of the battle!
> O Jonathan, thou wast slain in thine high places.
> I am distressed for thee, my brother Jonathan:
> Very pleasant hast thou been unto me:
> Thy love to me was wonderful,
> Passing the love of women.
> How are the mighty fallen,
> And the weapons of war perished!
>
> *II Samuel 1:19–27*

But of course Saul's death changed the whole picture. David had now nothing to fear. On the credit side, he had his romantic story and his reputation as a brilliant military commander. He was the only man who could rally his despondent countrymen and smash the Philistines. So step by step he made himself master of the situation. First of all, he got himself proclaimed king over the southern part of the country – presumably with Philistine permission. Then Saul's tough old commander-in-chief Abner, who had made one of Saul's younger sons nominal king over what was left of Israel, came over to David's side, and soon after the young king himself was murdered in his sleep. David was now in theory king of the northern territories as well. He had yet to make it a fact. Bit by bit he nibbled at the Philistine hold over the country. Battle after battle was won. He now had the people behind him, he had the cream of the army and all his own skill and leadership. At length he could say that Israel was once again an independent nation. The Philistines had been vanquished.

But now came the master stroke that showed David to be not only a brilliant general but also a brilliant statesman. The northerners and the southerners in Israel had lived for centuries in uneasy association. If David was to be king of a united people where would his capital be? In the north or in the south? Either way would perpetuate ancient rivalries and jealousies.

Between the two, however, there had stood ever since the Israelites came into the land of Canaan the city and fortress of Jerusalem – an apparently impregnable island citadel in the hands of a non-Israelite power. It was a mark of David's genius not only to see the advantages of having a neutral capital – neither in the north nor in the south – but to take by a stratagem a mountain stronghold which was overpowered only twice in the next millennium.

So about a thousand years before Christ, David installed himself in his new capital, surrounded it with a great wall, built himself a fine palace and called Jerusalem the 'city of David'. But he was determined that it should be more than the centre of government. It must be the centre of the religious life of the people as well, for this was no ordinary nation, but Israel, the People of God. It was a people that through all its ups and downs – and there had indeed been many – had never doubted that from the time of the Exodus under Moses its destiny had been in the hands of God.

David, for all his faults, was a deeply religious man, conscious that he held his kingship in trust and that it was only by the providence of God that he had become king. He knew too that in these warlike clans that together made up Israel, with their feuds and rivalries, the only bond between them was their common roots in the past, their epic escape from slavery in Egypt which had now become a saga and their toughening experience in the desert under Moses before they reached the land of Canaan.

The memory of the Exodus and the desert wanderings, the recollection of the pledge at Sinai, the hard austere life of those nomadic days, all this found its religious symbol in the Ark of the Covenant – the simple portable box which contained the stone tablets on which Moses had carved the Ten Commandments. When it had fallen into enemy hands there had been national lamentation; for more than two hundred years it had been the sacred palladium of Israel, the symbol of the continuing presence of God in their midst, a reminder that they were not like other nations but a people under obedience to divine law, kings and people together under the authority of God. David won it back from the Philistines, and now brought the Ark to Jerusalem and housed it in a tent, again a reminder of the desert days. As the procession entered the city, with the sound of trumpets and the shouts of the people, with the king himself leading the dancing throng, this must have been David's greatest hour.

So, from his splendid new capital at Jerusalem David proceeded to enlarge his kingdom. One after another the small principalities that surrounded him were defeated and their territories annexed. The plunder of victory flowed into Jerusalem. David's frontiers soon stretched from beyond Damascus in the north to the Red Sea in the south, from the Mediterranean in the west across the Jordan into the eastern desert. Brilliant generalship abroad and wise statesmanship at home made David's little empire secure and solid, a model kingdom ruled by a strong and successful king.

But the Bible says relatively little about all this. It is more interested in David the man than David the monarch. It draws attention to his concern to help any survivors of Saul's family for the sake of his old friendship with Jonathan and tells how he sought out Jonathan's crippled son and treated him as one of his own family. But it draws attention equally to the seamy side of David's character and shows him as the idol of the nation who turns out to have feet of clay. The account of his adultery with Bathsheba and how he had her husband killed so that he might have her as his wife is also part of David's story.

If this had been any other middle-eastern country in those days that would have been the end of it. A king could do as he liked with his subjects. But this was no ordinary country. This was Israel and Israel had a greater king than David, the Lord God himself who had said, 'You shall not commit adultery. You shall not murder.' Whenever kings or commoners failed in their obedience to the Ten Commandments, there were always men of God in Israel to remind them of their obligations. Such a one was the prophet Nathan who now took his life in his hands and confronted the king with his crimes. He told the king a story: 'There were two men in one town, a rich man and a poor man. The rich man had many sheep and cattle; the poor man had nothing but a single ewe lamb which he had bought; he fed it, and it grew up with him and his children, it used to eat his own morsels and drink from his cup and nestle in his bosom, just like a daughter. Now a traveller came to visit the rich man, and the rich man spared his own sheep and cattle when he had to make provision for the traveller who had come to visit him; he took the poor man's lamb and prepared that for his visitor.'

David's anger blazed furiously against the man. 'By the life of the Eternal!' he said to Nathan, 'the man who did that deserves to die.' . . . Nathan said to David, 'You are the man!'

Then Nathan in the name of God pronounced judgement. In any other country with any other king such an action would have cost him his life. But David was stricken with shame and remorse. For all his success as a king he had failed as a man. Humbly he confessed: 'I have sinned against the Lord.' His cry for God's forgiveness came from a contrite heart.

But Israel's most glorious and successful king had yet to drain the cup of bitter failure to the dregs. Strong and ruthless with his nation's enemies, David was soft and weak with his own family. His handsome son, Absalom, vain as a peacock, was working steadily behind his father's back to undermine the king's popularity and win the throne for himself. He pulled out all the stops and created a dazzling public image of himself as a royal sportsman, the poor man's friend, the prince with the common touch and the heart of gold. As a 'con-man', Absalom has had few equals.

His tactics were successful and when he raised the banner of revolt and proclaimed himself king, popular support was with him. David had to flee from Jerusalem with his family and the part of the army that remained loyal. There is a pathetic picture of him making his way up the Mount of Olives, weeping, with his head shrouded and his feet bare. Jonathan's son whom he had taken into his own family deserted to the side of Absalom. Stones were flung at the man who had once been the popular hero. Absalom occupied the royal palace at Jerusalem while David fled across the Jordan.

But there was still enough fire and still enough astuteness in the old warrior to turn the tide of his fortunes. David rallied his supporters and a decisive battle was fought in which Absalom's forces were routed. Despite David's order that at all costs Absalom's own life should be spared, the handsome young rebel met a macabre end. As he fled on his mule through the forest he was caught by the neck in the overhanging branches of an oak tree and stabbed to death. When news was brought to David that the revolt had been crushed, his first question was for Absalom's safety. When he heard that he was dead the king was inconsolable:

'He wept as he went up to the chamber above the gateway, and as he wept he cried, "O my son Absalom! My son, my son Absalom! Oh that I had died instead of you, Absalom, my son, my son!"'

So, back in his capital at Jerusalem, David was once again the unchallenged ruler of his people. But his long reign of forty years was nearly at an end. We are left with the picture of a tired old man, with little zest for life, surrounded by palace intrigues to determine his successor. Bathsheba, who had marked the turning point in his life from success to failure, engineered affairs to get the old man to promise his throne to her son, Solomon. So David died, harried, careworn and disappointed, and was buried in the city that he had made his own.

His memory lived on in Israel. And strangely enough what was remembered was not just his military victories but the striking blend of triumph and tragedy that characterised his life. His achievements had been on the grand scale but so had his failures. He was a strange mixture for a man who stands next to Moses in the hierarchy of Israel. Yet the biblical chroniclers judged this particular character as having more than made the grade.

That wise old prophet Samuel, when he picked out David as Saul's successor had said, 'Man looks at the outward appearance but the Eternal looks at the heart.' This might well be the final verdict on David. For it was the memory of a big-hearted man who could take the measure of his successes and his failures, his triumphs and his tragedies, that made him the David of legend and saga. He had the root of the matter in him. He was essentially a man of God, and however much he fell from grace he always came back to the God to whom he had pledged his life.

Surely one of the reasons why the psalms of David still awaken a response in the minds of twentieth-century men and women is that in so many of them we hear the cry of a man who had tried and failed, loved and lost, and stumbled and fallen, but who knew in his heart of hearts that he was involved in a far bigger assignment than he could ever understand or fulfil.

As time went on and Israel's fortunes declined until little or nothing was left of these spacious days except a memory, his reign was looked back on as the Golden Age. Even centuries later, when there seemed to be no future for the Jews except extinction, they still harboured the hope in their hearts that one day a 'Son of David' would appear, a Messiah who would deliver them as David had done in days gone by. When the

Messiah did come he was more than a second David, but there must surely have been much in the life of this very human man of which Jesus the friend of life's failures approved.

12. Solomon the Magnificent

THERE are two verdicts on Solomon in the Bible. One comes from the narrator of his story in the Old Testament: 'King Solomon exceeded all the kings of the earth for riches and for wisdom.' The other came from Jesus when he said that Solomon in all his regalia was less impressive than a wayside flower. On the evidence, Jesus was the shrewder judge. Solomon was certainly astute. He transformed David's rustic kingdom into a centre of spectacularly successful commercial enterprise, with a flourishing industry and a thriving foreign trade. As a tycoon he was brilliant but as a king of Israel he was a disaster.

In the eyes of later historians, his greatest achievement was the building of the Temple at Jerusalem. For this they were prepared to overlook his glaring failure as a man and to credit him with a wisdom which he certainly did not possess. The one example of his so-called 'wisdom' which is quoted shows him to have had typical oriental quick-wittedness in unravelling knotty problems but little more than that. When two wrangling women claimed the same child as their own, he offered to cut the infant in two, giving a half to each, knowing that the real mother would rather surrender the child to her rival than see it killed.

On his father David's death he had reached the throne by a palace intrigue. He then proceeded to assassinate any other potential claimants, including his older brother, and settled down to a reign of peace and prosperity. Peaceful it certainly was. There is no record of any military expeditions whatever and no record even of threats to the safety of the realm. Solomon was not a soldier like his father. He had apparently no ambition to extend the frontiers of his kingdom. His policy was to be one of consolidation and commercial expansion. He safeguarded himself by alliances with foreign states, —sometimes by marriage—by strengthening his border fortresses and by increasing his standing army.

But above all his ambition was to rebuild his capital, Jerusalem. In David's time the Ark of the Covenant had been housed in a tent as a symbol of the old nomadic life. Now it must be installed in a temple. The arrangements for the construction of this temple, with its furnishings and its specifications, occupy a wholly disproportionate amount of space in the Old Testament. To later generations who included these details it was the most noteworthy single achievement to Solomon's credit. Yet when all is said and done, the tabernacle which he built to house the Ark was a comparatively small building, less than a hundred feet long and fifty feet high. It was considerably smaller than Solomon's elaborate palace to which it was attached as a kind of royal chapel.

Nevertheless, the great Temple enclosure which contained palace, tabernacle and other buildings must have impressed people who were still not far distant from the time when Saul had had to fight for every inch of Israelite soil. Some of the stone came from a quarry just under the Temple itself but the expensive cedarwood, cypress, gold and bronze for the furnishings and decorations had to be brought from a distance, and paid for. Phoenician workmen had to be employed since the Israelites were unskilled in this kind of work. They, too, had to be paid. So in addition to Solomon's normal expenditure on his household staff, which was considerable, and on his army which was a large one, he had to find money for these lavish building projects.

Part of the cost was met by taxation, which is always unpopular, part was avoided by forced labour, which is even more unpopular. The old tribal areas were divided up into districts which were made responsible in turn for maintaining the king's household, overseers were appointed and a chief labour organiser was put in charge of the whole scheme. Taxation and forced labour did not produce enough to meet the king's ambitious plans. So he levied heavy tolls on caravans, using the great trade route between Asia and Africa which passed through his territory. He became a trader in horses, buying from Egypt and selling to Syria. He sold part of his land to the Phoenicians for gold and it looks as if he even sold some of his subjects to Egypt in exchange for horses and chariots, which he then retailed.

But his master-stroke was the exploitation of his iron and copper mines. It is only recently that archaeologists have discovered the chief source of Solomon's income. At the top of the Red Sea remains of mines and blast-furnaces were found, indicating, in the words of Nelson Glueck who conducted the excavations, that Solomon had built the seaport of Ezion-Geber and turned it into the 'Pittsburgh of Palestine', a remarkable industrial site with copper refineries and shipbuilding yards from which he exported the products of his factories. Solomon's merchant navy sailed from there to Ophir, probably Somaliland, trading his wares for 'gold and silver, ivory, and apes, and peacocks'. Since the Hebrews were no sailors, the ships were manned by Phoenicians. When the Queen of Sheba, from the 'land of spice' in South Arabia, paid her notorious visit to Solomon to 'prove him with hard questions', it was no doubt more of a trade mission than a state occasion and these two astute oriental rulers did some hard bargaining to their mutual economic advantage.

The effects of this dramatic expansion of Israel in so short a time were, however, disastrous. No one would have complained if all this activity and enterprise had been for the good of the people as a whole. But it was, on the contrary, serving merely to gratify Solomon's love of ostentation and to support an ever-increasing entourage. David left a kingdom contented, united and solvent. Solomon's extravagance not only reduced it to near bankruptcy but cut at the very roots of the relationship between king and people which David had established and on which the unity of the kingdom depended.

The Hebrews had too much of the nomadic spirit of independence still left in them to suffer gladly an autocrat such as Solomon. When that autocracy was combined with a policy

that imposed hardships on them for no other purpose than to satisfy the luxurious whims of the monarch and his courtiers, the justification for monarchy as such had in the people's eyes disappeared. In the later years of Solomon's reign, revolts among subject nations that David had bequeathed to him lost him both useful territory and, even more, useful income. The 'copper-king' was either unwilling or unable to recover them.

He was able to quell a revolt among his own people but the storm broke after his death. The kingdom split in two. Ten of the tribes refused to recognise Solomon's son as king and he was left with a fraction of the legacy which his father had inherited. The unwisdom of this legendary wisest of all the kings of the earth had brought its own retribution. It may be that Solomon had always had things too easy. He knew nothing of the hardships and struggles that had kept his father David essentially a humble man and always a people's man. In the royal court when David was in his dotage Solomon had been brought up by a fond mother who engineered his accession to the throne. His magnificence was paid for by the sweat of his people for whom he showed his contempt. His harem was enormous, though some of his marriages were political. Even the benevolent recorder of his story, who can see little fault in Solomon's behaviour, is forced to admit that his foreign wives may have been his undoing and that he was not the man his father had been.

He seems to have dabbled in natural science and lyric poetry, and may have coined some of the proverbs that are attributed to him. He was certainly not the author of all the wisdom literature in the Old Testament which was traditionally associated with his name. It was anything but wisdom that led him to alienate the affection and loyalty of his people and to bring about the destruction of their unity which had been so painfully achieved. No one, however successful as a tycoon, could more woefully have misinterpreted the character of the Hebrews than to try to set himself up as a typical little oriental despot over men who had still in their blood the desert nomad's passion for freedom.

13. Kings and Prophets

THE end of the reign of Solomon, about 930 BC, sounded the death-knell of Israel's attempt to become a competitor in the game of power politics. This was not the role that had been cast for the descendants of Abraham, 'the friend of God'. Unless the whole Bible is nonsense from beginning to end, we have to recognise that God chose to disclose the meaning and purpose of human life through the unlikely channel of one particular racial group, the Jews. But perhaps the whole process makes sense when we learn to accept the fact that what is nonsense to us in our human pride is indeed the way God works.

There is nothing more nonsensical, humanly speaking, than that God should have selected Israel to be the means of communicating the truth about life, unless it is that he should have chosen a Galilean carpenter to be the fullest expression of what we can understand about him, or that the record of his dealings with mankind should be committed to such an apparently haphazard composition as the Bible. No doubt this is why St Paul who was more farsighted than most of us said that God's foolishness is wiser than the wisdom of men.

If all this makes human nonsense but divine sense, we shall recognise in the story of Israel the story of mankind seen through the wrong end of the telescope, so that on that tiny stage of the Levant there was enacted a veritable divine comedy, in which all the issues that affect the world for good or ill were presented for our edification. In the failure of her kings, Israel was being taught, as we are being taught through her, that the people whom God had chosen could not fulfil their role in the world by aping the standards and values of other nations. It was not by the might of armies, or by territorial expansion or by economic progress that Israel would accomplish her mission of bringing the world to the knowledge of the truth about God and the purpose of man's existence.

Whatever virtues, Saul, David and Solomon may have had, and they had many, they were not the kind of men to lead the People of God along the way to their appointed destiny. Nationalistic and imperialistic dreams had to be shattered before Israel found her true vocation, not because these things were bad in themselves but because the kind of kingdom the People of God had to build would come not by might and not by power but by the spirit of God.

So Israel had to experience the disintegration of her little empire. The chroniclers who record the story in the Bible show that, for all their gifts, Saul, David and Solomon were essentially failures as leaders of the kind of community that Israel was meant to be. Their successors are given shorter shrift and treated with scant sympathy. When the kingdom broke in two after Solomon's death, the divided states of Israel and Judah remained separated for two more centuries, until the northern half which had retained the name of Israel, fell before the ruthless war-lords of Assyria. A century and a half later, the southern half, Judah, was likewise ravaged and destroyed in its turn by the new world-power of Babylon. Jerusalem was sacked and by 587 BC the kingdom founded by Saul had ceased to exist.

The tale of the thirty-nine monarchs who reigned over the severed halves of Israel during these three and a half centuries is dismissed in thirty-six short chapters of the Bible. In the eyes of the recorders of the story, this is all they were worth. Once or twice one or other of them comes in for a word of praise, but in the main it is a depressing tale of petty warfare, intrigue and political manoeuvre. Israel's end as a nation was in sight.

So it was that Israel had to learn to look for her leadership not in her kings but in her prophets. For from now on, the Bible spotlights a series of remarkable figures who emerge as critics of the kings and keepers of the nation's conscience. Taken together the prophets of Israel are a unique phenomenon in the history of religion. It was they who taught Israel to see that it was not in the purpose of God that she should be a nation like other nations, questing for power, prestige and material

progress, and that God was teaching her through the disasters that befell her where her true vocation lay.

The first and greatest of the prophets had been, of course, Moses. He it was who had given Israel a new understanding of her role in the world, together with a new insight into the nature of the God who had given her this assignment and the standard of behaviour that he demanded. Lesser men who came after Moses had to some extent shared his insights. God did not ever leave himself without a witness, and through these queer and fanatical wandering prophets who appear in Israel's story after she settled in Canaan, as well as through the more striking contribution of men such as Samuel and Nathan, God was constantly reminding his people of what they stood for, and ensuring that Israel should not forget her high calling.

In the period of her history between the end of Solomon's reign and her final, or apparently final, disappearance as a recognisable national unit, when her kings were by and large unfit to be her leaders, Israel was kept in awareness of her destiny by prophets of the calibre of Elijah, Amos, Hosea, Isaiah and Jeremiah. These were not by any means the only prophets but they were the greatest of them. Each had a distinctive contribution to make and it was due to them that, when the final crash came, Israel did not perish in despair and disillusionment but rose again to a new beginning, chastened but enlightened, convinced that God had still a mighty purpose for his people which they were only then beginning to understand.

The prophets of Israel conformed to no set pattern. They were priests or statesmen, counsellors of kings or ordinary working men. Some of them behaved as oddly as the wandering 'holy men' in the time of Saul, some of them brought about changes in national policy, some of them paid for their honesty with their lives. Essentially they were men of God who, out of their deep personal commitment to God, spoke to the people of their day, to kings and commoners alike, in protest, warning, comfort or encouragement as the need arose and as the situation demanded.

Some of the things they said have been collected by their

followers in the books that bear their names, and these prophetic books in the Old Testament – Amos, Isaiah and the rest – provide a running commentary on the events and experiences that the prophets shared with their countrymen, but which from their own deep religious convinctions they were better able to interpret than their rulers or their neighbours. What they said they claimed to be the Word of God: 'Thus saith the Lord', not 'Thus saith Amos or Isaiah'.

They were not infallible. Sometimes their forecasts of events proved to be wrong and their limitations were as great as those of anyone else at the time. But on the issues of right and wrong, of justice and injustice, of religious insincerity and political chicanery their judgement was sound and fearless. It was due to them that the faith and standards of Israel were moulded into the legacy which Jesus and Paul inherited and which they in their turn passed on with their own distinctive contributions to Christianity.

It is a complete misunderstanding of the prophets to think of them primarily as prognosticators of future events. Their chief function was that of spokesmen of God and what they had to say dealt with the past and the present as much as with the future. They looked at the world as they found it and saw behind the things that were happening the pattern of God's activity in human affairs and the response that man must make. As often as not, what they said was not what men wanted to hear. Often their protests fell on deaf ears. Often they were ill-treated and humiliated, attacked and vilified.

They did not speak in a vacuum but always in the situation of their day, involving themselves in the political, economic and social movements of the time and taking part in the arguments that raged around the particular issues of the moment. They spoke out in the name of God on questions of peace and war, public and private morality, the rights of the common man and the obligations of the common man, without fear or favour, because they believed that it is the whole of life that God is concerned with and not merely public worship and private piety.

14. Elijah and Queen Jezebel

BEFORE the days of the classical prophets, that is, those whose teaching has been collected and made into books of the Bible which bear their names, there are two prophets who feature in the story of Israel not so much for what they said about God and man as for how they reacted to particular issues in their time. Both of them illustrate in different ways what the prophets stood for and how they contributed, by their intervention in the affairs of their day, imperishable insights into what the Bible is all about.

The story of Elijah takes us back to the ninth century BC when Ahab was king of the northern part of the kingdom over which Solomon had reigned, and which after his death had refused to recognise his son as its ruler. Solomon's son had announced that whereas his father had beaten his people with whips, he would beat them with loaded scourges, and his already restive subjects had, rather naturally, decided to secede. Now about a hundred years later they had Ahab as their king but it was clearly his wife Jezebel who was the power behind the throne.

She had been a princess of Tyre, the prosperous island principality on the Phoenician coast, which lived by trade and commerce and whose ships were seen in every foreign harbour. Now she was queen of Israel where she found a way of life very different from that of Tyre. The god the Tyrians worshipped was called Melkart and was a comfortable kind of god who made few demands. A king could be a proper king in Tyre and do what he liked with his subjects; their lives were in his hands and what he wanted he took. The priests and prophets of Melkart were likewise paid to do as they were told. They carried on the worship of the state religion – the ceremonial of the temples, the sacrifices, the feasts and holy days – but they knew better than to interfere in politics or to question the authority of the royal house.

This was how Jezebel had been brought up and when she became Ahab's queen she was appalled to find how different everything was. The Israelites had always been at heart a desert people with the bedouin's love of independence. They had never taken kindly to kings and they had never hesitated to show their disapproval of those who tried to be dictators. Their ideal king had been David, who looked on himself as the servant of his people, and in Jezebel's day his memory was fresh in their minds.

The queen was a much stronger character than her husband Ahab, and she was determined that the king of Israel, and of course through him the queen, should have the kind of power over his subjects that she had been brought up to believe every king should have. No subject should have the right to criticise the monarch's actions or thwart the royal will. It did not take her long to discover that what stood in the way of her ambitions was the state religion of her adopted country.

Outwardly, it was in many ways not unlike her own. Prophets and priests, festivals and sacrifices were much the same. But it had been built on a different foundation. The religion of Israel went back to the Exodus, when under the leadership of Moses the people had pledged themselves to Yahweh, the God who had saved them from a living death in Egypt, who had led them to the Promised Land, and who had always after that been regarded in a special sense as the God of Israel.

Even though many Israelites had adopted the pagan practices of their neighbours, there had always been a protesting minority to remind them that Yahweh was not like other gods and that Israel was not like other peoples. Israel was bound to observe the commandments of God. What was right and what was wrong was not decided by her kings, but by the terms of the covenant that God had made with Israel. Prophets of the calibre of Samuel and Nathan in earlier days had never been afraid to challenge rulers who abused the people's rights or flouted the will of God.

All this was anathema to Jezebel. With such a God as Yahweh the power she craved in Israel would never be hers. So she determined that the state religion should be changed. She would not rest until she had replaced Yahweh as God of Israel by Melkart her own god. Systematically she went ahead and the easy-going Ahab tamely acquiesced. She built a temple to Melkart in the capital, encouraged large numbers of Israelites to change their faith, and supported out of the royal purse several hundred prophets, pledged to propagate the new religion. Those prophets who remained loyal to the old faith were persecuted and those who did not escape were killed. It looked as if Jezebel had won the day. But she had reckoned without Elijah.

This striking and impressive figure was a man of the desert who, even in the way he dressed, showed how strongly he clung to Israel's desert upbringing. Like Samuel and Nathan, he was a prophet who was not afraid to tell his rulers in the name of Yahweh, God of Israel, where they had gone wrong. He was passionately concerned that the Israelites should remain faithful to the God of Moses, not only because of what he had done for Israel, but because Elijah saw that with any other god or any other state religion the rights of the common man would be in jeopardy.

So he set himself to fight Jezebel's attempt to destroy the old religion of Israel. It was a conflict of two iron wills. Jezebel had behind her the power and authority of the monarch; Elijah could only urge the people to be loyal to the faith of their fathers and to judge for themselves whether Yahweh or Melkart best deserved their allegiance.

The Bible describes an epic contest on Mount Carmel between Elijah and the prophets of Melkart. Whether the details are accurate or merely picturesque, it means that Elijah succeeded in persuading the people that Yahweh and Yahweh alone must be the God of Israel. In the end Jezebel's prophets were wiped out, and even though Elijah had to flee for his life from the wrath of the queen, Jezebel's attempt to foist her own religion on Israel had failed.

The Bible shows us quite plainly what was at stake, and what Elijah was fighting for, in the story of Naboth's vineyard. King Ahab wanted this ground which lay beside his palace.

Naboth refused and the king was still enough of an Israelite to recognise a man's right to his own property. Jezebel, however, was aghast that a mere peasant should be allowed to defy a king and she had Naboth executed on a trumped-up charge. There is a dramatic scene where Elijah confronts the king in the vineyard, gloating over his ill-gotten prize, and accuses him of being a murderer and a thief.

We may take it that this was only one instance out of many. Elijah's fight to preserve Yahweh as the God of Israel was also a fight to ensure the right of the common man to be treated as a person and not as a puppet to be manipulated by any king or government that chose to exploit him.

15. Micaiah and King Ahab

THE second story is also about a prophet who faced up to King Ahab. The scene is set in Samaria, the capital of the northern kingdom and on the day in question the king was in high spirits. His neighbour and ally, Jehoshaphat the king of Judah, was paying a state visit and Ahab had every reason to think that the political talks they had been having over the last few days were going the way he wanted. It had been a long-standing grievance and a blow to national pride that the old desert fortress of Ramoth-Gilead was in enemy hands. This ancient Israelite town was occupied by the Syrians and for prestige reasons, if nothing else, Ahab felt that now was the time to get it back.

Jehoshaphat was sympathetic and pledged to help. To gain moral support for their action the two kings took the advice of the court prophets – four hundred of them – and with one accord the prophets urged them on to battle and promised them success. Yet something about these religious yes-men made Jehoshaphat uneasy. Were they saying what they believed or what they knew the kings wanted to hear?

So Jehoshaphat asked if there were no other prophet in the

place who might be consulted. This put Ahab in a fix. There was indeed one man, Micaiah the son of Imlah, not one of the regular court prophets but a man of independent judgement who spoke his mind without fear or favour. Ahab had good cause to hate him, for every time he had asked his views the verdict had always been the opposite of what the king wanted to hear. Micaiah had paid for his boldness and was at that very moment in the palace dungeon.

However, Jehoshaphat insisted that Micaiah's voice be heard, so an officer was sent to fetch the troublesome prophet from the jail. Meantime there was a splendid performance for the visiting king's benefit. The two monarchs sat on their thrones at the city gates, arrayed in their royal robes, while the four hundred court prophets processed in front of them, vying with each other to shout the loudest that victory was as good as won and that God was on their side. One of them donned a pair of iron horns and thrust right and left like a bull to show how the enemy would be routed.

While all this was going on, Micaiah was being given advice by his escort: 'Take your cue from the rest of the prophets. They've all foretold success and victory. Don't spoil the king's day.' Micaiah's grim reply was that he would say what the Lord told him to say, no more and no less, whether it pleased the king or not.

So Micaiah was brought before the two monarchs, the bedraggled, emaciated prisoner confronting the regal splendour of Israel and Judah. At first, when Ahab asked him: 'Should we embark on this enterprise or stay where we are?', Micaiah with biting irony replied: 'By all means. On to victory. The Lord is on your side.' He might have added: 'Your four hundred godly advisers have told you to go on and win. Who am I to contradict them?'

Then Ahab, dominated by his forceful wife Jezebel, but still with far more respect for this awkward prophet of the God of his fathers than for the four hundred paid lickspittles of his court retinue, said to Micaiah: 'How many times must I charge you on your solemn oath to tell me nothing but the truth in the name of the Lord?'

Ahab knew that from this one man and from him alone he would get the truth. And every time he got an answer it was an answer that he did not want to hear. He hated Micaiah for it but in his heart of hearts he knew that this was a man of God who would speak as God prompted him. So on this occasion too he demanded the truth, knowing that he would get it and already hating what he was certain he would hear. For Ahab knew in the secret of his soul that he had been a failure as a king of Israel. He had betrayed the faith of Abraham, of Moses and of David. He had used his power for his own advancement and not for the good of his people. How, on this expedition which was meant to further nothing but his own prestige, could he expect blessing and victory from the God he had spurned. He knew Micaiah's answer before it came.

Then the floodgates were opened and this man of God said what was given him to say. Who can tell what went into a prophet's vision? Micaiah said that he saw Israel scattered on the mountain as sheep without a shepherd. It meant disaster for the expedition and death for Israel's king. Perhaps he saw things with an insight and a perception that were denied to ordinary folk. Perhaps what he said was based on his appraisal of the political situation and his estimate of Israel's chances. Who knows?

What we do know is that, however he came to that assessment of the result of the assault on Ramoth-Gilead, he had the courage to say so to the king, knowing full well that his honesty would send him back to jail. Ahab's reaction was prompt and decisive: 'Take this man back to the dungeon and keep him on bread and water until I return victorious.' Micaiah's wry comment may have gone unnoticed: 'If you return victorious God has not spoken through me.'

But Ahab was not to be deterred. The armies marched on Ramoth-Gilead and were completely routed. Ahab paid enough heed to the prophet's warning to disguise himself as a common soldier. But even that could not save him and he fell mortally wounded by an arrow from an unknown bowman. Before the day was over his body was brought back to the capital for burial.

And what of Micaiah? With Ahab dead and his army defeated, Micaiah must either have been put to death or died of starvation. But he stands out in the story as a man who was ready to face death rather than compromise with his conscience. Micaiah obeyed a higher law than the law of self-preservation. He had committed his life to God and his supreme loyalty was to the God who had called him. With heart and mind and all his senses he was ready to receive the messages that God sent him, and what God said to him was truth that must be told, whatever the consequences.

What Micaiah was showing – like Moses, Nathan, Elijah and after his day Amos, Isaiah and the rest of these Old Testament prophets – was that things do not happen by chance. The Lord God is in control of all that happens. There is a supreme power in charge of life and history. Ahab was on any normal showing a reasonably competent, efficient king. But as the sovereign of the People of God, the people of the Covenant, the people of the Ten Commandments, he was a failure. And Micaiah was not afraid to say so.

We cannot see the story of Ahab's downfall isolated from his past. In a sense he was a pathetic figure. But this was the man who had weakly submitted to Jezebel's ambition to substitute her own brand of paganism for the historic faith of Israel. This was the man who had allowed his queen to murder Naboth, a peasant who had insisted on his right to independence. From Micaiah's point of view, the king was a failure and the Lord God had no further use for him.

Surely what emerges from this story is that when a man lives close to God, as Micaiah did, and listens to what God says to him, he has no choice but to speak the truth as he sees it, even if it brings him disaster or even death.

16. Amos and the Affluent Society

So far the stories of the prophets have been told in the Bible as part of the record of the kings. Samuel and Nathan appeared as characters in the stories of Saul and David. Elijah and Micaiah featured in the account of the reign of Ahab and Jezebel. They have all been remembered more for what they did than for what they said; for their courage, for their defence of the rights of ordinary citizens against despotic monarchs, and for their influence on the political and religious developments of their day.

In the case of Elijah, and even more so of his successor Elisha, legends grew up around them, as they always do around men of outstanding calibre, especially when their stories are passed on verbally and not written up until long after they are dead, sometimes centuries later. When we read, for example, that Elijah had a magic cloak with which he could divide the waters of the river Jordan or that at his death he was carried into the skies in a chariot of fire, this is not history but folklore. But it does show that Elijah was regarded as something more than a mortal. Or when Elisha miraculously recovered an iron axehead which had fallen into the Jordan in order to save the skin of the poor man who had had it on loan, we can recognise the type of story that followers of holy men in all religions have delighted in inventing. Yet the same Elisha undoubtedly played a very big part in public affairs as well.

But although all these earlier prophets fought valiantly to maintain the difference between the People of Yahweh and all other nations, reminding kings and commoners alike that the kind of behaviour that was good enough elsewhere was not good enough in Israel, nevertheless their understanding was limited by the times they lived in. Elijah risked his life to oust

Jezebel's god and root out all that he stood for from the life of Israel, but it does not seem to have worried either him or Elisha that the state religion of Yahweh in their day was little different in practice from that of the old Canaanite gods. They fought to make Yahweh the only God in Israel, but they did not question the existence of other gods in other nations, nor do they seem to have realised that what went on in the temples and shrines of Israel would have made Moses turn in his grave.

It was not until a hundred years later, in the middle of the eighth century BC, that the first of the great prophets, Amos, heralded a breakthrough in the understanding of the nature of God and the kind of service he demands. It was due to Amos and the other major spokesmen of Yahweh who followed him that the faith and moral standards which Moses had established in outline were fashioned into the imperishable legacy which the people of the Old Testament handed on to Christianity.

Again we must be careful not to claim too much. The great prophets were children of their time, as we all are, with limited insights and restricted knowledge. But we have in the Bible in their own words, collected by their disciples in the books that bear their names, a testimony to their profound assessment of the meaning and purpose of life and of the kind of God who controls the universe. Unlike their predecessors their outstanding contribution came from what they said rather than from what they did. They were no less courageous, no less ready to intervene in public affairs, no less men of action. But they are altogether more comprehensible. They are no longer rather bizarre figures from an unfamiliar ancient past, but men who grapple with problems that are as real today as they were then. Their background is certainly still that of the world as it was eight centuries before Christ, but their message has a relevance that is timeless.

When Amos came on the scene about 750 BC, the two little kingdoms of Israel and Judah were basking in a deceptive Indian summer of prosperity and peace. Israel was only thirty years from her downfall, but for the time being the great world powers were too busy trying to exterminate each other to bother about the small fry in the Levant. So Israel had taken the opportunity to extend her frontiers at the expense of her neighbours and was now sitting back to enjoy the reward of her efforts. Wealth was pouring into the country from the plunder of conquest. Trade and commerce were enjoying an illusory boom. The picture we get from Amos himself is one of unbridled luxury and extravagance. It looked as if the affluent society had come to stay.

It was not just the court, as in Solomon's day, that profited from the flow of easy money. A new class of merchant prince had arisen who had quickly learned to cultivate expensive tastes – costly palaces, rich furnishings, lavish tables, rare delicacies, choice vintages, gorgeous robes, expensive jewellery. Here is Amos' caustic description:

> You who lie on beds of ivory,
> And sprawl upon your couches,
> Eating choice lambs and farm-fed veal.
> Who croon to the music of the harp,
> And compose melodies as though you were David himself!
> You who drink wine by the bowl-full,
> And anoint yourselves with the finest oils.
>
> *Amos 6: 4–6*

But it was no affluent society for the great mass of the people. Little or nothing of Israel's prosperity came their way. Poverty and starvation sat at the palace gates. Peasant farmers found themselves evicted by absentee landlords or condemned to work as slaves on their own farms to pay their debts. This concentration of all the wealth in the hands of a few men was bad enough but in addition the merchants cheated and judges could be bribed; dishonesty and perjury walked hand in hand with squalor. Amos in biting words condemns the acquisitive society that Israel had become:

> Listen to this, you who trample upon the needy,
> And grind the faces of the poor!
> You who say, When will [the festival of] the new moon
>   be past,

So that we may sell our grain?
When will the sabbath be over,
So that we may offer our corn for sale?
While you make your measure short
And your prices high,
And cheat with biased scales.
And all to possess the poor for silver,
And the needy for the price of a pair of shoes,
Selling for grain the sweepings from your floor.

For I know how wilful are your crimes,
And how determined are your sins –
You browbeat honest men, you take bribes,
And ignore the poor man's claim for justice.
Therefore a wise man keeps his mouth shut,
For the days are full of menace.

Amos 8: 4–6; 5: 12–13

On the other hand the state religion was, like the national economy, on the crest of the wave. Places of worship were crowded out. The holy festivals were observed with enthusiasm. People were falling over each other to demonstrate their zeal for God. Tithes were paid punctiliously and free will offerings were made with a maximum of publicity. No one seemed to be asking what all this religiosity added up to or what kind of God was being honoured. Still less did they seem to worry that the austere God of the Ten Commandments, whose servants they were supposed to be, might not approve of the pagan practices which they had incorporated into the state religion of Yahweh – where lust, dishonesty, and drunkenness flourished under the very roof of the house of God:

Father and son use the same temple-girl,
And so defile my holy name.
Beside every altar they lounge on garments which
    they took in pledge,
And in the houses of their gods they drink away
    the money they imposed in fines.

Amos 2: 7–8

This was the situation – social inequality, flagrant injustice and corruption of religion – which Amos denounced. He was a blunt shepherd from the hills who disclaimed any connection with the well-paid official prophets of the state religion. But what he had seen in the market towns and at the annual fairs cried out for protest from a man who still believed in the God of Moses. Amos made no secret of his passionate hatred of this travesty of what was expected from the people whom Yahweh had chosen.

He proclaimed his protest in season and out of season, in the market place and in the temple, unsparingly, without mincing his words. He lashed with his tongue the nations that surrounded Israel for their crimes of inhumanity, but even more he accused Israel itself of its failure to be the People of God. Because they had been set apart at the Exodus, and marvellously guided throughout their long story, this did not mean that they could do as they liked and trust in Yahweh to protect them. Their responsibility was greater, not less, and they would feel the weight of God's judgement and punishment like all the rest.

They need not rely on their religiosity to save them. This was not the kind of service God demanded. Amos pronounced God's verdict on the religion of his time:

> I loathe and despise your festivals;
> Your meetings for sacrifice give me no pleasure.
> You may bring me your burnt-offerings, your meal-offerings,
> Or your thank-offerings of fat cattle,
> And I shall not so much as look at them.
> Let me have no more of your noisy hymns;
> My ears are closed to the music of your harps.
> Instead, let justice roll on like a mighty river,
> And integrity flow like a never-failing stream!

Amos 5: 21–24

Justice in the community, integrity in the individual, sincerity in religion – these according to Amos were the marks of the People of God. Responsibility not privilege was the meaning of Israel's calling. Amos' powerful message was too unpalatable for the authorities and he was banished to his farm

in the hills. The disaster that he predicted and which he saw as the judgement of God on a corrupt society came thirty years later when Israel's leaders were taken into captivity by the Assyrians and the country was laid waste.

17. Hosea and his Unfaithful Wife

AMOS had been the first of the great prophets of Israel to spell out the basic truth which the Old Testament as a whole stands for, that religion and morality, faith and conduct, belief and practice are two sides of the same coin. He had been a harsh critic of his times. He had seen the failure of Israel to live up to the high standards which were required of the People of God and he had, with perfect logic, drawn the obvious conclusion. Israel was doomed; God had no further use for her. In terms of practical politics this meant her extinction as a nation.

The next in the sequence of spokesmen of God who moulded Israel's understanding of her vocation in the world was Hosea. He flourished about twenty years later than Amos, only ten years or so before Israel's downfall. What had been clear to Amos, namely that Israel's days were numbered, had now become apparent to politicians and people as well, as the Assyrians swept one little state after another off the map. Hosea was no less trenchant than Amos in his denunciation of the society of his day, of the failure of kings, priests and people.

Yet Hosea had a deeper understanding of God and of human failings than Amos had. Hosea also saw disaster ahead and, like Amos, looked on it as the just punishment that Israel deserved. But, unlike Amos, he did not believe that God would finally write off what had been for him a costly experiment. He had chosen Israel and from her infancy had been trying to teach her, despite her failures, what it meant to be the People of God. Could he now, as Amos seemed to think, turn his back upon the child of his choice because she had become wayward and wilful? Was there no future for the bride to whom Yahweh had plighted his troth in the long-distant days of Moses and the Covenant?

It is in poetic imagery of this kind that Hosea conceived the relationship between God and his people. But undoubtedly the conclusion he reached, that Yahweh had still a purpose for his people and that, after a time of discipline, there would still be an Israel, a People of God, to stand for truth in the world at large, was founded upon his own experience and upon what he had learned from it. Hosea's contribution to our understanding of God springs from the tragedy of his own unhappy marriage.

The contents of the book that bears his name are very disjointed. We are not told anything about Hosea's background, what sort of a family he came from, or what he did for a living. But so far as we can make out, as a young man he had married Gomer, the girl of his choice, and to begin with their marriage had been a happy one. There was nothing to suggest the tragedy that lay ahead. Their first child, a boy, was born into a home where husband and wife found in each other the perfect kind of love and companionship that marriage was meant to provide. Then something went wrong. Gomer began to tire of her husband. We are not told why, so we can only guess.

Hosea clearly loved his wife but perhaps not in the way she wanted. Perhaps life with an earnest and serious-minded young prophet was a bit of a strain for a light-hearted, lively young girl. So Gomer had an affair with another man and had a child by him – this time a daughter. How much Hosea knew about the affair we do not know, but he certainly knew that the child was not his. In those days adultery was a capital offence. According to the law the penalty was death for both parties.

But whatever Hosea thought about the law or his wife's lover, the one thing he knew was that he still loved his wife. We can if we like fill in the picture – the shock of discovery, Hosea's anger, Gomer's tears. It cannot have been any different in ancient Israel from today when a husband or a wife feels

betrayed and humiliated. Whatever went on inside the home, the world outside knew nothing of it. Whatever stormy scenes there may have been, Hosea's love for Gomer won the day. He acknowledged the child as his own and set out to rebuild the broken home.

For a time all went well. Gomer knew that she had wronged her husband and that he had forgiven her simply because he loved her. This would have been enough for most women but it was not enough for Gomer. Psychologists would no doubt suggest a reason, but the Bible as usual does not go into detailed explanations. It simply says that she had another affair with someone else and became pregnant once more. This was the last straw as far as Hosea was concerned and he threw her out. Gomer drifted from bad to worse and became a common prostitute. Hosea nursed his grief in an empty home.

But however much he plunged himself into his public work and busied himself with the great issues of his day, there was always an ache in his heart. He could not forget the girl with whom he had found such happiness in the early years of his marriage. She had let him down and treated him disgracefully, yet to his own astonishment he found he still loved her and wanted her back.

So he sought her out and at last found her, a piece of human wreckage, up for auction in a slave market. What he had to pay for her was not a vast amount but it was a lot to him. He took her back to his home and began the weary slow process of recovering the happiness they had lost. But it took a long time. Old habits die hard and for a while Hosea kept his wife not only under his eye but under his thumb. Yet what brought Gomer back to being the woman she once had been was not so much her husband's severity as his love and forgiveness, and the end of the story is once again a happy home and a husband and wife reconciled and facing life together in a true partnership of affection and trust.

But of course the Bible would not be the Bible if that was all there was to it. Remember that Hosea was a prophet of Israel. Like the other great figures of the Old Testament Hosea saw God's hand in everything and heard God speaking to him in the affairs of every day. He knew of course from his boyhood that the God he had been taught to believe in was a God who hates sin but has mercy on even persistent sinners. He knew that sin brings its own punishment but that the greatest truth about God is his care and concern for men and women.

But somehow his own experience made this all come to life in a new way. He remembered that no matter how his wife had wronged him he had never ceased to love her. And if he, a mere man, could feel this ache in his heart for the wife who had deserted him, how much more must this be true of God? And so Hosea, as we can see from his book, has a depth of understanding of God's love and compassion for the wayward and the wandering which brings him very close to the mind of Jesus. He does not gloss over sin any more than Jesus did, or pretend that it does not matter, but his own suffering had taught him that the ultimate truth about life is the infinite patience and infinite love of God.

18. Isaiah of Jerusalem: Confidant of Kings

NONE of the books of the prophets makes for easy reading. Apart from the fact that these great moulders of Israel's faith were so deeply involved in the politics of their day, with which we are quite unfamiliar but which play a large part in their message, what they had to say about the affairs of their time generally took the form of short oracles, poetic in character, delivered on a particular occasion and subsequently collected into book form by their disciples. Thus a single chapter in one of the prophetic books might consist of a variety of these short utterances, spoken at different times and with no obvious connection or continuity.

But, to add to the difficulty, a single book of prophecy may well contain not only the words of the prophet himself but also prophecies spoken by his followers. A prophet's disciples regarded themselves as echoing their master's thoughts, and therefore their contributions could properly be included under his name. The supreme example of this is the book of Isaiah, which contains not only oracles spoken by Isaiah himself but even more which come from members of his school. In the case of this particular book the collection covers a period of three hundred years and includes prophecies which relate to vastly different situations.

As sometimes happens, the work of one of the apprentices turns out to be more impressive than that of the master himself, although it appears in the Bible under the master's name. For convenience, therefore, we may single out two 'Isaiahs' who made a distinctive contribution to Israel's thought and therefore eventually to Christianity. The first, with whom we are concerned here, was the original Isaiah, founder of the school, whom we may call 'Isaiah of Jerusalem'. The name of the second, perhaps the greatest of the Old Testament prophets, is unknown, but his teaching is included under Isaiah's name and it is simplest therefore to call him 'Isaiah of Babylon', which is where he flourished about two centuries after 'Isaiah of Jerusalem'. We shall return to him later.

The last two prophets we looked at, Amos and Hosea, were men of the people. Isaiah of Jerusalem was of aristocratic birth. He lived about the same time as Amos and Hosea, in the second half of the eighth century BC, but while they were concerned with what was happening in the northern kingdom, Israel, Isaiah was involved in the affairs of the smaller southern kingdom of Judah. In his lifetime he saw the end of the northern kingdom, and the threat from the dreaded Assyrian war-machine hanging over his own country.

Like Abraham, Moses and, later, Jeremiah, Isaiah had a distinctive religious experience in which he recognised that he was being called by God and given a particular assignment. He himself describes what happened on this occasion. He was in the Temple at Jerusalem when he had a sudden vision of God enthroned in majesty and surrounded by angelic figures who proclaimed his glory. This ecstatic glimpse of the sovereignty of God over his whole creation, and of his utter holiness, left its mark on Isaiah's subsequent preaching, but the essence of his vision was not so much a sense of the otherness and remoteness of the divine Being, as of his direct concern that the lives of men should reflect the holiness of their Creator. Isaiah was overwhelmed by the contrast between the God who had revealed himself to him and the pitiful inadequacy of his own life and that of his countrymen.

In contrition and penitence he acknowledges his own failure and that of the whole People of Yahweh, and by a symbolic act one of the winged seraphs in his vision assures him of forgiveness. Isaiah hears the voice of God saying: 'Whom shall I send? Who will be our messenger?', and he makes the simple answer: 'Here I am, send me.' It was this dramatic act of consecration and self-dedication that launched Isaiah on his career as a prophet and determined the content of his message.

For forty years he was in the thick of public affairs, advising a succession of kings and statesmen who in this period sought to come to terms with the Assyrian menace. But behind the practical shrewdness of Isaiah's advice on foreign policy was his deep appreciation of the moral issues that were at stake. Like Amos and Hosea, he denounced the evils of a society that claimed to be the People of Yahweh but behaved like pagans. He pictures Yahweh as the farmer who plants a vineyard, tends it, guards it, and gives it all his care, only to find that instead of producing grapes it produces sour berries.

Oppression of the poor by the rich, drunkenness and luxurious living, bribery and greed, these are the characteristics of Isaiah's Judah as they had been of Amos' Israel. Superstitious belief in the value of religious ceremonial for its own sake, the endless offering of sacrificial animals in the Temple, festivals, pilgrimages and meaningless prayers – all this Isaiah declares is sheer hypocrisy when it is not matched by right conduct. In the prophet's words Yahweh is saying to his people:

When you stretch out your hands
I turn my eyes away.
You may multiply your prayers,
I shall not listen.
Your hands are covered with blood,
wash, make yourselves clean.

Take your wrong-doing out of my sight.
Cease to do evil.
Learn to do good,
search for justice,
help the oppressed,
be just to the orphan,
plead for the widow.

Isaiah 1 : 15–17

Solemnly Isaiah warns his people that they will have to answer to God for the travesty of religion and morality of which they are guilty, and like all the prophets he sees God as executing his judgement through political and natural disasters. The ordinary man thought of Assyria as the incarnation of evil, the ultimate enemy of Yahweh, since it was a threat to the life of his people. Isaiah, on the contrary, declares that Assyria, for all its godlessness, is the means the Lord will use to discipline his disobedient children.

Yet Isaiah could not believe that God would utterly annihilate his people. Beyond the impending disaster he still saw grounds for hope. There would be a 'remnant' who would survive, a faithful minority who would carry on the name and the mission of the People of God. This was an important insight which in the long run proved to be true. When Judah and its capital, Jerusalem, were finally devastated, a 'remnant' was in fact preserved to maintain the faith and standards that had been revealed to Israel. Centuries later St Paul had no doubt that Isaiah's prophecy about the 'remnant' had been further fulfilled in the emergence of the Christian Church.

But perhaps Isaiah's greatest contribution lay in his intuitive perception that the providence of God would eventually overrule the follies of men. He had no particular reason to

be optimistic about the future, caught up as he was in the political intrigues of a tiny nation heading for collapse. Yet he believed in better things to come because he believed in the sovereignty of God and in the ultimate triumph of his purpose. Isaiah looked forward to a new Golden Age, with a new and greater David to bring it into being. He believed that one day, beyond all the changes and chances of history, 'the earth shall be full of the knowledge of the Lord as the waters cover the sea.' It was this kind of hope that encouraged subsequent generations to pin their hopes on God despite the disasters that beset them, and it was words like these which led the first Christians to believe that with the coming of Christ Isaiah's Golden Age was beginning to come true.

19. Jeremiah: The Reluctant Prophet

WE have moved on a hundred years. The little state of Judah is now within a few decades of the final catastrophe, the sack of her cities and the exile of her people. From their ancient capital, Jerusalem, her rulers looked out upon dramatic changes in the world-scene. The old scourge and terror of the small principalities of the Near East, Assyria, was to the vast relief of all of them herself within sight of her end. The prophet Nahum celebrated on everyone's behalf the fall of her capital, Nineveh, 'the city soaked in blood'. Another old enemy, Egypt, was riding for a fall. But all this brought little lasting comfort to the small states of the Levant. The new world power of Babylon was sweeping everything before it and the turn of Judah came in 587 BC when the redoubtable Nebuchadnezzar laid waste Jerusalem.

Jeremiah lived through all of this in his long ministry of forty years. He is perhaps the most tragic figure in the Old Testament. Michelangelo has immortalised him on the ceiling of the Sistine Chapel where he still sits, a sad-eyed craggy giant of a man, slumped forward with hand on chin, brooding over mysteries that are beyond human understanding. He saw his country hurtling to its doom, and while his heart bled for it and for his people, his conscience compelled him to maintain that this was the will of God. He was hated for his message, ill-treated and vilified, yet like all the prophets he felt compelled to speak the Word of God.

No man was ever more reluctant to occupy the role of prophet for which he had been cast. In his resistance to the summons which came to him as it had come to Moses and to Isaiah, he pleaded his youth and inexperience. He may have been no more than twenty at the time, a country lad from near Jerusalem who would probably have spent his days as a village priest. But the call from God was unmistakable and he had no choice but to obey. Shy and sensitive, distrustful of himself, a constant prey to the fear that he might be mistaken – all this, which is recorded in his own words, was the private agony of a man who in his public utterances spoke with a certainty and an assurance that deceived everyone but himself. The story of his heart-breaking assignment of preaching a message that he hated to deliver has left us a picture of a man 'cast in brass, dissolving in tears', and what he suffered for his loyalty to the God who had called him to be one of his prophets has justly earned him the title of Father of the Saints.

He was born in the reign of one of the worst kings that either Israel or Judah had ever known. As if the travesty of the worship of Yahweh that Amos and Isaiah had denounced as a mockery of the God of Moses was not enough, idolatry, astrology, black magic and human sacrifice had been intro-duced into the state religion. Soon after Jeremiah received his call to be a prophet, a drastic reformation under a new king swept away all overt traces of paganism and abolished all centres of worship except the Temple at Jerusalem. This was a heartening sign to Jeremiah – he had been too young to contribute towards it himself – that Yahweh was still at the centre of the nation's life. But he was soon disillusioned when he found that, although the ecclesiastical arrangements had

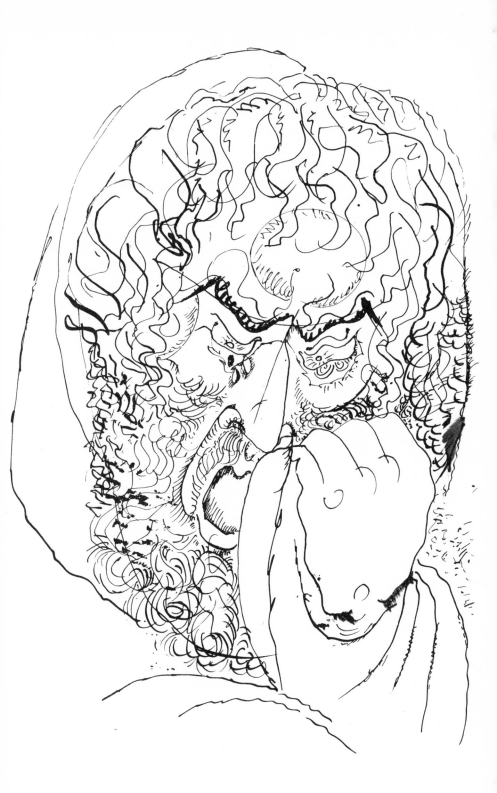

improved, there had been no real change in the lives of the people.

Perhaps it needed this experience to convince Jeremiah that the mark of a religious people is not any outward compliance with correct ceremonial or properly organised religious institutions but individual commitment to God. At all events this becomes the burden of his message. Convinced as he was that Israel had a unique role to play in the world, he maintained that the People of God could only persuade the world at large of the truth of their convictions and lead others to the knowledge of God, if they themselves showed by their lives that they were in the right relationship to God. It was not by claiming to be the descendants of Abraham, or by paying lip-service to the laws of Moses, or by any hallowed forms of worship, but by personal integrity and personal faith and trust in God that his people would be worthy ambassadors of the Lord they claimed to represent.

Jeremiah's understanding of the nature of God and of our proper response is expressed in a variety of ways but the essence of it is summed up in words such as these:

Thus says the Lord: 'Let not the wise man glory in his wisdom, let not the mighty man glory in his might, let not the rich man glory in his riches; but let him who glories glory in this, that he understands and knows me, that I am the Lord who practise steadfast love, justice and righteousness in the earth; for in these things I delight, says the Lord.'

Jeremiah 9: 23–24

We have seen how each of the great prophets adds some memorable insight to the composite picture of God which the people of the Old Testament bequeathed to Christianity. Thus through all the variety of his pronouncements on the state of society Amos had stressed as a dominant theme the justice of God, just as Hosea had emphasised God's mercy and Isaiah his holiness. Jeremiah has no new light to shed on the picture of God which his predecessors had handed on. But his whole life was an example of how a man behaves when that is the kind of God he believes in.

He did, however, make a striking contribution to Christianity in his idea of the New Covenant. The whole of the Old Testament faith and practice was based on the Covenant, the pledge of loyalty to Yahweh as God of Israel with all that that involved, which dated back to Moses and the Exodus. It was because she knew that she was a nation committed to certain beliefs and standards which affected the whole of life, that, despite the follies of kings and statesmen and the failure of the mass of the people to live up to these beliefs and standards, Israel throughout the centuries had never ceased to regard herself as a covenanted people.

But now Jeremiah saw that this was not enough. No nation, composed as all nations are of the virtues and vices of ordinary human nature, can establish a claim to be the People of God on the basis of a written constitution. In the case of Israel this was the Law of Moses – not simply the Ten Commandments, but the whole body of legislation that had grown out of them. Jeremiah maintained that only when every man accepted in his own heart the obligation to serve God and committed his life to that service, could there be in any real sense a People of God who would represent God in the world at large. This he could not see happening in his own day but he believed that, in the providence of God, the day would come when God would make a New Covenant with Israel, a new relationship no longer written on tablets of stone like the Law of Moses, but written on men's hearts.

When Jesus at the Last Supper took bread and wine in his hands as the symbol of his broken body and outpoured blood, he claimed that through him this New Covenant of which Jeremiah had spoken had now been made possible. Now at last men could be at one with God in a new personal relationship based on commitment to him as they had come to know him through Jesus. The first Christians believed that by the death of Christ the forgiveness of sins which Jeremiah had promised as part of this New Covenant had become a reality for all who accepted it in faith and penitence. The Church saw itself as the new Israel, the Israel of God, no longer a nation but a community of all who believed in all nations, and acknowledged its continuity with the people of the old Covenant by calling its sacred scriptures the New Covenant, which is the same word as Testament.

But, of course, it was not so much for saying things like these that Jeremiah suffered. Like the other prophets he maintained that God spoke through the everyday events that happen in society, through political changes, through the rise and fall of nations and empires. In his own day he claimed that God was speaking in no uncertain terms to Israel. They had been false to the covenant which he had made with them as a people, they had flouted his laws; they had put their trust in the wrong things: in their holy land, their holy city, the outward trappings of Temple ceremonial and correct ritual, instead of in personal devotion and moral obedience.

The People of God must learn to serve him without these artificial props to piety. This meant in practical terms that they must accept the devastation of their land, the loss of their holy city and the destruction of their Temple as the judgement of God. God was using the new world power of Babylon, evil though it was and answerable to God for its own crimes, to discipline his people. When Nebuchadnezzar made his first attack on Jerusalem in 598 BC and carried off the king and the leaders of the people into exile, Jeremiah declared this to be the beginning of the end and a foretaste of worse things to come.

He maintained that Babylon should not be resisted and that Israel should accept the total loss of her land and the exile of her people, for only in exile, far away from the temptation to worship their land, their holy city and its Temple instead of God, would they learn in reflection and penitence what the service of God really meant. They must suffer the loss of all they held dear in order to gain something far more precious; they must in effect pass through the valley of the shadow of death in order to reach their true life. Although Jeremiah maintained that, after their period of exile, they would return cleansed and renewed to rebuild their community life on more wholesome lines, this part of his message received less attention than his claim that the impending Babylonian invasion should be accepted as the will of God.

In the eyes of everyone but Jeremiah this was blasphemy, defeatism and treason. No patriotic Israelite could believe that this was what God was saying. Even Jeremiah, as we have seen, was himself often uncertain that this could possibly be part of the divine plan for Israel. Yet the inward voice that had always been stronger than his own doubts pressed him to proclaim his unpopular message. He was put in the stocks, flogged, imprisoned, thrown down a pit and left to die.

Rescued from the death-pit by a compassionate African, he lived through the devastation of his country. When all but the poorest who survived the sack of Jerusalem had been finally carried off in chains to Babylon, Jeremiah chose to remain among the wreckage rather than live in comfort under the protection of the Babylonians. But even the role of salvager of what was left was denied him. He was carried off to Egypt by Jewish partisans who had murdered the regent the Babylonians had appointed over their new province of Judah and had then fled for fear of reprisals. When last we hear of him in Egypt he is still a lonely spokesman and defender of the God whose service had brought him so much unhappiness. Tradition says that the partisans stoned him to death.

20. 'By the Waters of Babylon'

THE fall of Jerusalem in 587 BC was a traumatic experience for the Jews. It must have seemed to many to mark the end of their story. The glorious prospects that had opened up under David and Solomon of the country expanding in power and importance and indeed becoming as significant as any of the great nations of the world were not to be fulfilled. First the kingdom had split in two, then the northern part of the country had been devastated by the Assyrians, its citizens carried off to exile and for all practical purposes lost for ever. So long as the south had remained more or less intact with its ancient capital at Jerusalem, there was still a link with the past and hope for the future. But now that had gone.

It must also have seemed to make nonsense of all that the Jews had been told of their unique vocation as the People of Yahweh. What had become of the faith of Abraham that Canaan was their promised land, of the confidence of Moses that Israel was not destined to perish in Egypt but that the Exodus was part of the divine plan that Israel should be preserved to witness to Yahweh in the world? Had Yahweh failed at last, vanquished by the more powerful gods of Babylon who had made their people everywhere victorious?

Many Jews came to this conclusion as they found themselves stateless exiles in a foreign land. Yahweh had either deserted them or proved himself useless. They discovered that the Babylonians were humane in their treatment of racial minorities in their empire. Life was on the whole tolerable, Babylon was civilised and wealthy, prospects were opening up for trading with their new masters and of being well rewarded for their skill. Let the past look after itself! Forget Jerusalem! Forget Yahweh!

But there were some exiles who could forget neither Yahweh nor Jerusalem. One of them put their feelings into words:

> By the waters of Babylon,
>   there we sat down and wept,
>   when we remembered Zion.
> On the willows there
>   we hung up our lyres.
> For there our captors
>   required of us songs,
> and our tormentors, mirth, saying,
>   'Sing us one of the songs of Zion!'
>
> How shall we sing the Lord's song
>   in a foreign land?
> If I forget you, O Jerusalem,
>   let my right hand wither!
> Let my tongue cleave to the roof of my mouth,
>   if I do not remember you,
> if I do not set Jerusalem
>   above my highest joy!
>
>   *Psalm 137 : 1–6*

This was not nostalgia or impotent patriotism. It was the cry of men, perhaps not many, who knew in their hearts that Abraham, Moses, Hosea and Isaiah had not been wrong. Yahweh was still their God and his purpose would not be defeated. Babylon, for all its wealth and beauty, was a land of pagans. Israel, despite her collapse, had been entrusted with a faith and a moral code which were infinitely superior to the beliefs and practices of her conquerors. Had not Isaiah foreseen that, despite the disaster to Jerusalem, there would be a 'remnant' who would keep the faith of Yahweh alive; and what above all had Jeremiah said?

It was now that the message of this lonely and much abused spokesman of God began to make sense. Most of what Jeremiah had predicted had in fact come true. He had been right about the impending catastrophe; might he not also have been right about why it had happened? His claim had been that it was not Yahweh who had failed but Israel, and that this time of exile was an opportunity for rethinking and renewal. He had maintained that Israel had herself to blame for the decline and fall of her country. She needed to go down into the depths of despair in order to find her soul, she must renew her life through penitence and suffering. The exile in Babylon was no accident, but an opportunity to learn from past mistakes. If the exiles could only see their plight as a necessary discipline imposed by God for their own good, they would find that God would open up a way for their return to the homeland where they could rebuild their community life on better foundations.

But now among the exiles themselves two great prophetic voices were raised in support of what Jeremiah had said. These were Ezekiel and the anonymous disciple of Isaiah whose words are found included in the book that bears his master's name and who for convenience may be called Isaiah of Babylon. It is not too much to say that under God these three men, Jeremiah, Ezekiel and Isaiah of Babylon, changed the history of the world. It was because these three great spokesmen of Yahweh succeeded in persuading a sufficient number of exiles that Israel had a future, that, when the opportunity arose, enough Jews returned to Palestine to rebuild their city and their community, out of which five centuries later were to come Christ and his Church.

The uniqueness of Israel's role and the providential ordering of her affairs is at no point in her history more clearly seen than now. Historically speaking there was no reason why the exiles in Babylon from the southern kingdom should have followed a different course from the exiles of the northern kingdom who simply dissolved their identity among the mixed races of Assyria. That this did not happen can only have been because in the divine plan the People of God were destined to be preserved in order that out of Israel should emerge in the fullness of time what St Paul called the Israel of God, the Christian Church. Jeremiah, Ezekiel and Isaiah of Babylon were the three men whom God, at this critical stage in Israel's story, chose to lead the way.

With the best will in the world, it is difficult for us today to be attracted by Ezekiel as a man. Perhaps he suffers from being sandwiched in history between Jeremiah and Isaiah of Babylon – Jeremiah whose warm-hearted sympathy shines through his sombre predictions, and whose courageous stand for the truth against all opposition has been described so movingly by his devoted friend and disciple Baruch; and Isaiah of Babylon whose sublime insight into the compassion and tenderness of God brings him very close to the mind of Jesus. It is noticeable that both these men had a profound influence both on Jesus and the early Church, as we can see from the record of the New Testament.

Ezekiel, on the other hand, belongs almost exclusively to the world of the Old Testament. Yet the Old Testament is part of the Christian story and there is no question but that in his day Ezekiel made a major contribution, and that it was he more than the other two who shaped the religious life of Israel between the Exile and the coming of Christ. He was a priest, who must have been sufficiently influential to be included among the first batch of Jews who were banished to exile in 598 BC. Five years later, in the Jewish settlement in Babylon to which he had been deported, he had an overwhelming vision of the Lord God enthroned in majesty, which

convinced him that Yahweh was still in the midst of his people and that he himself was being summoned to be one of his prophets.

From then until the fall of Jerusalem he poured out his soul in condemnation of the People of God for their failure to be worthy of that name and inexorably proclaimed the impending disaster as the just judgement of God. Not only in words but in actions of a most bizarre kind he pressed his message home. He was undoubtedly abnormal, on the border-line between genius and madness. His visions have a night-marish quality. Yet behind all this is the intense conviction that there is meaning and purpose in all that is happening. God speaks through catastrophe as much as through pros-perity.

Accordingly, when he heard that Jerusalem had fallen, Ezekiel struck a new note. His message was now one of hope and encouragement. Yahweh had not deserted his people. He still had a mission for them in the world. If in exile they would learn the lesson that they were being taught, accept this disaster as a call to new endeavour, turn their backs upon the follies that had brought this havoc upon them, reset their compass and plan their programme on different lines from the past, they would find themselves in God's good time back in their homeland with a more glorious prospect stretching before them than they had ever known in what they thought of as their more spacious days.

Ezekiel's vision of the Valley of Dry Bones is justly mem-orable. He saw a valley littered with dry bones. This was Israel scattered in exile and spiritually dead. Then at the Lord's command the dry bones sprang together, took on flesh and received the breath of life. This was Israel renewed, alive and alert, ready to build the new Jerusalem and fulfil her historic mission. The centre of the new community would be the Temple, and Ezekiel saw every detail of its fabric in his mind's eye. Israel would be a holy people, the Lord would dwell in her midst, Jerusalem would be at last truly the city of God.

Ezekiel was outstanding as prophet, priest, theologian and

as a moulder of history. As prophet he insisted, like all the prophets, that we live in a world which is governed by moral law. The difference between right and wrong is a real one and we disregard it at our peril. If we choose to flout the will of God we pay the price, as individuals or as societies. Every man lives his life under the judgement of God. But, unlike some other prophets, Ezekiel, as a priest, saw that life under God did not merely mean 'doing good'. It also meant being aware of the presence of God, and so he stressed the value of public worship and an ordered liturgy, of going to particular places at particular times where we are confronted by God through eye and ear and heart and mind.

As a theologian, Ezekiel's influence on the thought of subsequent generations was far-reaching indeed. We shall see how many of his ideas were perverted in ways which he never intended by lesser men who lacked his genius. We cannot but be challenged, however, by this strange man's sense of the complete transcendence and sovereignty of God. For him God was no comfortable father-figure, but the awe-inspiring Lord of the universe, unfathomable and shrouded in mystery. This is certainly part of the truth about God, and Ezekiel does not allow us to forget it.

The Exile lasted about fifty years, longer than many had hoped but not as long as Jeremiah had warned them to expect. It came to an end when Babylon met the fate of Assyria and was herself ousted from world supremacy by the new power of Persia under her dynamic ruler Cyrus. The Persians swept westwards, Babylon capitulated, and the Jews in exile had a new master. One of the first acts of this wise statesman, Cyrus, was to give the various racial minorities in his new empire the opportunity to return to their homelands. No doubt for him it meant the elimination of possible troublemakers. For one Jew at least it was again the hand of God.

As Cyrus drove onwards in his meteoric advance towards Babylon, an anonymous disciple of the school of Isaiah boldly affirmed that the day of liberation was at hand. Cyrus was but a tool in the hands of Yahweh, who had now determined that his people had been disciplined enough, and who was using

the Persian's victories to open the way for their return to the
holy land. The sublime effrontery of this unknown and insignificant exile under a foreign yoke, as he dismisses the
conquest of the world as almost irrelevant, and sees the
formidable conqueror as a mere instrument of Yahweh (of
whom Cyrus had doubtless never heard), could only have come
from a prophet of Israel.

It was, however, a much needed message that Isaiah of
Babylon delivered. His words suggest that, although many
Hebrews were weary of captivity, many others had no great
desire to leave Babylon. Isaiah tried to whip up their enthusiasm
by telling them that a new and greater Exodus lay ahead.
Cyrus would take Babylon, its mythical gods would be power-
less to stop him, for the irresistible strength of Yahweh was
behind him. The captives would be set free; a miraculous
highway would open up for them across the desert; they would
return with joy and gladness to the holy city with Yahweh at
their head; Jerusalem would be too small to hold her children
of whom she had so long been bereft.

It is possible that there was a resistance movement among
the Jews in Babylon, to which Isaiah belonged, and which
had some contact with Cyrus in his advance and some knowledge of his intention to liberate the racial minorities in his new
empire after the inevitable collapse of Babylon. This might
account for Isaiah's confidence in asserting that the day of
freedom was close at hand, but it would not account for the
magnificent flight of the prophet's imagination as he clothed
the whole idea of the return to Jerusalem in such splendid
imagery. The very fact that Jerusalem was again to be the
home of the People of God was to the prophet such a miracle
of God's forgiving mercy that Isaiah could not speak of it in
anything but miraculous terms.

In the course of his moving call to his countrymen to be
worthy of this great moment in their history, Isaiah reached
a conception of God which is the loftiest and most perceptive
in the whole of the Old Testament. He saw God as Creator and
sustainer of the universe, as Lord of all history, ruler of kings
and nations, yet as a God who cares for all his children as

tenderly as a shepherd gathers his lambs in his arms and gently leads the mother ewes. To those who thought that God had forgotten them, Isaiah declared:

> Have you not known? Have you not heard?
> The Lord is the everlasting God,
>   the Creator of the ends of the earth.
> He does not faint or grow weary,
>   his understanding is unsearchable.
> He gives power to the faint,
>   and to him who has no might he increases strength.
> Even youths shall faint and be weary,
>   and young men shall fall exhausted;
> but they who wait for the Lord shall renew their strength,
>   they shall mount up with wings like eagles,
> they shall run and not be weary,
>   they shall walk and not faint.
>
> *Isaiah 40 : 28–31*

For Isaiah there was only one God, Yahweh, who had called Israel to be the means of light and life for all nations. His purpose was nothing less than that this tiny people, through no merit of their own, should be his instrument for the salvation of the world. We have come a long way indeed from earlier days when Yahweh was the warrior god of Israel, fighting her battles for her, showing himself from time to time to be more powerful than the gods of other nations, unpredictable in his actions, capricious in his moods, but solidly committed to Israel's material advancement. Yet Isaiah's picture of God, a distillation of the insights of many prophets who had seen one or other of the aspects of the truth about God which he so marvellously unites, is merely the climax of the unique understanding of God which had been progressively given to the people of the Old Testament through their prophets beginning with Moses.

In terms of practical results, Isaiah's mission must be counted a failure. When Cyrus issued his edict in 538 BC, allowing the Jews among others to return to their homes, there was no eager response on the part of the exiles, no massive, far less miraculous, march back to the holy land. The few who did go back at that point found when they reached Jerusalem that they were hard enough put to it to eke out a living among its ruins, without thinking of rebuilding the Temple, or the city, or of constructing a brilliant new way of life. Isaiah's message bore fruit in the end, but it took a century and a half and the energy and enthusiasm of many others besides himself before his vision of the new Jerusalem was realised, and when that happened its character had more of Ezekiel than Isaiah in it.

His legacy is much more to be seen in the imperishable quality of his thought which survived and surmounted the rather arid period that we have next to consider, and made a deep impression on the minds of the first Christians. This is particularly true of Isaiah's so-called Songs of the Servant of Yahweh. It has been thought by some that these songs were composed by the prophet in a spirit of disillusionment when his great hopes of a spectacular return to the homeland were unfulfilled and when Cyrus, instead of giving Yahweh credit for his victories, accepted the gods of Babylon.

The songs strike a note unique in the Old Testament. It seems most likely that what Isaiah had in mind was that Israel's future role in the world would have nothing to do with her own material advancement, but that it would be through humiliation, suffering and death that the People of God would yet bring the nations to the knowledge of the truth. He must have known that this programme would not attract his countrymen as a whole. Perhaps he hoped that some of them would see their vocation along these lines. In fact there is no indication that the generations that came after him paid the slightest attention.

But Jesus did, and who can say that Isaiah might not have had it in mind that when Messiah came, whoever he might be and whenever he might appear, this was the role that God had planned for him as representative of his people? At all events, as we shall see, it was as the Servant of God who through his suffering and death would bring men to God that Jesus conceived his own mission, and the early Church had no doubt that when this prophet of the Exile spoke words which

went unheeded for five hundred years he was pointing his
finger directly at Jesus:

'Who could believe what we have heard,
and to whom has the power of Yahweh been revealed?'
Like a sapling he grew up in front of us,
Like a root in arid ground.
Without beauty, without majesty (we saw him),
no looks to attract our eyes;
a thing despised and rejected by men,
a man of sorrows and familiar with suffering,
a man to make people screen their faces;
he was despised and we took no account of him.

And yet ours were the sufferings he bore,
ours the sorrows he carried.
But we, we thought of him as someone punished,
struck by God, and brought low.
Yet he was pierced through for our faults,
crushed for our sins.
On him lies a punishment that brings us peace,
and through his wounds we are healed.

We had all gone astray like sheep,
each taking his own way,
and Yahweh burdened him
with the sins of all of us.
Harshly dealt with, he bore it humbly,
he never opened his mouth,
like a lamb that is led to the slaughter-house,
like a sheep that is dumb before its shearers
never opening its mouth.

By force and by law he was taken;
would anyone plead his cause?
Yes, he was torn away from the land of the living;
for our faults struck down in death.
They gave him a grave with the wicked,
a tomb with the rich,
though he had done no wrong
and there had been no perjury in his mouth.

Yahweh has been pleased to crush him with suffering.
If he offers his life in atonement

he shall see his heirs, he shall have a long life
and through him what Yahweh wishes will be done.

His soul's anguish over
he shall see the light and be content.
By his sufferings shall my servant justify many,
taking their faults on himself.

Hence I will grant whole hordes for his tribute,
he shall divide the spoil with the mighty,
for surrendering himself to death
and letting himself be taken for a sinner,
while he was bearing the faults of many
and praying all the time for sinners.

Isaiah 53: 1–12

21. Jerusalem after the Exile

RACIAL minorities in a foreign land have always tended to
stick together and maintain their customs and traditions,
particularly if they are allowed or compelled to settle in specific
areas. Chinatown in San Francisco and the Warsaw Ghetto
are outstanding modern examples, and it was no different with
the Jews in Babylon. They had been permitted to settle in
communities and on the whole they were not interfered with.
This meant that they could to a large extent shape their own
way of life in their day-to-day activities and cultivate their own
religious beliefs and practices.

What happened during the Exile was the reverse of what
happened after the Exodus. On their arrival in Canaan the
Israelites had found themselves among a people with a recog-
nisably higher standard of living from which they had much
to learn. This included, as we saw, adopting the religion of
Canaan as well as its culture. Until the days of the great prophets,
there was little to distinguish the state religion of Yahweh from
the state religion of any other small nation in the Near East.
The process of assimilation had been almost complete, despite
the protests of early prophets such as Nathan and Elijah.

Now, however, the sustained witness of Amos, Hosea, Isaiah of Jerusalem and other prophets had left its mark. The Jews knew that the Babylonians had nothing to teach them as far as the arts and graces of civilisation were concerned. They remembered Solomon's Jerusalem. Babylon was certainly wealthier, but as archaeologists have discovered from clay tablets recording the transactions of a great Jewish banking and insurance concern Murashu and Sons, enterprising Hebrew exiles could divert some of the wealth into their own pockets. They were, however, profoundly conscious that in the field of religion and morality their own heritage was vastly superior to that of their masters.

They had lost their Temple, the centre of their religious life, but even in exile they could continue many of the practices which had religious significance for them. In this way some of the practices acquired a new importance; circumcision, for example, unknown among the Babylonians, and abstaining from certain types of food and observing the sabbath. These were the outward signs of a people who were inwardly committed to Yahweh and called to be a nation like no other nation. The synagogue where the laws of Yahweh were read and expounded now took the place of the Temple.

The intention was admirable. Jews must be seen to be different from other men, since they must demonstrate their unique vocation. In practice what tended to happen was that the outward observance, being easier, bulked more largely than the inward commitment. It became the mark of a 'good' man to observe the sabbath and ostentatiously to avoid pork. It was during the Exile that the seed was sown of that exclusive, intolerant, legalistic attitude of mind which flowered later into the Judaism which produced the Pharisees of the gospels. It was then that Israel, no longer a nation, began to think of herself as a Church, a community organised on a religious basis, dominated by the priesthood, regulated by the Law.

Since the days of Moses, the Law of Israel had grown as a result of individual decisions by kings and priests. In the best biblical tradition, whereby all the psalms are attributed to David although many of them date from after his time, all

the Law was attributed to Moses although much of it dates
from the Exile and later. When, with the edict of Cyrus in
538 BC, a start was made to return to the holy land, it was the
beginning of a process which ended with the rebuilding of
Jerusalem and the surrounding area into a tightly knit theocracy, governed by high priests, controlled by the Law,
hostile to any foreign influences, rigid, self-centred and, not
surprisingly, generally disliked.

It is a tragic commentary on human nature, but also an
essential part of the experience of Israel – and through her,
of the world at large – that, from the Exile onwards, having
turned their backs in penitence on the blatant sins of the past
which the prophets had rightly condemned, the People of
God should now substitute for the sins of the flesh the sins of
the spirit. The road to hell is indeed paved with good intentions.
Nothing could have been more laudable than this effort to
show the world what it meant to be a people committed to
God, nothing could be more unlovely than the result.

The pious author of the books of Chronicles, Ezra and
Nehemiah, writing two centuries after the events he describes,
sees through rose-tinted spectacles the return to Jerusalem after
the edict of Cyrus as the kind of triumphal procession that
Isaiah of Babylon had hoped for, culminating in an enthusiastic tackling of the rebuilding of the Temple. The contemporary evidence of the two short books of the prophets
Haggai and Zechariah gives a more sober account of what
actually happened. According to them those exiles who took
the opportunity of returning to their homeland were too busy
keeping themselves alive to worry about rebuilding the
Temple.

It was not until 520 BC, seventeen years after the first batch
of exiles had reached Jerusalem, that a second batch, including
Haggai and Zechariah, who seem to have glimpsed something
of Isaiah's vision, returned to Palestine from Babylon, set to
work on the reconditioning of the Temple and completed its
reconstruction in four years. After that there was a lull, and
again contemporary evidence from the prophet Malachi and
another anonymous disciple of the school of Isaiah, whose

words are included in the final chapters of the book that bears
his name, suggests that once more through lack of leadership,
there was apathy and drift. In 445 BC the leader appeared.

This was Nehemiah. He was descended from an exiled
Jewish family, had made good in the service of the king of
Persia, but had never forgotten the land of his fathers. It
irked him that the ancient capital Jerusalem should still be in
a ruinous state and subjected to attack from her old enemies
who surrounded her. With the king's permission and material
help he visited Jerusalem, which was now part of a Persian
satrapy, with a view to rebuilding the city walls. Uncertain
of the local reactions, he first inspected the state of the walls
under cover of darkness. But soon he rallied the people to the
task, arming the builders against opposition from jealous
neighbours who viewed any resurgence of Jewish nationalism
with suspicion. Thanks largely to Nehemiah's enthusiasm, the
walls were rebuilt.

But Nehemiah was building more than a wall of stone and
lime; he was fencing Israel in as a holy people, protecting her
from contamination by the outside world. He shared the view
that had developed through the Exile that the only way to
avoid the heathenism which had brought disaster upon the
old Jerusalem was to reconstruct the life of the new Jerusalem
as a people 'separated from all strangers'. This meant no
mixed marriages, an emphasis on racial purity, and meticulous
observance of Jewish religious practice.

This policy of segregation was carried a stage further by
the arrival in Jerusalem in 398 BC of Ezra, who was a priest
from Babylon, and whose main concern was that the Jews
should become visibly a holy people governed by the Mosaic
Law. He not only denounced marriage with non-Jews, but
insisted that all who had married Gentile wives must divorce
them, and disown their children. It was Hitler's Aryan Laws
in reverse. In a solemn ceremony Ezra read to the people 'the
book of the Law of Moses' and the whole community solemnly
pledged itself to observe it. Among its contents were the Ten
Commandments, and much that bore the imprint of the great
prophets' insistence that justice, mercy and humility were the

true marks of the People of God. But there was also the new emphasis, which had developed as a result of the Exile, on correct ceremonial, sabbath observance, racial purity and ritual obligations. And inevitably it was this emphasis that dominated the life of the Jerusalem community from then on.

Before we dismiss this development as a tragic blunder and a betrayal of the memory of the great prophets, it is well to remember that no other policy would have ensured the survival of the prophetic witness. Between the time of Nehemiah and Ezra and the birth of Christianity, cross-currents of pagan thought and practice swept through every corner of the Near East except Jerusalem. There, within the hard shell of institutional religion based on the Mosaic Law, the warm humanity of the prophets lay embedded until Jesus made it live again. If much of the Law was nonsense, it was at least moral nonsense. However trivial some of the details of Jewish ceremonial and ritual practice in this period may have been, the same Law of Moses still enjoined each Jew to love God with heart and mind and soul and strength and to love his neighbour as himself. It needed Jesus, however, to sort out the priorities.

22. Ruth and Naomi

THE narrowly nationalist policy of Ezra and Nehemiah did not pass unchallenged. There were still men in Israel who saw that racial and religious apartheid had no place in the purpose of God for the world. However necessary it may have been for the Jewish community after the Exile to fence itself in with restrictive practices, it needed those raised voices to remind it of the dangers of exclusiveness and intolerance. Such were the unknown authors of the two short books of Ruth and Jonah, who in effect build a bridge from the great prophets, especially Isaiah of Babylon, over the forbidding barricades of the intervening centuries, to the broad horizons of Jesus and the early Christians.

The book of Ruth is a splendid short story with a message of compassion and charity far removed from the orthodox policy which prevailed when it was written. Like the book of Jonah, its aim is to underline the claim which had been made by the greatest of the prophets that God cares for all his children, whether Jews or Gentiles, and that to exclude the majority of mankind by some national or religious yardstick is a travesty of the will of the Creator who loves the world that he has made and everybody who lives in it.

The story tells of a man of Bethlehem in the days before Israel was a kingdom. During a time of famine he fled with his wife and two sons to the land of Moab which, though not far away, nevertheless seemed to narrow Jews like Ezra a heathenish country and the home of a defiled race. In Moab the man and his family found food and work and decided to stay. When his sons grew up they married Moabite women, again a thing that would stink in the nostrils of the apostles of racial purity. Then by a series of accidents the father and both sons died and the Jewess Naomi was left with her two Moabite daughters-in-law, Ruth and Orpah.

Naomi had nothing to keep her in Moab. She longed for the homeland and for her own kith and kin. But by the same token her daughters-in-law were at home in Moab. In Judah they would be strangers. So she besought them to allow her to return alone and advised them to marry again among their own people. They accompanied her so far on her way and then with much emotion she bade them farewell. Orpah wept bitterly and turned to go back but Ruth clung to Naomi and swore that she would never leave her:

> Whither thou goest, I will go;
>   and where thou lodgest I will lodge:
> Thy people shall be my people,
>   and thy God, my God:
> Where thou diest, will I die,
>   and there will I be buried:
> The Lord do so to me, and more also,
>   if aught but death part thee and me.
>
> *Ruth 1: 16–17*

With these moving words Ruth pledged herself to share Naomi's life, her faith and her home, and the older woman knew that she could not dissuade her. So Naomi the Jewess and Ruth the Moabitess came to Bethlehem at the beginning of the barley harvest. They had little enough between them, and Ruth went out to the fields to glean what the humane law of Israel demanded should be left by the reapers for the benefit of widows and folk in need. With some justice Keats could speak of the 'sad heart of Ruth when, sick for home, she stood in tears amid the alien corn'.

By chance it happened that she landed in a field belonging to a wealthy farmer, a relative of Naomi's late husband. This kindly man, Boaz, saw the stranger and having found out who she was made her welcome, not only inviting her to continue gleaning on his land but privately whispering to the reapers to leave some handfuls of corn specially for her, as if by accident. When she got home and told her mother-in-law where she had been and how well she had been treated, the old lady at once scented a romance and started to plot accordingly.

Here was poor Ruth, a penniless young widow. There was Boaz, a wealthy middle-aged bachelor, not only obviously needing a wife but also almost one of the family already. But how could the unforthcoming Boaz be persuaded to ask Ruth to marry him? Naomi's plan was original, and was certainly not suggested by *Aunt Kate's Book of Etiquette*. When the harvest was over and the threshing had started, Ruth was to go down to the threshing floor, an open courtyard, and more or less ask Boaz herself. Naomi knew the law of the land and was anxious to keep in the family what little property Ruth's late husband had owned. If it was not taken over by a near kinsman it would go to strangers. But if Boaz could be persuaded to take Ruth he might take the land too.

So according to plan Ruth waited until nightfall and when Boaz had rolled himself in his cloak for the night she slipped along and lay down at his feet. When he awoke during the night and found her there she asked to be taken under his cloak, in other words asked him to marry her. Boaz was secretly flattered that she preferred him to younger and more dashing swains, but he told her to lie still till morning because there was a nearer kinsman than he who must be given first chance.

Next morning he put the proposition to the relative, who turned it down. This man was quite willing to take the land, and probably Ruth, until he realised that the old Jewish law of inheritance was going to complicate his own family affairs. The upshot was as Naomi had hoped and planned. Boaz married Ruth and they both lived happily ever after. So far so good. It is a pleasant little story, but where is its point?

Well, the sting, if such a praiseworthy motive may be called a sting, was in the tail. In a dozen words this admirably subtle propagandist set by the heels all the disciples of Ezra and Nehemiah with their theory of blood and soil. The oldest son of Ruth and Boaz, he added quietly, was called Obed, and Obed was the father of Jesse, and Jesse was the father of David. Which reminds us, he is implying, that our great king David, the noblest and most glorious monarch in our history, was the grandson of a man whose mother was a Gentile. In modern terms, it is as if Pastor Niemoeller had discovered that Frederick the Great had had a Jewish grandmother.

The law of Israel was plain. No descendant of a Moabite might enter the congregation of the Lord even to the tenth generation, and the rigid fanaticism of men like Ezra was prepared to enforce it. So with gentle irony the author of this little broadsheet posed the dilemma. Either the blessed David and his magnificent son Solomon had no right to the throne of Israel or else this narrow nationalism must be scrapped. Either David's honour must be tarnished, which was unthinkable, or there must be room for Gentiles as well as Jews among God's chosen people.

23. Jonah and the Whale

ABOUT the same time as the story of Ruth and Naomi was written in protest against racial intolerance, another skilful propagandist wrote a humorous little story with the same purpose. This was the tale of Jonah and the Whale, which has become famous for quite the wrong reasons. It is not so long ago that fundamentalists were prepared to argue that, if you did not believe that Jonah was swallowed by the whale as the Bible says, it meant that you did not really believe in God. One staunch defender of the verbal infallibility of the Bible went so far as to say that if the Bible said that the whale was swallowed by Jonah he would believe that too.

What nonsense people make of the Bible and of this story when they either solemnly claim that it is impossible for a man to emerge alive from a whale's inside after three days, or equally solemnly maintain that some whales have been found with gullets big enough for a man to slip in and pop out again. Perhaps what would have annoyed the author of the story most in all this dreary disputation would be that his joke had fallen flat. For the whole tale is full of fun and fantasy and the bit about the whale is only one of the places where the story-teller expected his audience to laugh.

But, of course, behind his fun the author is in deadly earnest. What he is really writing is a passionate plea for racial tolerance and compassion at a time when the official policy introduced by Ezra and furthered by his disciples was that anyone but a pure Jew was a second-class citizen in the sight of God. He tells this tale of a dour unlovable man in the hope that his countrymen will recognise it as a caricature of themselves. When he pillories Jonah he pillories the whole Jewish community in his day. All the characters are as fictitious as those in Jesus' parables of the Good Samaritan and the Prodigal Son. The author might have prevented his story from becoming the centre of much stupid controversy if he had made his hero anonymous, as Jesus did. People would not then have been tempted to regard this amusing tale as true in fact, though it is undoubtedly, like the parables of Jesus, true to life.

The story tells how a prophet called Jonah is commanded by Yahweh to go to Nineveh, the great Assyrian city which was one of the wonders of the ancient world, but whose name was for the Jews a symbol of all the worst vices of heathenism. When he gets there, he is to warn the Ninevites that Yahweh has heard about their goings-on and that their wickedness will not go unpunished unless they mend their ways. This was the last thing Jonah wanted to do. He hated foreigners and he was terribly afraid that if he did as he was told the Ninevites might repent and then soft-hearted Yahweh would certainly forgive them. So he decided to run away from Yahweh and boarded a ship which was going in the opposite direction from Nineveh. But the hound of heaven was on his trail. Yahweh sent a tempest that almost wrecked the ship. The pagan sailors threw out the cargo and prayed to all their gods to save them. In the midst of the turmoil, the boatswain found Jonah fast asleep in the hold. Angrily he roused him and ordered him to say his prayers like everyone else to whatever god he believed in, in the hope that one or other of the gods might come to their rescue. Meantime the sailors have reached the conclusion that there must be a hoodoo on board. They draw lots to find out who it is and Jonah is identified as the cause of their plight.

He tells his story and the superstitious pagans are horrified at the thought of this rash mortal defying his god's command. Jonah assures them that, unless they throw him overboard, the wrath of Yahweh will wreck the ship. This the decent sailors are unwilling to do except as a last resort. They row like mad but the storm grows worse. At last they have no choice but to throw Jonah over the side. At once the sea becomes calm, much to the sailors' wonder and dread at the power of Yahweh. But Jonah is not to escape Yahweh even by drowning. Yahweh has an enormous fish laid on for the occasion which swallows him and carries him in its belly to land. The journey lasts three days during which time Jonah sings a psalm, a surprisingly good composition for such an odd place. At the end of the three days the fish is told by Yahweh to vomit up Jonah on to the shore which it dutifully does. ('Beachcomber' caught the spirit of the story when he suggested that this was a case of small prophets and quick returns.)

Jonah can continue his battle with Yahweh no longer. He

gives up the unequal struggle and sets out for Nineveh in accordance with instructions. He reaches the vast city and it takes him three days to walk across it. It was clearly not called the Great City for nothing. He delivered his message and sure enough it happened just as he had feared. The people repented. From king to commoner, even to the beasts of the field, all Nineveh donned sackcloth and fasted as a token of penitence and to avert the wrath of Yahweh. Having noted this change of heart with approval, Yahweh relented and stayed his hand. Nineveh would be spared.

Jonah flew into a rage and took Yahweh to task. He told him he was far too soft-hearted. He had always known that he would give these unspeakable heathens a second chance. That was why he never wanted to go to Nineveh at all. He wished he were dead rather than live to see such folly. Yahweh's only answer was a little gentle banter: 'Are you very angry with me, Jonah?' Jonah goes off in the sulks, makes himself a little leafy shelter overlooking the city, and sits there hoping against hope that Yahweh will still change his mind and destroy the city as he had threatened.

As Jonah sits there brooding, Yahweh waves his magic wand again and up comes a great castor-oil plant which shades Jonah beautifully from the hot sun. Jonah is delighted. But next morning with another wave of his wand Yahweh sends a worm which eats the heart out of the plant so that it promptly withers, and he throws in for good measure a scorching heat which almost gives the poor man sunstroke. The loss of his shady bower is the last straw for Jonah and again he prays for death to put an end to his misery.

Yahweh now thinks Jonah is ready to learn his lesson. He asks him playfully: 'Are you sure you are right to be angry about the castor-oil plant, Jonah?' Jonah says: 'Certainly I have every right to be angry, every right to wish I were dead.' 'There,' says Yahweh, 'you are sorry about the loss of a castor-oil plant, which cost you nothing in time or effort. It sprang up in a night and died in a night and you have had nothing to do with it. Am I not to feel sorry for Nineveh, this great city which is full of my own blind and stupid children, to say nothing of all these poor animals?'

And there abruptly but perfectly the story ends. The bitter intolerant Jonah is Israel. As Jonah sulks in his bower waiting for God's judgement on the wicked heathens, so the narrow orthodoxy that dominated Jewish thought in the author's day shut itself up within the walls of Jerusalem, clutching its faith to its bosom and viewing the pagan world with cold disfavour. But the hated pagans are the only good people in the story, the kindly charitable sailors and the repentant people of Nineveh. The writer not only contrasts his own people unfavourably with the foreigners but shows them how, like Jonah, they are missing their opportunity. Their vocation and responsibility as the People of God was to bring light into pagan darkness, to tell the nations of the love of God and to set them an example. The world was waiting and ready to respond. Instead of that, Jonah-like, the Jews were full of nationalist pride and hatred of all Gentiles. As Jonah had been engulfed by the whale, they had been engulfed in the Exile. But, like Jonah, they had learned nothing from their experience.

So this little manifesto, portraying once more, like the story of Ruth, the true message of the great prophets in opposition to the narrowness that had supervened, is a challenge thrown down by the author to his countrymen. Its spirit of broad tolerance, its picture of the love of God, its deep human sympathy and its attitude to the animal world make it unique in the Old Testament and bring it very close to the heart of the Gospel. It ends with a question mark because the author could not tell how Israel would respond to his plea.

24. Songs of Grief and Glory

I T would be wrong, however, to think of the period between Nehemiah-Ezra and the coming of Christ as one in which religion had been turned solely into a kind of strait-jacket, where joyless obedience to the Law was all that was open to people and there was no place left for a living faith. This

would be to overlook the Psalms which became the hymn book of the Jewish Church after the Exile, when the services of the Temple at Jerusalem with their colourful pageantry, choral singing and orchestral accompaniment spoke to men's hearts and minds of the glory of God, and when the words that were sung clothed the legacy of the prophets with the warmth and devotion of unknown poets who had learned the truth of their message through their own experience.

The name of King David has been traditionally associated with the psalms. Probably he did write some of the early ones but most of them are the work of nameless devout souls after David's day, who had learned from Amos, Hosea, Jeremiah and Isaiah to know something of the majesty of the Creator, his power and purpose, his compassion and forgiveness. As in any modern hymn book, not all the psalms are of the same quality, but they cover the whole range of the human spirit – its aspirations, its hopes, its fears, its doubts. For this reason they are timeless and speak as directly to Christians in the twentieth century as they did to the Jews of olden days who shared the same faith in God's providence and who were as often perplexed as we are by the mystery of his ways.

Many of the psalms seem to have been written for national occasions – such as special days of thanksgiving – and for the great festivals of the Jewish Church. Others, however, seem to be much more personal, expressing one man's sense of the burdens and cares that weigh him down, his consciousness of failure, or on the other hand his sense of the companionship of God and of his presence amid the chores of every day. More than anything else the psalms are songs of praise, of thankfulness to God for his goodness, of delight in his worship and of glad wonderment at his never-failing love.

The psalms were sung not only in the splendid setting of the Temple but in the simpler services of the synagogues and in the homes of the people. They were both hymn book and prayer book to be read and thought about in private reflection and meditation, to be taught to children and memorised by them. Jesus must have learned many of them by heart in the synagogue school at Nazareth and in the house of Joseph and

Mary, as in all religious families they would form part of family prayers.

Everyone who gets to know and love the psalms has his own favourites but some of them might be regarded as universal because they bridge the centuries, break down the barriers of race and social background, and speak of matters that concern all men everywhere. Such a psalm as the twenty-third, for example, breathes a message of trust and confidence which we can still take to ourselves in an industrial society, far removed from the simple country setting of the poet who wrote it:

> The Lord is my shepherd; I shall not want.
> He maketh me to lie down in green pastures:
>   he leadeth me beside the still waters.
> He restoreth my soul: he leadeth me in the
>   paths of righteousness for his name's sake.
> Yea, though I walk through the valley of the
>   shadow of death, I will fear no evil:
>   for thou art with me; thy rod and thy staff
>   they comfort me.
> Thou preparest a table before me in the presence
>   of mine enemies: thou anointest my head with oil;
>   my cup runneth over.
> Surely goodness and mercy shall follow me all the
>   days of my life: and I will dwell in the house
>   of the Lord for ever.

The man who wrote the fortieth psalm spoke for everyone who has come through some shattering experience and reached solid ground at the end of it. The agony is past and on reflection the psalmist sees how the hand of God has guided him to a safe haven:

I waited patiently for the Lord; and he inclined unto me, and heard
   my cry.
He brought me up also out of an horrible pit,
   out of the miry clay, and set my feet upon a rock, and established
   my goings.

And he hath put a new song in my mouth,
    even praise unto our God: many shall see it, and fear, and shall trust
    in the Lord.
Blessed is that man that maketh the Lord his trust, and respecteth
    not the proud, nor such as turn aside to lies.
Many, O Lord my God, are thy wonderful works which
    thou hast done, and thy thoughts which are to us-ward: they cannot
    be reckoned up in order unto thee: if I would declare and speak of
    them, they are more than can be numbered.

Tradition has always associated the fifty-first psalm, a heartfelt cry of penitence, with King David's confession of guilt after his adultery with Bathsheba and shameful treatment of her husband Uriah. Whether this is so or not, it is a prayer which is wrung from a grieving heart that pleads for forgiveness:

Have mercy upon me, O God, according to thy
    lovingkindness: according unto the multitude
    of thy tender mercies blot out my transgressions.
Wash me throughly from mine iniquity, and cleanse
    me from my sin.
For I acknowledge my transgressions: and my sin is
    ever before me.
Against thee, thee only, have I sinned, and done this
    evil in thy sight: that thou mightest be justified
    when thou speakest, and be clear when thou judgest.
Behold I was shapen in iniquity; and in sin did my
    mother conceive me.
Behold, thou desirest truth in the inward parts: and
    in the hidden part thou shalt make me to know wisdom.
Purge me with hyssop, and I shall be clean: wash me,
    and I shall be whiter than snow.
Make me to hear joy and gladness; that the bones
    which thou hast broken may rejoice.
Hide thy face from my sins, and blot out all mine iniquities.
Create in me a clean heart, O God; and renew a right
    spirit within me.

Cast me not away from thy presence; and take not
  thy holy spirit from me.
Restore unto me the joy of thy salvation; and
  uphold me with thy free spirit.
Then will I teach transgressors thy ways; and
  sinners shall be converted unto thee.
Deliver me from bloodguiltiness,
    O God, thou God of my salvation:
    and my tongue shall sing aloud of thy righteousness.
O Lord, open thou my lips; and my mouth shall show
  forth thy praise.
For thou desirest not sacrifice; else would I give it:
  thou delightest not in burnt offering.
The sacrifices of God are a broken spirit: a broken
  and a contrite heart, O God, thou wilt not despise.

As an expression of thanksgiving to God, in which the
psalmist feels himself caught up with the whole of creation in
praise and exultation, it would be difficult to surpass the
hundred and third psalm:

    Bless the Lord, O my soul: and all that is
      within me, bless his holy name.
    Bless the Lord, O my soul, and forget not
      all his benefits:
    Who forgiveth all thine iniquities; who
      healeth all thy diseases;
    Who redeemeth thy life from destruction;
      who crowneth thee with lovingkindness
      and tender mercies;
    Who satisfieth thy mouth with good things;
      so that thy youth is renewed like the eagle's.
    The Lord executeth righteousness and judgment
      for all that are oppressed.
    He made known his ways unto Moses, his acts unto
      the children of Israel.
    The Lord is merciful and gracious, slow to anger,
      and plenteous in mercy.
    He will not always chide: neither will he keep his
      anger forever.

He hath not dealt with us after our sins; nor
   rewarded us according to our iniquities.
For as the heaven is high above the earth, so great
   is his mercy toward them that fear him.
As far as the east is from the west, so far hath he
   removed our transgressions from us.
Like as a father pitieth his children, so the Lord
   pitieth them that fear him.
For he knoweth our frame; he remembereth that we are
   dust.
As for man, his days are as grass: as a flower of the
   field, so he flourisheth.
For the wind passeth over it, and it is gone; and the
   place thereof shall know it no more.
But the mercy of the Lord is from everlasting to
   everlasting upon them that fear him, and his
   righteousness unto children's children;
To such as keep his covenant, and to those that
   remember his commandments to do them.
The Lord hath prepared his throne in the heavens;
   and his kingdom ruleth over all.
Bless the Lord, ye his angels, that excel in strength,
   that do his commandments, hearkening unto the voice
   of his word.
Bless ye the Lord, all ye his hosts; ye ministers of
   his, that do his pleasure.
Bless the Lord, all his works in all places of his
   dominion: bless the Lord, O my soul.

25. 'But Where Shall Wisdom Be Found?'

AFTER the time of Ezra and for the last few centuries of the
Old Testament period, Israel, as we have seen, became the
'people of the book'. The Law of Moses was paramount and
what went on in public and private life was governed by it

just as much as was what took place in the Temple and in the synagogues. Only the psalms show that personal faith was still very much alive and that many found in the festivals and ceremonial of the Temple a real sense of joyful communion with God.

There was, however, in this period another antidote to the rigid legalism imposed on all aspects of life by the priestly rulers of Israel. This was the contribution of a group of writers known as the wisdom scribes. Three books in the Old Testament came from their pens – Proverbs, Ecclesiastes and Job. These sages were primarily concerned with the nature of the good life. They were content to leave institutional religion in the hands of the priests, and deeper questions about the spiritual life in the hands of the psalmists. They were more concerned with the humdrum routine of day-to-day existence.

Their chief interest was in the human situation, the things they wrote about were men's virtues and vices, and the pursuit of happiness. They made it their business to translate the great insights of the prophets into everyday terms, to show how what Amos and his successors had said about God, the world and ourselves could be worked out in practice in the ups and downs of human affairs. They have sometimes been called the humanists of Israel, and in a general sense this is a good description of them, so long as we recognise that their humanism was firmly anchored in God.

The book of Proverbs is the least interesting of the three wisdom books in the Old Testament. By the same biblical convention which attributes all the laws to Moses and all the psalms to David, all the proverbs are ascribed to Solomon. It may indeed have been in his day that the type of moral axioms that we find in the book of Proverbs began to be collected. They are obviously the work of expert teachers of morality and not, like our own 'a stitch in time saves nine', the casual products of folklore. But like the laws and the psalms most of the proverbs come from a much later date than that of the man to whose name they have been loosely attached. Most of the wisdom writings, including the book of Proverbs, come from after the Exile.

The answer to the question at the head of this chapter, 'Where shall wisdom be found?' is given by the writer of the book of Job, but all the wisdom scribes would have agreed with him when he says: 'The fear of the Lord, that is wisdom: and to depart from evil is understanding.' In the eyes of the authors of Proverbs the wise man is the man who organises his life in accordance with the will of God as it has been shown to us. He does not need to be a clever man to be wise in this sense, nor is a fool, according to these sages, an ignoramus. He is a man who cheats and lies, who is at the mercy of his own hot temper, who drinks too much, who is sexually promiscuous. Such a man is a fool, they say, because he brings disaster on his own head. In other words it pays to be good.

Some people are inclined to sneer at this and tell us that this is not the best reason for trying to live a good life. We should love goodness for its own sake, they say, or we should seek after goodness because God himself is good. The writers of Proverbs would probably have agreed with them but they would have gone on to say that in this workaday world the ordinary man needs to hitch his wagon to something a bit closer to earth than a star. They would perhaps have added that if we feel that the Creator has made the kind of world that runs properly only when moral principles are observed, goodness is bound to pay in the sense that we are managing our lives in harmony with the Creator's will and not in opposition to it.

So the writers of Proverbs give us page after page of sanctified common sense, urging the case for cultivating the virtues of honesty, sobriety, kindness, diligence and chastity. As an alternative to self-interest or a 'couldn't care less' attitude, it is undoubtedly good advice and in line with what philosophers and teachers of the good life in all religions have always said. Where we may question the writers of Proverbs is in their claim that the good man will always prosper in this world, for this is obviously not true. No one saw this more clearly than the author of the fascinating little book called Ecclesiastes, which is also part of the wisdom literature of the Bible.

This consists of the reflections of an elderly man who had

sought happiness in one way after another. But whether it was by acquiring knowledge or amassing wealth, or by ringing the changes on the ancient recipes of wine, women and song, he found that it all ended in disillusionment. His verdict is 'Vanity of vanities, all is vanity.' He does not share the easy optimism of the writers of Proverbs who argued that honesty is always rewarded and that crime does not pay. He is too much of a realist for that.

He has seen wickedness crowned with honour and prosperity, and simple, honest men crushed against the wall. Crooks grow fat on their ill-gotten gains and good men are hated and envied for acts of kindness. He does not doubt that Providence holds the reins but he is mystified by the fact that luck seems to play so large a part in life. 'I have seen servants upon horses,' he says, 'and princes walking as servants upon the earth.' So, he goes on, in this grey and so often meaningless world the best we can do is to make the most of life when we can. There is a time for tears and a time for laughter, a time for mourning and a time for dancing, a time for loving and a time for hating, a time for war and a time for peace. We cannot hope to understand the mystery of life; the one thing of which we can be certain is death.

Despite this melancholy assessment, Ecclesiastes still ends his book on a note of courage. While life remains, he says, 'eat your bread with joy and drink your wine with a glad heart . . . spend your days with the woman you love . . . whatever work you have to do, do it while you can, for there is neither achievement, nor planning, nor knowledge, nor wisdom in the grave where you are going.'

No one would pretend that Ecclesiastes gives us a wholly satisfactory philosophy of life. It has been called a gospel of moderation in all things for tired men in chaotic times. There is no suggestion that we should attempt to do anything about the mess the world is in except to grin and bear it. Perhaps if Ecclesiastes had been less concerned with finding happiness for himself and more concerned with helping others, he would not have felt so strongly that 'all is vanity'. But it is a brave and honest book and one which reflects the mood of

all of us when we are depressed by the number of things in life that we simply cannot understand and for which we see no explanation.

Perhaps this is why the book of Ecclesiastes is included in the Bible. There are times when there seems to be no other solution than to echo Ecclesiastes' closing words: 'Let us hear the conclusion of the whole matter: Fear God and keep his commandments: for this is the whole duty of man.' It may well be, as Dean Bradley said, that the Bible in its capacity as a looking-glass of life has kept here a place 'for the sigh of defeated hopes, and for the gloom of the soul vanquished by the sense of the anomalies and mysteries of human life.'

The third of the wisdom books in the Old Testament, the book of Job, is the greatest of the three and in the Authorised Version of our English translation is one of the master-pieces of world literature. It faces up to the problem which has always vexed men's minds: why does an innocent man suffer? It tells the story of a worthy character, Job, whose conduct was above reproach, who was renowned far and wide for his integrity and benevolence. If the writers of the book of Proverbs were right he should have been blessed with this world's goods and should have enjoyed to the full the rewards of his virtues. So indeed it was to begin with.

Then one disaster after another fell upon him. Calamity upon calamity robbed him of his property and possessions, his family perished in a hurricane and he himself was afflicted with a loathsome type of leprosy. According to the orthodox teaching of the time, such adversity was the result of sin, since prosperity was the reward for virtue. Job's three friends, the notorious 'Job's comforters', try hard to persuade him that if he will only turn to God in penitence he will find that God is ready to forgive. Job angrily denies that he has anything to repent of, certainly nothing that would account for his present plight.

His friends are convinced that Job must be guilty, and pass from insinuation to accusation, wildly inventing charges which they know to be untrue, so determined are they to defend religious orthodoxy. Job's problem is an agonising one. The one thing he is sure about is his own innocence and this he will not compromise. He accuses God of playing cat and mouse with helpless mortals like himself, calls God the great spy who will not leave men in peace, using his power to strike them down, allowing rogues to flourish and victimising the weak and helpless. In his heart Job does not doubt that there is an overruling Providence but he sees no reason or justice in what has happened to himself. At times he even wonders whether there is a God of justice at all and whether the world is not in the hands of some blind Fury.

The climax of the drama comes when Job and his friends have exhausted each other with their arguments. Job still maintains that he has done nothing to deserve the disasters that have overtaken him, his 'comforters' are equally convinced that he must have done some great wrong. Their inability to reach a solution is a confession of the bankruptcy of human wisdom and its complete failure to find an answer to this great problem of why a good man should suffer.

The author of the book insists that the orthodox view that was current in his day was wrong. Suffering is not necessarily the result of sin, though it may be a test of a man's character. In Job's case he stood up manfully to the test and refused to betray his conscience. Before the drama ends, he reaches peace of mind in the recognition that prosperity or adversity has nothing to do with a man's relationship to God, and that none of us can hope to understand more than a fraction of the mystery that surrounds us. Certainly, as Job saw at last, we are not entitled to question the way God runs the universe on the basis of what happens in our own experience.

In the end of the story Job is restored to health and prosperity but by now this is incidental. Job might have died in misery as countless good men have done throughout the ages, but he had come to terms with life and learned that to some questions there are no answers except to trust in a God who we believe knows the answers. Like the rest of the people of his time Job believed that death was the end of everything. In the midst of his agony he wistfully hoped that perhaps this might not be so, but he did not know. It was not until New

Testament times after the Crucifixion and Resurrection of Jesus that the whole problem of innocent suffering was seen in a new light.

26. Pogrom in Reverse

THE Jews have always been a persecuted race. Belsen and Auschwitz are the horrible climax to a long story of oppression and cruelty which dates back to before the Christian era. Sometimes it has seemed to the Jews as if suffering was all that they could expect. Sometimes, however, they have dreamt that the boot was on the other foot and when this happened there was little to choose between their tactics and those of their persecutors. The book of Esther tells of one such dream. It is unlikely that it was more than a dream, but the story was highly popular as we might expect among people who liked to think that on one occasion at least the tables had been turned. Before we condemn the book as sub-Christian let us remember that most of the persecution of the Jews has been carried out by so-called Christian nations.

The scene is laid in Susa, the capital of the great Persian Empire in the days of the notorious Xerxes, called by the Hebrews Ahasuerus. He had arranged a kind of Empire Exhibition which lasted about six months and which was designed to impress officials from all over his far-flung dominions. At the end of it he staged an enormous and magnificent open-air all-male banquet which went on for seven days. At the same time his queen Vashti entertained the ladies correspondingly well inside the palace.

The king's choicest wines were on tap and towards the end of the feast Xerxes, in a state of alcoholic exaltation, began to boast of the queen's beauty. In a misguided moment he ordered the court chamberlain to produce the queen so that her charms might be exhibited and praised by the whole company.

Vashti, who had more sense, refused to come, whereupon the king flew into a drunken rage. He took counsel with his guests as to what should be done and they unanimously decided that some drastic action must be taken. Vashti was setting their wives a very bad example indeed. What was going to happen to a husband's authority if a wife could snap her fingers at a direct command?

So Vashti must be deposed. Not only that but a royal decree should be sent round the empire ordering that every husband should be master in his own house – which is the kind of fatuous resolution that one would expect to issue from a drunken spree. The next step was to find a new queen. So a beauty competition was held to decide who was to be the Miss Persia of 483 BC. The prize in this case was to be the royal throne. Among the entrants was a certain Esther, a Jewess, of the same clan as King Saul. This beautiful orphan girl had been brought up by her cousin Mordecai, who was apparently one of the exiles of Nebuchadnezzar's first deportation. (This would make him well over a hundred years old, but dates do not matter to the fiction writer.)

Among other pieces of advice which Mordecai had given Esther was a strict instruction not to reveal her nationality, since the Jews at the time were none too popular. The lovely Esther took the king's fancy and was promoted from the royal harem to be queen in Vashti's place. Soon after this, old Mordecai, who had taken up his post outside the palace gate to keep an eye on Esther, discovered a plot against the king's life. He told Esther of this; she told the king and the conspirators were hanged.

Then the king appointed a new prime minister, Haman, who was a pompous ass. Everybody had to prostrate himself as he went past. The only man who refused to do so was old Mordecai. Haman took this as a personal affront and determined to be revenged not only on him but on all Jewish people who were to be found within the bounds of the Persian Empire. He obtained the king's consent to a wholesale massacre of the Jews for an appointed day, and notices were sent out accordingly. The reason given by Haman for the extermination of the Jews was that they were different from anyone else and lived by their own laws.

Then there went up a universal wailing and lamentation from the Jews throughout the land. Mordecai sent a message to Esther in the harem that the fate of the whole Jewish race was in her hands. She must approach the king and get the massacre cancelled. 'Who knows?' he said, 'perhaps you have come to the throne for such a time as this.' But according to the laws of Persia it was as much as even the queen's life was worth to appear uninvited before the king, so while all the Jews in Susa fasted in sympathy, Esther and her maids-in-waiting fasted inside the palace in preparation for the ordeal.

Finally, taking her life in her hands and robed in her royal attire, Esther ventured unsummoned into the king's presence. She caught him at the right moment. He was in a mood to give her half his kingdom. All she asked, however, was that the king and Haman should come to a little dinner party with no other guests apart from themselves. The king agreed and Haman was beside himself with delight. He ran home to tell his wife and even the sight of surly old Mordecai sitting tight and not even standing up as he passed through the palace gates could not spoil his pleasure as he told Zeresh, his wife, what a wonderful chap he was, how the queen had singled him out, and how she was repeating the invitation on the following day.

'Yet,' as Haman said, 'all this availeth me nothing, so long as I see Mordecai the Jew sitting at the king's gate.' This was the one fly in the ointment. What could he do about it? His wife and friends had a splendid idea. He must set up an enormous gallows, about a hundred feet high. Then tomorrow he must tell the king about Mordecai and his repeated insults and get the fellow hanged on it. Then he could really enjoy the dinner.

That night the king could not sleep. Having presumably tried all the traditional recipes for insomnia, he sent for the royal annals to be read to him. This would surely lull him to sleep. But when the courtier reached the point that told of the plot to kill the king that Mordecai had discovered, the patient suddenly sat up in bed and asked what had been done

to reward this faithful subject. The reply was: 'Nothing, Sire.'
The king demanded action at once. Who was in attendance?
As it happened, Haman, who could not wait to see his private
plan for Mordecai mature in the morning, was pacing up and
down in the courtyard waiting for the dawn.

So Haman was brought in and the king asked him what he
thought would be a fitting reward for someone whom the king
wished to honour. Haman, thinking this could be no one but
himself, recommended a triumphal procession on horseback
through the city, clad in the royal robes and wearing the
imperial crown, with a herald in front proclaiming what it was
all about. Judge the poor man's shock when the king told
him that the person to be honoured was Mordecai and that
Haman's job was to lead the horse.

After the procession Mordecai came back to his seat at the
palace gates and Haman went home with his spirits at zero to
glean what comfort he could from the wife who had such bright
ideas. All he got was the chilling advice to expect the worst.
In the midst of his forebodings the royal envoys appeared to
convey him to Esther's little party. When the wine was flowing
freely, the king asked the queen what favour she had to ask and
Esther begged for the lives of her people: 'For we are doomed,
I and my people, to destruction, slaughter and annihilation.'

The king, still apparently not aware that Esther is a Jewess,
asks the name of the villain of the piece and Esther replies:
'This wretch Haman!' The king rushes out to the garden to
cool off. Haman falls on the queen's couch, a suppliant for his
life. One of the eunuchs standing by reminds the king on his
return that there is a fine new gallows conveniently erected
in Haman's garden, to which the king's reply is: 'Hang him
on it.' So up went Haman instead of Mordecai and the king
felt a lot better.

Then the tables were completely turned. Mordecai was made
prime minister and the Jews, instead of being massacred on
the appointed day, were authorised by Xerxes to turn on their
enemies instead. They had such a field-day of slaughter that
Esther gained permission for another day's killing in the
capital, and as a special titbit for her the ten sons of Haman

were hanged like their father. So there was great rejoicing among the Jews and they kept the day in annual remembrance as a happy festival.

The story of Esther is much more like something out of the *Arabian Nights* than out of the Bible. It was viewed with grave suspicion by the learned rabbis and almost did not get into the Bible at all. Luther wished it had never been written. It is intensely nationalistic and vindictive and the name of God is never even mentioned. There was undoubtedly a king called Xerxes but there is no evidence outside the story itself that anything of this kind ever happened. The Jewish festival of Purim seems to date from the period when the Jews were part of the Persian Empire and this story may simply have grown up round it to explain its origin.

27. *'Dare to be a Daniel'*

THE Bible gets its message across in a variety of ways. Sometimes by recording things that actually happened and showing how God speaks to us through them. Sometimes by preserving the inspired writings of psalmists, prophets and sages, where God has used the minds of men attuned to listen to what he is saying to convey to us different aspects of the truth about himself and ourselves. Sometimes by telling stories of things that did not actually happen but which nevertheless have something to teach us, like the books of Ruth and Jonah. The last book to be written in the Old Testament collection, the book of Daniel, is one of these.

Some of the stories about Daniel are almost as well known as the tale of Jonah and the Whale. Daniel in the Lion's Den, the Three Men in the Fiery Furnace, and Belshazzar's Feast have always been popular with painters and story-tellers. Yet like the book of Jonah the book of Daniel has often been sadly misunderstood. Part of the trouble is that much of it, like the book of Revelation in the New Testament, deals with visions of the future and with mysterious symbolism with which we are unfamiliar. As a result the book of Daniel, like the book of Revelation, has often become a happy hunting ground for religious cranks who treat it like *Old Moore's Almanac* and find in it all sorts of crazy nonsense never intended by the author.

The book of Daniel was written at a time when the Jewish people were in the throes of a severe crisis which threatened their whole existence. The Persian Empire, under which they had lived as a tiny provincial backwater since their return from Exile, had been swept aside by the spectacular conquests of Alexander the Great, who became virtually master of the world in 331 BC. On his death his empire was divided and Palestine came under a succession of foreign rulers, until in 175 BC it found itself part of the territory of Antiochus IV, king of Syria.

The legacy of Alexander the Great had been to bequeath to the civilised world the language, customs and culture of Greece. Alone within his empire, the Jews in their little bastion of Jerusalem and its environs, faithful to the tradition of the Law of Moses and fortified by the exclusive policy of Nehemiah and Ezra, preserved their identity intact and refused to compromise the faith and practice of their forefathers by allowing any infiltration of Greek customs or, as they would have said, heathen ideas. Their new overlord, Antiochus IV, was, however, a progressive ruler who felt it to be his duty to bring the Jews into line with the modern world.

There was some support for his policy among the priestly aristocracy in Jerusalem – the forerunners of the Sadducees of the gospels – but determined opposition from the rank and file of the people. National pride and religious loyalty alike called for resolute resistance to this threat to obliterate the tradition of Moses and the prophets, and to submerge the unique vocation of Israel in the advancing tide of pagan 'progress'. The patriots at this time, who developed into the Pharisees of the gospels, were in effect defending all that Israel had ever stood for.

Antiochus would not tolerate this opposition from people

whom he regarded as obscurantist backwoodsmen and he proceeded to occupy Jerusalem. Obviously the root of Jewish stubbornness was their religion, therefore this must be stamped out. Accordingly the worship of Yahweh was forbidden, the Jewish scriptures were publicly burned, and possession of a copy of the Torah, as the Jews called the Law of Moses, was made punishable by death. In addition sabbath observance was abolished and circumcision of infants was made illegal. Pagan altars were set up throughout Jewish territory, and in the sacred Temple itself an altar to Zeus was consecrated by the sacrifice of swine, and priests and people were compelled to drink pig broth.

Nothing so frightful had happened to Israel in all its history. Outraged religious feelings and patriotic fury burst into flames in 167 BC. The revolt was led by a priest and his five sons, the most notable being Judas Maccabaeus. Rebellion became widespread and developed into a war of independence, known as the Maccabaean War, as a result of which Antiochus and his troops were driven out of Jerusalem, and the Temple was cleansed and dedicated anew to Yahweh.

It was during the rebellion that the book of Daniel was written. It was not so much a call to arms as a passionate plea to resist to the death Antiochus' attempt to suppress the historic faith of Israel. Daniel was a traditional hero and perhaps these stories were already familiar. Here, however, they are retold with a slant to make them fit the occasion. The scene is laid back in the days of the Exile in the reign of the redoubtable king Nebuchadnezzar, whose black record as far as the Jews were concerned would immediately suggest a parallel with Antiochus.

Daniel and his three friends had been deported from Jerusalem to Babylon where they were now employed in the royal palace. Rather like Joseph at the court of the pharaoh, Daniel had the gift of being able to interpret dreams, and he too reached dizzy heights in the royal favour. One tale is of how Daniel and his friends refused to eat the meat and drink the wine which was provided from the king's bounty. They insisted on eating nothing but vegetables and drinking nothing but water. Despite this they put on more weight and looked better than the meat-eaters, who had of course been feeding on flesh which had been dedicated as a sacrifice to a heathen god. The moral was clearly that if the Jews stuck to their own food laws and avoided the forbidden meat that Antiochus insisted on they too would have the Lord's approval.

Another story was designed to encourage resistance to Antiochus' attempt to force the Jews to worship pagan gods. Nebuchadnezzar had set up a massive golden image and at a given signal everyone was to prostrate himself before it in reverence. The penalty for refusal meant being thrown into a 'burning fiery furnace'. Daniel's three friends stoutly stood their ground. When they were threatened with this horrible death they defied the king to his face, making the splendid reply: 'Whether our God delivers us from the furnace or not we shall not worship this heathen image.' In a fury the king ordered the furnace to be heated to seven times its usual intensity so that the men who threw the three young captives into the flames were themselves burned to death. To the king's astonishment Daniel's friends were joined in the furnace by a guardian angel who protected them from the flames and they emerged unscathed without a hair of their heads being even singed.

Then there is the tale of Belshazzar's feast. Belshazzar was Nebuchadnezzar's son and at his banquet he rashly provided as drinking cups the sacred gold and silver vessels which had been looted from the Temple at Jerusalem. In the middle of the feast a mysterious hand appeared and wrote an inscription on the wall of the banqueting hall. Not all the astrologers or wise men of Babylon could interpret the words despite the king's promise of a lavish reward. On the queen's suggestion, Daniel was sent for and after denouncing the king for his sacrilege he interpreted the writing on the wall as a message from the God of Israel pronouncing judgement on Babylon and its king. That very night, the story ends, the king was murdered and the Persian army swept into Babylon. The point of the story is the obvious parallel between the profanation of the sacred vessels by Belshazzar and the desecration of the Temple by Antiochus. The fate of the Babylonian king would

encourage the rebels to toughen their resistance in the hope that a like judgement might speedily fall upon the unspeakable king of Syria.

The best-known of all the stories is the tale of Daniel in the lions' den. Jealous of Daniel's success and royal patronage his rivals contrived to persuade the king to pass a decree forbidding the worship of any god apart from his own divine majesty for a period of a month. Daniel however continued to kneel in prayer to the God of his fathers as he had always done. When this was reported to the king he saw that he had been tricked, but his nobles insisted that 'the law of the Medes and Persians', which could not be altered, required Daniel to be thrown to the lions. Next morning to the king's great joy Daniel reported that all was well. The Lord had sent an angel who had sealed the lions' mouths and Daniel emerged unhurt. His wicked accusers were, however, consigned to the lions with their wives and families, and this time there was no angel. The message was clear. Antiochus had forbidden the public worship of Yahweh but let the people continue their devotions in private. Should they be found out, let them take heart from Daniel's example.

Throughout the stories, the implication is that God was watching over his people and that in face of evil, such as the policies of Antiochus, resistance, if need be to the death, was the only course for men of faith and principle. In a series of visions the writer, assuming the guise of Daniel looking forward from the time of the Exile, shows the unfolding pattern of history with the rise and fall of empires, culminating in the catastrophic destruction of Antiochus and his monstrous regime. In fact of course the author, living under the tyranny of this Syrian persecutor, was writing history in retrospect and drawing lessons from the past. It was none the less his conviction that God would shortly bring the nightmare of terror to an end and this was a major part of his message to his afflicted countrymen.

The stories of the lions' den and the fiery furnace are more than fairy tales. Their point is not that Daniel and his friends escaped by some kind of magic but that God was with them in their ordeal and because of this they were able to survive what, by all human standards, was the certain death of their bodies. It is therefore not surprising that towards the end of the book of Daniel we find the clearest expression so far in the Old Testament of belief in a life beyond death. It has already been hinted at in the book of Job and the book of Psalms, but here in Daniel it crystallises into something more concrete, which leads on to the New Testament belief in a resurrection.

28. Between the Old and New Testaments

IN a normal copy of the Authorised Version of 1611, which is the Bible most people have in their homes, we turn the page from the last chapter of the Old Testament in the book of Malachi to the first chapter of the New Testament in the gospel according to St Matthew. Some editions of the Revised Version of 1885 and the New English Bible have a section in between called the Apocrypha and sometimes the Apocrypha are printed as a separate book. Protestant readers of the new Roman Catholic English translation called the Jerusalem Bible find no section labelled Apocrypha, but instead various books, whose names are perhaps unfamiliar, cropping up at different points in the Old Testament. What is the explanation of all this?

The Old Testament was written largely in Hebrew but as time went on this became a dead language for ordinary purposes and was replaced in Palestine by Aramaic, which was the spoken language in the time of Jesus. The Hebrew version was still used in the synagogues as being the original sacred language in which the Law and the prophets had been written, but an Aramaic translation was always given and the sermon was in the language of the day. By the end of Old Testament times, however, there were far more Jews living outside Palestine than inside it and for ordinary purposes they spoke Greek which was then the international language throughout the civilised world. About 250 BC it was felt that a Greek translation of the Hebrew scriptures should be made for the benefit of Jews living overseas who were no longer familiar with their ancient tongue.

The largest colony of Jews living outside Palestine was in Alexandria in Egypt and it was here that the Greek translation, known as the Septuagint, first appeared. The Old Testament as we know it had been built up over the centuries, but it was never finally decided either inside or outside Palestine what should be included in it until AD 90. By this time the Romans had overrun Palestine, Jerusalem with its Temple had been destroyed, and the Jews had lost their ancestral home. Moreover, Christianity was emerging as a distinct religion and it was imperative that a decision should be reached as to what constituted the sacred writings of the Jews.

At the Synod of Jamnia in AD 90 the leaders of the Jewish Church fixed the contents of the Old Testament as we know them in our Authorised Version. There was a difference of opinion about some books, for obvious reasons – for example, Ecclesiastes because of its sceptical tone, and Esther because of its bloodthirsty character – but finally the decision was taken in their favour. Some other books, however, were left out. These were religious writings which had become popular among Greek-speaking Jews and which they regarded as part of the sacred scriptures, but which, largely because they were considered 'modern', were treated with reserve by the more conservative Palestine rabbis. It was decided to group these in a class by themselves and to call them the Apocrypha, meaning 'hidden', in the sense of being withdrawn from public use and not included in the regular services of the synagogues.

The Greek Septuagint, however, contained them and it was this that became the Old Testament of the early Christian Church. When Latin succeeded Greek as the world language, the Old Testament part of the Vulgate, as the Latin translation of the Bible was called, included these extra books as the Septuagint had done. The Roman Catholic Jerusalem Bible, although it is a fresh translation from the original languages, keeps the Apocrypha not as a separate section but interspersed with the other books of the Old Testament as it was in the Vulgate.

At the Reformation the Protestants decided to follow the more conservative line of the Jewish rabbis at Jamnia and relegated the Apocrypha as a kind of appendix to the Old Testament. There is some difference of attitude and practice among the various Reformed churches, but by and large the Apocrypha are not treated as being on the same level of importance as the Old Testament. Most people would, however, agree that the great words which are read in churches on national occasions beginning: 'Let us now praise famous men', and which come from the Apocrypha, are considerably more significant for Christians than some of the dreary stretches of Leviticus, and the same could be said of many other passages.

The contents of the Apocrypha are as varied as the Old Testament itself. There are fourteen items in all, some being complete books, some merely additions to existing Old Testament books, such as Daniel and Esther. History, poetry, wisdom writings, prayers and some excellent short stories are included in this littler known part of the Bible which forms a bridge between the Old Testament and the New. As it happens, the writers of the New Testament books do not quote from the Apocrypha as they do from the Old Testament, but on the other hand Jesus and the apostles must have known and read these books as part of their religious upbringing.

They would read there in the two books of the Maccabees the stirring story of the revolt of the Jews against the attack on their cherished faith and traditions by Antiochus IV, which provoked the book of Daniel. Judas Maccabaeus is the hero of the story as Antiochus is the villain. It is indeed only here that the dark tunnel of Jewish history from the days of Nehemiah and Ezra bursts into broad daylight. Here is the story of the valiant struggle of the Maccabees against the oppressor, the restoration of religious liberty and the establishment once more of an independent Jewish state for the first time since the fall of Jerusalem and the Babylonian exile.

Two splendid wisdom books, Ecclesiasticus and the book of Wisdom, belong to the same class as Proverbs, Ecclesiastes and Job. Much of Ecclesiasticus reminds us of the book of Proverbs but the immortal words of its great hymn of commemoration must be quoted:

Let us now praise famous men, and our fathers that begat us.
The Lord hath wrought great glory by them through his great
    power from the beginning.
Such as did bear rule in their kingdoms, men renowned for
    their power, giving counsel by their understanding, and
    declaring prophecies:
Leaders of the people by their counsels, and by their
    knowledge of learning meet for the people, wise and
    eloquent in their instructions:
Such as found out musical tunes, and recited verses in writing:
Rich men furnished with ability, living peaceably in their
    habitations:
All these were honoured in their generations, and were the
    glory of their times.
There be of them, that have left a name behind them, that
    their praises might be reported.
And some there be, which have no memorial; who are perished,
    as though they had never been; and are become as though
    they had never been born; and their children after them.
But these were merciful men, whose righteousness hath not been
    forgotten.
With their seed shall continually remain a good inheritance,
    and their children are within the covenant.
Their seed standeth fast, and their children for their sakes.
Their seed shall remain for ever, and their glory shall not be
    blotted out.
Their bodies are buried in peace; but their name liveth for
    evermore.

Ecclesiasticus 44: 1–14

The book of Wisdom, which was universally popular in the early Christian Church, contains some of the finest writing in the whole Bible. Unlike some of his more bigoted countrymen, the author is a Jew who recognises that God has also spoken to men through the pagan philosophers. As St Paul was to do at a later date, he sees the minds of the Greek thinkers reaching out towards the truth that God had revealed to Israel. Wisdom is for him the highest activity of the human spirit, akin to the wisdom of God, so that a man who possesses it has something of God within him which lifts him above the changes and chances of life. In a great passage he refutes the sombre view of Ecclesiastes that death is the end of all human effort, good and bad alike.

> But the souls of the righteous are in the hands of God,
>   and there shall no torment touch them.
> In the sight of the unwise they seemed to die: and their
>   departure is taken for misery,
> And their going from us to be utter destruction: but they
>   are in peace.
> For though they be punished in the sight of men, yet is
>   their hope full of immortality.
> And having been a little chastised, they shall be greatly
>   rewarded: for God proved them, and found them worthy
>   for himself.
> They that put their trust in him shall understand the truth:
>   and such as be faithful in love shall abide with him:
>   for grace and mercy is to his saints, and he hath care
>   for his elect.
>
> *Wisdom 3: 1–5, 9*

People who are familiar with the Anglican order for morning prayer will know that the splendid canticle which begins: 'O all ye works of the Lord, bless ye the Lord', and is generally known as the *Benedicite,* comes from the Apocrypha, but mostly this collection of borderline writings is known for its lively short stories. On the whole they have more entertainment value than religious value. Among the additions to the book of Daniel, which include the *Benedicite,* is the famous story of Susanna and the Elders, which tells how Daniel outwits two nasty old men who try to seduce the virtuous Susanna. His skill in cross-examination gave rise to Shylock's famous words about 'a Daniel come to judgement'. There is also an amusing

piece of folklore in the tale of how Daniel was too smart for the priests of the Babylonian god Bel, and how he coped with a sacred serpent. This is described as 'The History of the destruction of Bel and the Dragon' and includes the story of how Daniel is visited in the lions' den by an air-borne prophet who flies in from Palestine with some dinner for him.

The heroine of the story of Judith and Holofernes – which was highly popular with classical painters – is a more estimable character than Esther. She rescues her beleaguered townsmen by tricking the general of the besieging army. When he thinks he has her in his clutches he gets hopelessly drunk, whereupon Judith cuts off his head. The enemy is routed and Judith becomes the toast of her people. It is a gripping tale, skilfully told, illustrating with its strongly nationalist temper, its stress on meticulous observance of the Law and its hatred of Gentile oppression, the trend of popular Jewish thought at the dawn of the Christian era. Its saving grace, unlike the story of Esther, is its intensely religious emphasis.

Another side of the Jewish legacy is reflected in the equally fanciful story of Tobit, more popularly known to playgoers under the title of Tobias and the Angel. In contrast to the military atmosphere of Judith, which like the book of Daniel would have an inspiring message for a nation fighting for its independence from a powerful oppressor, as was the case in the Maccabaean War, this little tale of domestic life with its stress on family loyalty, neighbourly charity and simple piety points forward to the type of ordinary Jewish homes in the time of Jesus, of which that of Joseph and Mary at Nazareth would only be one among countless others. The details of the story are delightfully far-fetched and amusing – a girl whose seven bridegrooms had been killed by a demon on their wedding night, a great fish that sounds like the Loch Ness monster, and a highly resourceful angel in disguise. But kindly old Tobit and his wife, his son Tobias who sets out on a journey with his dog, and, with the help of Raphael his ingenious but mysterious travelling-companion, breaks the wicked demon's spell and comes back in triumph with a wife as the eighth and only surviving bridegroom, all contribute to leave us with an impression less of fantasy and more of the splendid people who feature in the story – which is presumably what the author intended.

29. Israel's Legacy to Christianity

I T cannot be said too often that the Bible is one book and not two. Strictly speaking, Christianity begins with Christ, and the New Testament is the story of how it started, but the Christian

Church goes back to Abraham, and the Christian faith has its roots firmly embedded in the experience of the people of the Old Testament. The word 'testament' means 'covenant' and the idea of a covenant or relationship between God and man is common to both Jews and Christians. Jews believe that in the pages of the Old Testament we can find all that we need to know about God's purpose for the world and the meaning of life. Christians believe that the Old Testament leaves so many problems unsolved that it ends in a large question mark, and that the answer to the question has been given in Christ.

From the beginning of the Church, Christians have always looked on the Old Testament as the preparation for the gospel, the book that points forward to Christ and is incomplete without him. In the happier state of affairs that exists within the Christian Church today, Catholics and Protestants recognise that what they have in common is far more important than the issues that still keep them apart. Similarly, despite much misunderstanding and bitterness in the past, thinking Christians are readier than they have been for centuries to recognise how close Jews and Christians are in their approach to God. They differ on the question of the status of Jesus but they share the same rich legacy of God's revelation of himself and of the truth about life through the prophets, psalmists and sages of Israel.

Before it became a world religion, Christianity had taken on a Western character, largely because its expansion was dictated by the extent of the Roman Empire, which was the civilisation in which it grew up. But its origins are wholly oriental and outspokenly Jewish. It came into being in Palestine and its founder and his first followers were exclusively Jews. It is therefore impossible to think of Christianity or of Jesus himself without linking them both with the background from which they came. Jesus lived and thought like a first-century Jew and not like a twentieth-century European. We cannot make sense of what the New Testament says about him unless we remember that both Jesus and the writers of the New Testament were steeped in the history, ideas and stories of the Old Testament that we have been talking about. This was their sacred book, their guide to life and to the knowledge of God long before the New Testament came to be written.

Far from being something that Christians can dispense with, the Old Testament is thus an integral part of our story and is as important for us as it is for Jews. The teaching of Jesus is based on the teaching of the Law and the prophets; what he says about God, himself and us ties up directly with what the Old Testament had already said. Jesus did not claim to be the founder of a new religion. What he claimed to do was to revitalise an old religion, to cut away its dead wood, to bring to light again the living faith and practice of Israel as it had been handed down from Moses onwards, and to show its true meaning. He did not, therefore, as it were, swallow the Old Testament whole. He discarded some of it as no longer relevant and put its various lines of thought in their proper perspective.

When we remember that the Old Testament is a collection of the religious writings of a nation, gathered up over a thousand years and written in a variety of different situations by men who never saw the whole truth but only part of it, it is obvious that it needed the master mind of Jesus to distinguish between what was of lasting value and what was out of date or mistaken. What he did not stamp with his own seal from the Old Testament heritage is obviously of less importance for Christians than what he made his own, but as we look at what Jesus had to say about the meaning and purpose of life, and what the New Testament writers following his lead have to say about it, we shall find over and over again how much the faith and practice of Christianity owe to their Jewish origins as they are recorded in the Old Testament.

We have seen how since the time of the Exodus the best minds in Israel had been conscious that their people had been singled out for a special purpose. Israel was not meant to be a nation like other nations. It was to be a community which by precept and example would convince the world that the God who had revealed himself to Israel, through the things that had happened, through the words of prophets and psalmists, was the only true God, Creator of all that is, the Lord of history who held the destinies of men and nations in his hands. Yet this was no remote and inaccessible potentate but a God of mercy and compassion, tender and forgiving, who hated sin but who was always ready to pardon the penitent sinner.

No one has expressed this faith of Israel more finely than the unknown prophet of the Exile, whom we call Second Isaiah, or Isaiah of Babylon, as he dwells on the majesty and tenderness of God:

> Who has measured the waters in
>   the hollow of his hand
>   and marked off the heavens with
>   a span,
> enclosed the dust of the earth in a
>   measure
>   and weighed the mountains in
>   scales
>   and the hills in a balance?
> Who has directed the Spirit of the
>   Lord,
>   or as his counsellor has instructed
>   him?
> Whom did he consult for his enlightenment,
>   and who taught him the path of
>   justice,
> and taught him knowledge,
>   and showed him the way of understanding?
> Behold the nations are like a drop
>   from a bucket,
>   and are accounted as the dust on
>   the scales;
>   behold, he takes up the isles like
>   fine dust.

Isaiah 40 : 12–15

> Have you not known? Have you not
>   heard?
>   Has it not been told you from
>   the beginning?
>   Have you not understood from the
>   foundations of the earth?

It is he who sits above the circle of
      the earth,
   and its inhabitants are like grasshoppers;
who stretches out the heavens like
      a curtain,
   and spreads them like a tent to
      dwell in;
who brings princes to nought,
   and makes the rulers of the earth
      as nothing.
Scarcely are they planted, scarcely
      sown,
   scarcely has their stem taken root
      in the earth,
when he blows upon them, and
      they wither,
   and the tempest carries them off
      like stubble.
To whom then will you compare
      me,
   that I should be like him?
      says the Holy One.
Lift up your eyes on high and see:
   who created these?
He who brings out their host by
      number,
   calling them all by name;
by the greatness of his might,
   and because he is strong in power
      not one is missing.

Have you not known? Have you not
      heard?
The Lord is the everlasting God,
      the Creator of the ends of the
         earth.
He does not faint or grow weary,
      his understanding is unsearchable.
He gives power to the faint,
      and to him who has no might he
         increases strength.

> Even youths shall faint and be
>   weary,
>   and young men shall fall exhausted;
>   but they who wait for the Lord
>   shall renew their strength,
>   they shall mount up with wings
>   like eagles,
>   they shall run and not be weary,
>   they shall walk and not faint.

Isaiah 40 : 21–31

> He will feed his flock like a shepherd,
>   he will gather the lambs in his
>   arms,
> he will carry them in his bosom,
>   and gently lead those that are
>   with young.

Isaiah 40 : 11

The proper response of men to a God of this kind has been summed up by another of Israel's prophets: 'This is what Yahweh asks of you: only this, to act justly, to love tenderly and to walk humbly with your God.' Justice and charity between a man and his neighbour, humility and thankfulness to God for all his goodness – this was the high calling of any Israelite who took his faith seriously. In the course of his defence of his integrity against the charges levelled against him by his 'comforters', Job puts into words the standard of behaviour which was expected of a devout Jew after the impact of the great prophets. It is a standard of which any nation could be proud at any stage in its history:

> Surely he sees how I behave,
>   does he not count all my steps?
> Have I been a fellow traveller with falsehood,
>   or hastened my steps towards deceit?
> If he weighs me on honest scales,
>   being God, he cannot fail to see my innocence.
> If my feet have wandered from the rightful path,
>   or if my eyes have led my heart astray,
>   or if my hands are smirched with any stain,

let another eat what I have sown,
  and let my young shoots all be rooted out.
If I ever lost my heart to any woman,
  or lurked at my neighbour's door,
let my wife grind corn that is not mine,
  let her sleep between others' sheets.
For I should have commited a sin of lust,
  a crime punishable by the law,
and should have lit a fire burning till Perdition,
  which would have devoured all my harvesting.
If ever I have infringed the rights of slave
  or maidservant in legal actions against me –
what shall I do, when God stands up?
  What shall I say, when he holds his assize?
They, no less than I, were created in the womb
  by the one same God who shaped us all within our mothers.
If my land calls down vengeance on my head
  and every furrow runs with tears,
if without payment I have eaten fruit grown on it
  or given those who toiled there cause to groan,
let brambles grow where once was wheat,
  and foul weeds where barley thrived.

Have I been insensible to poor men's needs,
  or let a widow's eyes grow dim?
Or taken my share of bread alone,
  not giving a share to the orphan?
I, whom God has fostered father-like, from childhood,
  and guided since I left my mother's womb,
Have I ever seen a wretch in need of clothing,
  or a beggar going naked,
without his having cause to bless me from his heart,
  as he felt the warmth of the fleece from my lambs?
Have I raised my hand against the guiltless,
  presuming on my credit at the gate?
If so, then let my shoulder fall from its socket,
  my arm be shattered at the joint.
God's terror would indeed descend on me;
  how could I hold my ground before his majesty?

Have I put all my trust in gold,
  from finest gold sought my security?

Have I ever gloated over my great wealth,
  or the riches that my hands have won?
Or has the sight of the sun in its glory,
  or the glow of the moon as it walked the sky,
stolen my heart, so that my hand
  blew them a secret kiss?
That too would be a criminal offence,
  to have denied the supreme God.
Have I taken pleasure in my enemies' misfortunes,
  or made merry when disaster overtook them,
I who allowed my tongue to do no wrong,
  by cursing them or vowing them to death?
The people of my tent, did they not say,
  'Is there a man he has not filled with meat?'
No stranger ever had to sleep outside,
  my door was always open to the traveller.
Have I ever hidden my sins from men,
  keeping my iniquity secret in my breast?
Have I ever stood so in fear of common gossip,
  or so dreaded any family's contempt,
  that I have been reduced to silence, not venturing out
                                    of doors?

Who can get me a hearing from God?
  I have had my say, from A to Z; now let Shaddai answer me.
When my adversary has drafted his writ against me
I shall wear it on my shoulder,
  and bind it round my head like a royal turban.
I will give him an account of every step of my life,
  and go as boldly as a prince to meet him.

Job 31: 4-37

Such then was the faith and practice of Israel at its best as it
has been handed on to Christianity from the Old Testament.
Such should have been the teaching that Jesus received in the
synagogue school at Nazareth where he grew to manhood.
It would seem from the gospels, however, that this was not
the case. What had gone wrong?

30. The World into which Jesus Came

BEFORE we look for an answer to the question at the end of the last chapter let us first try to see what the world looked like at the time of the birth of Jesus. The first clue is given in St Luke's account of the Christmas story when he says: 'Now at this time Caesar Augustus issued a decree for a census of the whole world to be taken.' The 'whole world' in this case meant the Roman Empire, which stretched from the Atlantic to Arabia, from Britain to the Sahara. The great Persian Empire had been overthrown by Alexander the Great, and his Greek Empire had now given place to the rule of the Caesars. This was what counted as civilisation. Beyond it were the 'barbarians'.

At the birth of Jesus, there was peace almost everywhere within the empire. The authority of Rome, backed by mobile legions and strategic garrisons, provided the world with a welcome respite from war for almost a century around this time. A man could travel from end to end of the empire without a passport by using the marvellous system of arterial roads. Merchants, officials, soldiers and private citizens passed along these highways in an endless stream. In due course Christian missionaries too had cause to be grateful for them as a means of spreading the gospel.

Yet the empire, although Roman in name and government, was still Greek in character. The legacy of Alexander the Great had been the culture and civilisation of Athens. The Roman conquerors had themselves been conquered by the power of Greek ideas. Most significant of all was the fact that basic Greek had become the international language. People still spoke their own native tongues, and Latin was the language of officialdom, but whether it was Asia Minor or North Africa, Italy or Spain, Greek was spoken and understood. Again this

was something which was of prime importance in the early
days of Christianity when St Paul, for example, was as easily
understood in Ephesus as in Rome. It was an educated world,
with schools and universities on the Greek pattern, and cities
where the architecture, dress and manners would have made an
old Athenian feel very much at home.

In Palestine, however, it was a different story. While the
rest of the world enjoyed the Roman peace, in Judaea there
was tension and guerilla warfare that led to open revolt. While
Greek culture was welcomed everywhere else, in Jerusalem it
was passionately resisted. The horror of the time of Antiochus
IV was still fresh in Jewish minds. Any sympathy which
progressive Jews had felt then towards Antiochus' attempt to
bring them into line with Greek civilisation had been killed
by his sacrilegious attack on their ancient faith and institutions.
The Maccabaean War of Independence had united patriotism
and conservative religion, and the orthodox Jews of the time
of Jesus were more strongly entrenched in their own ancient
tradition than they had been since the time of Ezra.

The high hopes of the early days of the War of Independence,
when every Jew rallied to the summons of Judas Maccabaeus,
had been shattered by the dynastic disputes of the Maccabaean
family. The noble cause which had called forth the book of
Daniel was now seen to be a self-seeking struggle for power on
the part of those who followed Judas as heads of state. At
length, in 63 BC, the Romans were invited to arbitrate between
the rival factions, and having once got a foothold in Palestine
they took good care not to be dislodged. The story of the next
hundred years is one of increasingly bad relations between the
Jews and their Roman masters, ending in the terrible war of
AD 66–70 which resulted in the destruction of Jerusalem and
the devastation of the whole country.

Jesus was born in a land about the size of Wales, a tiny part
of the far-flung Roman dominions. It was also, as far as the
Romans were concerned, the most irritating thorn in their flesh.
They had established a monarchy, subject of course to Rome,
under Herod the Great, who had adopted the Jewish religion
although not a Jew by birth. His allegiance was to Rome and

his sympathies were Greek, which was hardly a combination to endear him to his subjects. He undoubtedly won their approval by taking in hand the rebuilding of the Temple at Jerusalem, but this approval was tempered by the heavy taxation he imposed to pay for it and the Roman eagle which he insisted on putting above the door.

The Jews certainly did not approve of his new Greek-style towns with their pagan temples, or of his splendid marble and gold palace in Jerusalem, built at public expense, or of the theatre and amphitheatre for games and gladiatorial displays, which he erected just outside the city walls. The less militant members of the Jewish community confined their protest to passive resistance. More fiery characters expressed their feelings more violently and Herod's reign was marked by the ruthless suppression of disaffected elements by means of massacres and crucifixions. One can well understand how a man of this sort, who by the end of his reign had become quite mad, could have been responsible for the mass murder of the children of Bethlehem, from which the infant Jesus was saved. On his death in 4 BC the Jews besought the emperor to take the country under direct Roman supervision. They had had enough of Herod.

The emperor Augustus, however, preferred to divide the territory among Herod's three sons. As it happened, the one who was made ruler of Judaea, the most important section of the country with Jerusalem, the capital, in the heart of it, was the worst of the three. After ten years of riots, rebellion and merciless reprisals, the emperor yielded to Jewish pleas and placed Judaea under the control of a Roman procurator, who was to be responsible to the provincial governor of Syria and through him to Augustus himself.

Procurators were not officials of high standing in the Roman administration. They were sometimes appointed to trouble spots in the empire's more backward colonies, and Palestine was obviously one of these. The fifth procurator to be put in charge of Judaea was Pontius Pilate, who took office in AD 26 and thus had the power of life and death in his hands at the trial of Jesus. The Herod who features most in the gospels was Herod Antipas – son of Herod the Great – who was ruler of Galilee, the part of Palestine to which Jesus belonged. He was bent on getting rid of Jesus, who described him as 'that fox', and he had already caused the murder of John the Baptist, who had condemned him for his bigamous marriage with Herodias. Pontius Pilate's record too is a black one. His method of government was brutal repression and he was eventually tried in Rome for massacring civilians without sufficient cause and was banished to Gaul.

The gospel story is thus played out in a land which was seething with unrest, badly governed and stained with blood. Apart from the Herods, who, although powerful enough, were merely the nominal rulers, the real clash was between Roman authority and Jewish religious scruples. The Romans were on the whole just and tolerant, if unimaginative, masters of their subject peoples. So long as law and order were observed they held their provinces on a light rein and allowed the natives reasonable freedom. What they could not understand was what they regarded as the religious fanaticism of the Jews.

Complaints against heavy taxation were understandable. This was a crushing burden at the time of Jesus, and the *publicani*, or government tax collectors, who lived mainly by extortion in addition to their normal dues, were regarded as rogues, and bracketed with 'sinners' in popular thought. It was also understandable to the Romans that the Jews should yearn for the independence they had enjoyed under Judas Maccabaeus. Likewise Romans could understand unrest which sprang from poverty and malnutrition as a result of bad harvests. What they could not understand, however, was a people who regarded an image of the divine emperor as an affront to the God whose Law forbade the worship of all graven images, who denounced theatres and athletic stadia as hotbeds of immorality and rose in revolt at the use of money filched from the Temple treasury to pay for an aqueduct. Naturally all this was seen by the Romans as sheer obscurantism, and opposition which they could not comprehend they used increasingly sterner methods to suppress. It is not surprising that the pages of the gospels are studded with so many cases of mental disorder and disease.

Ever since their return from the Babylonian exile, the Jews had tended to become more and more a theocracy, governed by priests in accordance with the divine Law as contained in the sacred scriptures. The high priest in Jerusalem had become the effective head of state and under Roman administration this continued, subject only to the ultimate authority of the procurators. The two high priests who are mentioned in the gospels, Annas and Caiaphas, were obviously powerful figures in the community. Annas was in office from AD 6–15 and his son-in-law Caiaphas ruled from AD 18–36.

Under them the chief legislative body was the Sanhedrin, whose leading members are described in the gospels as the 'chief priests'. Judicial matters which could not be settled by local tribunals were referred to the Sanhedrin, which was in effect the supreme court in all Jewish affairs except in the case of capital offences. High priests and chief priests were recruited from the party of the Sadducees, who are linked in the gospels with the Pharisees as the two dominant religious groups in the time of Jesus. Both parties had grown up since the time of the Maccabaean War. The Sadducees were wealthy, aristocratic and highly unpopular. They had been in their early days the 'progressive' faction, favouring the adoption of Greek practices, and although Antiochus' policies had alienated their sympathies they were still regarded as tainted with foreign ideas. The popular view was that they were too friendly with the Roman government and avoided a clash in order to keep themselves in power.

The Pharisees on the other hand had a much better record. They were mostly laymen and included a wide range of people of differing types. They had always been identified with Jewish national aspirations and had always been stout defenders of the unique character of Israel's heritage of faith and practice. They numbered among them the more militant young Jews who kept up a running battle against the Romans or the Herods or whoever seemed to be standing in the way of freedom. These *maquis* called themselves Zealots, and one of them, Simon by name, became a disciple of Jesus. Their revolutionary tactics were deplored by the more moderate members of the com-

munity, who called them 'robbers', since not only the Romans but also the wealthy were their targets. Many of them ended on a cross by the wayside, like the two who were crucified at the same time as Jesus. On the other hand the party of the Pharisees included the solid middle class, patriotic but law-abiding, hating Roman oppression but avoiding open conflict.

Yet Jesus, according to the gospels, had little to say in favour of the Pharisees. It was not the young Zealots who roused his ire or the quiet middle-of-the-road men and women who belonged to this party. His strictures were directed at those Pharisees who claimed to be the public guardians of religion and morals, who set themselves up as examples of godly living, and made the warm humanity of Israel's historic faith a miserable matter of pettifogging adherence to a soulless code of legalistic observances.

We ended the last chapter, where we saw the massive legacy that Christianity has received from the Old Testament, with the question why Jesus should nevertheless have had so little to say in favour of the religious atmosphere in which he grew up. The answer is that although there were doubtless some worthy Sadducees and Pharisees in his day, the policy of both parties had resulted in a religion which was a travesty of what the psalmists, prophets and sages of the Old Testament had stood for. As we shall see, the Sadducees, who controlled the Temple at Jerusalem, where generations of Israelites had felt themselves to be in the very presence of God, had turned this great national shrine into a commercial racket and a public fairground. The 'scribes' or rabbis of the Pharisaic party, who influenced society powerfully through the synagogues, offered men a bleak and sterile creed and commended as the good life a dreary pattern of 'thou-shalt-nots', which had no relevance to the real needs of ordinary people who were looking for help and guidance in the daily battle of living in a frightening world.

31. The Herald of the Messiah

HOWEVER, while Jewish orthodoxy in the time of Jesus was offering such a sorry substitute for the full-blooded faith of Israel at its best, a new and challenging voice was heard which rang out like that of one of the old-time prophets. While the Pharisees side-tracked religion into trivial channels, fussing over sabbath observance, dietary laws, ritual fasting and such-like religiosity, an austere figure reminiscent of Elijah drew crowds to listen to him in the desert country down by the river Jordan as he sounded once again the traditional call for repentance and proclaimed God's judgement on the nation's sins. This was John the Baptist.

It is now clear that, although the gospels mention only Sadducees and Pharisees, the representatives of the religious orthodoxy with which Jesus came into conflict, there was a wide variety of nonconformist sects in Palestine at the time, which can roughly be called a 'baptist movement' since baptism was one of their common characteristics. The discovery of the Dead Sea Scrolls a few years ago has drawn attention to one particular group who lived a monastic life at Qumran beside the Dead Sea, and who stored their library for safety in the neighbouring caves during the Roman-Jewish War of AD 66–70. There the scrolls lay hidden for almost two thousand years until the now notorious goatherd Mohammed the Wolf came upon them accidentally in 1947.

The site of John the Baptist's mission lies so close to the monastery at Qumran that a connection has inevitably been made between the two. The Dead Sea sect almost certainly belonged to the Essene movement which had several monastic settlements in different parts of the country. These people were ascetic in their habits, and practised baptism, so that it is not impossible that John the Baptist had been a member of such a community in his earlier years, since these two features were prominent in his own campaign. If this was so, he must have broken away from the monastic life at some point to conduct his own distinctive type of religious revival.

Israel had traditionally looked to the desert for its inspired men of God. It was in the desert at the time of the Exodus that Moses had made the Ten Commandments the basis of the Law; it was from the desert that prophet after prophet had come to recall the people to this historic faith. Elijah too had been a man of the desert and there was much about John the Baptist that revived the memory of that stern keeper of the nation's conscience. Like Elijah he was dressed in a coarse habit of camel hair and lived on the sparse fare of the scrubland. Like Elijah's too his message was one of warning and denunciation, a call for national penitence and rededication to the God of their fathers. Men flocked to hear him and many were moved to enter the Jordan at John's invitation and to be immersed in its waters as an outward sign of their penitence and inward renewal through God's forgiveness. In contrast to the superficiality of orthodox teaching, the call of the Baptist was clearly an authentic message from God which demanded a decision.

But John did not merely summon men to repent of their sins and embark on a new life of integrity and obedience to God. There was a more dramatic urgency in his appeal which brings us back to an element in the story of the Bible which we have already seen emerging – the hope of a coming Messiah. It had always been at the heart of Israel's faith that God had singled her out for some great purpose. Sometimes this had been perverted into nationalistic hopes for the supremacy of Israel over the Gentile nations, but the best thought of the Old Testament, as for example in the Servant Songs of Second Isaiah and in the book of Jonah, had seen Israel's vocation in terms of bringing light into pagan darkness and of being the means of the whole world coming to the true knowledge of God.

So strong was the conviction that the destiny of mankind was in the hands of a wise, just and merciful God and not in the grip of blind Chance or inscrutable Fate, that Israel could not believe in anything other than a good outcome to the changing

scene of history. God would see to it that in the end goodness would prevail and evil be destroyed. The time would come when wars would cease, when peace would reign, when truth and justice would replace the cruelty and corruption of the world as they knew it. Thus prophet and psalmist alike looked forward to the Golden Age to come, when men would live together in unity as the Creator intended; and when, in Isaiah's words, 'the earth shall be full of the knowledge of the Lord as the waters cover the sea.'

Inevitably, being Jews, they thought of this Golden Age of the future as being a more splendid successor of the only Golden Age that they had ever known in their chequered history, the reign of King David. Time had blurred the memory of the flaws in David's character and the mischances of his times. What remained was an image of a great king whose piety, resolution and devotion to Israel's heritage had made his age a paradise compared with everything that had happened since. Accordingly, when this future paradise on earth was envisaged, it was thought of as being ushered in and governed by a king like David, a 'Son of David', who as God's anointed representative on earth, the Messiah, would fulfil the Lord's purpose for the world.

But the Messiah, when he came to deliver the world from its plight and to rule in the name of God, would be no mere earthly king as David had been. He could be described by Isaiah as Wonderful Counsellor, Mighty God, Eternal Father and Prince of Peace. And as the people of Israel found themselves more and more at the mercy of ruthless oppressors, a pagan Antiochus, a mad Herod the Great, or, now, the Roman legions, their thoughts turned more and more to the belief that God must act swiftly and decisively to bring evil men to book, to vindicate the righteous and to inaugurate a new order. As things went from bad to worse, many felt that the world had become too corrupt to be the scene of God's rule. They could see nothing ahead but a cataclysmic end to the present world and the advent of a new heaven and a new earth. This had been in the mind of the writer of the book of Daniel and of many others who had written in the same apocalyptic strain between his day and the birth of Christianity. Their writings were frowned upon by the orthodox Jews but they fanned popular expectation of a coming crisis and the appearance of the Messiah.

There was much variety of opinion as to what would happen and how it would happen. The more religiously minded thought in terms of a supernatural Messiah whose reign would be preceded by a catastrophic end of the world. They conceived of a Day of Judgement to be followed by the Golden Age, or, as it had come to be known, the Kingdom of God. The more virile elements in society, such as the young Zealots, looked rather for a Messiah who would overthrow the Roman oppressors, and as they fought and died for the cause of Jewish freedom, they believed that they were hastening his coming.

It was to a people in this frame of mind that John the Baptist's message came as the sign for which they had been waiting. For his call to national repentance was, he said, the prelude to the imminent appearance of the Messiah. He himself was merely the herald of the Coming One. When he came, he would be so much greater than John that the Baptist described himself as not even worthy to unfasten his sandals. Moreover when he came it would be in Judgement, sifting the wheat from the chaff. John's challenge to the crowds who flocked to hear him was thus to save themselves from the wrath to come. He made it plain that the advent of the Messiah would be no triumph for Jews over Romans. Messiah's judgement would fall on evil wherever it was found and no privilege of Jewish race would save the sinner. On those who repented, however, and returned to the obedience which God demanded, Messiah would pour out a rich blessing of God's spirit.

John the Baptist was in a sense the last of the Old Testament prophets. Unlike the shallow orthodoxy of his day, he recalled men to the big issues of right and wrong, of social justice and personal commitment to God. But his emphasis was on the wrath of God rather than the love of God. He sought to frighten men into the service of God, and his gloomy asceticism offered little joy or gladness for ordinary mortals. Yet his significance in the story of the Bible is profound for it was the news of his dramatic message which brought Jesus out of the remote little town of Nazareth in Galilee to hear this strange prophet by the Jordan, and it was through John's ministry that Jesus began his own.

32. 'Unto Us a Child is Born'

IT is obvious the moment we look at the gospels that their writers did not set out to write 'lives of Jesus' in the modern sense. There is no day-to-day or even year-to-year account of what happened. Nothing is said of what Jesus looked like, whether he was tall or short, dark or fair, bearded or clean-shaven. Any paintings that have ever been made of him are pure guesswork. It is not certain exactly when he was born, how long his public ministry lasted, or in what year he died. All that is recorded of his teaching would fill no more than a page or two of a newspaper and we are told nothing of his conversation about everyday affairs. Clearly the authors of the four gospels were not writing 'biography' as we understand the word now.

The name given to his book by the writer of the earliest narrative about Jesus, St Mark, gives us the clue to what he and his fellow-evangelists were about. He calls it, not a 'life of Jesus' but a 'gospel'. This is an old Anglo-Saxon word meaning the 'God-story' or the 'good story' and it was used in the English version of the scriptures to translate the word which Mark uses and which means 'good news'. This then was what all four writers were bent on doing – giving an account of the 'good news' of what God had done for the world through Jesus Christ. This is why they do not linger over what they would have called tittle-tattle about Jesus' boyhood days, details of his personal tastes and mannerisms – all of which we should of course dearly love to know.

They believed they were writing of things far more impor-tant, nothing less than God's greatest act for the salvation of the world. It is significant that in Mark's sixteen short chapters, about half of them are taken up with the events that led up to

Jesus' death and Resurrection. In short, right from the outset of any record of Jesus at all, of what he did and what he said, there is the basic conviction that this is no ordinary life of a great teacher, or rabbi, or prophet, but an account of a unique person, who, although quite obviously a man like other men, was in some strange way like no other man who ever lived. Later generations tried to express the enigma of Jesus in succinct terms in creeds and confessions, and succeeded as far as it is possible to express in words what is ultimately inexpressible, but as far as the gospel writers were concerned they were content to set down what they themselves had known or heard and to leave us to draw our own conclusions.

They give us no tidy picture which would answer all our questions. They give us rather a series of impressions, incidents and utterances, which taken together have fired men's imaginations, inspired their devotion, demanded their decision and won their allegiance for well-nigh two thousand years. Perhaps it is just because, in the providence of God, it is such an imprecise record that men and women of all races, geographically, temporally, and temperamentally remote from first-century Palestine still find in the gospel story the answers to their deepest needs and their quest for meaning and purpose in a sometimes terrifying world.

Oddly enough, Jesus must have been born before the Christian era which is supposed to date from his birth. The monk who in the sixth century first reckoned when BC ended and AD began got his calculations wrong. Jesus must have been born before the death of Herod the Great, who died in 4 BC, and his birth was probably between 8 BC and 6 BC. Two of the four gospels, Matthew and Luke, identify his birthplace as Bethlehem where, as Luke tells us, Joseph and Mary were temporarily resident for registration during an imperial census which was being taken for taxation purposes.

Round the birth of Jesus in the stable of the inn at Bethlehem, where Joseph and Mary found makeshift accommodation, has grown a wealth of picturesque stories and customs reflected in the celebration of Christmas. Some of this is sheer fantasy and has no basis in the gospel narrative. Yet if the gospels had not given us a solid foundation on which to build our Christmas festivities the world would be a sadder and gloomier place. No one, despite the commercialism and odd whiffs of paganism at Christmastide, would suggest that we should be better off without its message of peace and goodwill, or that because some people eat too much or drink too much we should abolish an occasion which gives rise to so much happiness and friendliness.

Yet at the heart of it all is the gospel claim that the child who was born in a stable and cradled in a manger was the Saviour of the world. We must not be deluded into thinking that because poetry and devotion have added their quota with angelic choirs and guiding stars we are dealing with a fairy-tale or a world of make-believe. The Jews had been expecting a Messiah for centuries; the appearance of a particularly brilliant star such as might have been produced by a conjunction of Jupiter and Saturn in 7 BC could have brought astrologers or 'wise men' from Babylon to Palestine to investigate. Shepherds in the fields around Bethlehem may well have made their way to the traditional home of David, where the 'Son of David' might be expected to be born, moved by something less dramatic than an angelic announcement.

But the homage paid to the infant Jesus by representatives of the learned world and of simple peasants, however much the stories may have been embroidered by the time they came into the hands of the Gospel writers, brings us to the heart of the Christmas mystery – the Virgin Birth. All sorts of arguments, some of them quite sound, have been produced to show how this belief could have grown up for doctrinal reasons. It has been pointed out that it is mentioned nowhere else in the New Testament outside the opening chapters of Matthew and Luke, and that the early Church did not make belief in the Virgin Birth of Jesus a condition of becoming a Christian. Yet when all is said and done, many of us, remembering all that Christ has meant for the world, will find it easier to think of the beginning of his life on earth as being no less unique than its ending, and will ask ourselves if it is more likely that the Saviour of the world was the son of two worthy Jewish villagers

than that a special creative act of God brought into being a new type of Man.

Not long after the birth of Jesus we are told that mad King Herod, alarmed at the rumours of the birth of the Messiah and fearful of a threat to his throne, ordered the massacre of all male children in Bethlehem under two years old. Jesus was taken by Joseph and Mary for safety to nearby Egypt until, with the death of the old king, it was prudent to return. They settled at Nazareth in Galilee where Joseph was the local carpenter, and apart from a visit to Jerusalem at the age of twelve, where Jesus was found by his harassed family in the Temple earnestly questioning the rabbis long after the rest of the party had begun the homeward journey to Nazareth, the curtain falls on him for the next thirty years.

This, to us, extraordinary gap in the story has exercised the ingenuity of many minds from the earliest centuries of the Church's history. What people do not know they often invent, and fantastic tales were conjured up of Jesus' boyhood prowess and feats of strength in young manhood in these 'hidden years'. More recently, since the discovery of the Dead Sea Scrolls, it has been suggested that he may have spent some of these years in the monastery at Qumran. It is unlikely that this happened, and there is not the slightest evidence to prove that it did. Nothing could be further removed from the attitude of the rigidly exclusive ascetics of the Dead Sea community, as we know them from their writings, than the warmly compassionate and sociable friend of all in need, as we know Jesus from the pages of the gospels.

The four evangelists regard the real beginning of the story of Jesus as his entry into public life as a preacher and healer after his encounter with John the Baptist. But from the stories, or parables, that Jesus himself told we can gather something of his life during these 'hidden years'. Nazareth was a quiet village lying among the hills of Galilee. The great caravan route from Asia to Africa by-passed it on the coastal plain. City life, apart from visits to Jerusalem, seems to have played little part in Jesus' early days. He was a countryman with a countryman's interests. When St Paul looked for illustrations to make a point in his letters he found them in the life of the Greek cities which he knew. Jesus, on the other hand, turned to the fields, the farms, the fisher-folk and the simple country homes of Galilee to find his images.

Joseph is not mentioned during Jesus' public ministry so it is reasonable to assume that he had died in the meantime and that Jesus as the eldest son carried on the carpenter's shop. Other brothers and sisters mentioned in the gospels may either have been younger than Jesus or may have been children of Joseph by a previous marriage. It is thus in the uneventful life of an unimportant village in a provincial backwater of the Roman Empire that the stage was set for events that have turned the world upside down. Two things can be said with certainty. Firstly, that it was in Nazareth, in the normal life of a small community, that Jesus got to know ordinary men and women in all their strength and weakness. And, secondly, that it was here that as a serious-minded young Jewish joiner, among all the chores and daily problems of his trade, he began to ask himself far-reaching questions.

His knowledge of the Old Testament scriptures was pro-found, as we can see from his teaching, and to one who so clearly saw into the heart of Israel's faith at its best, it must have been a cause of growing discontent and dismay that the current orthodoxy of his time, no doubt fully represented in the services of the synagogue at Nazareth, was such a shallow travesty of Israel's great religious heritage. Accordingly, when news came to Nazareth that a prophet with an arresting message, like the powerful Old Testament spokesmen of God, was drawing crowds to the Jordan's banks by announcing that the coming of the Messiah was at hand, and that something like a mass religious revival had begun, it is not surprising that Jesus took this as a sign that God was once again stirring up his people and that he must hear it for himself.

But there must have been a deeper reason than curiosity to make him forsake his home and his trade. It would not have needed even a hint from Mary his Mother that there had been something strange in the manner of his birth to make this deeply thoughtful young man hold a continuing audit of his soul. Unless Jesus was an entirely different man during his public life from what he had been in his quiet Galilean village, he must have become increasingly aware that his relationship with God was far more intimate than it seemed to be in the rest of his circle. This sense of living his life in constant awareness of the presence of God must surely also have been matched with a growing sense of power, power that must have been given to him to use in the service of God on a wider stage than Nazareth.

So he made his way south and joined the crowds that thronged round the Baptist. John's words came to him as a personal call, not indeed to return to a life of obedience to God, for he had never known anything else, but to dedicate himself anew to God in baptism, to identify himself with those who responded to the Baptist's summons, and to offer his own service on behalf of those who were indifferent to God's challenge. His baptism in the Jordan at the hands of John was a shattering experience. As he came out of its waters it was as if the heavens opened and as if God himself spoke to him. At that moment his self-questioning was answered. He knew he was the Messiah.

In turmoil of spirit he went off into the solitude of the wild region around the Jordan to think this through. The picturesque stories of his 'temptations by the devil in the wilderness' are the Bible's way of telling us – as Jesus himself must later have confided his experiences at this time to his disciples – how he rejected one possible course after another. What sort of Messiah was he going to be? How was he to use this increased sense of power that had come to him at his baptism? Was it given to him to create the kind of material paradise that many were looking for, or to startle men into faith with spectacular supernatural displays, or, as most people wanted, was he to set himself up as a new Judas Maccabaeus and raise the flag of revolt against the Romans? Jesus came back from his solitary agonising over his problem with his mind made up. As God's Messiah he must take no short cuts to success, and offer no second-bests. The path he had finally chosen was far harder, but he believed that it was the path God wanted him to follow.

33. Failure of a Mission

WHEN Jesus left the harsh Judaean hills and returned to his own northern Galilean land he was in his early thirties. He chose Capernaum on the shores of the Lake of Galilee as his centre and from there began a teaching and healing mission which lasted about two years. The west bank where Capernaum lay was lined with small towns and villages, busy with fishing, boat-building and fruit growing. This provided the audience, but what was the message? On the face of it, it seemed to be little different from that of John the Baptist. Jesus' theme, according to Mark, was: 'The time has come at last – the Kingdom of God has arrived. You must change your hearts and minds and believe the Good News.' What did he mean?

It is typical of Jesus throughout his ministry that he should have taken old words that were familiar to everybody and given them a new meaning. He was speaking to people who believed that when Messiah came the hopes and prayers of prophets and psalmists for a different kind of world would be realised, a world where God would be everywhere acknowledged, where truth and justice, mercy and peace would reign, instead of oppression, cruelty and hatred. It would mean the end of the tyranny of evil and the triumph of the good purposes of God. The name they gave to all this was the Kingdom of God, meaning the Rule or Reign of God on earth.

John the Baptist had also announced that the time for all this to begin to happen was close at hand. But he had said that before the Kingdom of God could become a reality Messiah must appear with fire and judgement. The wrath of God must be endured before his Rule could begin. On the other hand, the Zealots and their friends believed that the Rule of God would be the triumph of Israel over the Romans and that Messiah would come to bring this about, while the teaching of the orthodox rabbis was that Messiah would appear and the Rule

of God would begin only when the people repented of their sins and obeyed the Law.

The message of Jesus was quite different and this is why it was good news. He said that indeed the time had come for which men had been hoping and praying, but it was not going to mean the end of the world and fiery vengeance on evildoers as John the Baptist had predicted, nor was it going to be the triumph of Israel over her enemies as the Zealots expected. The Rule of God, said Jesus, has already begun: the power of God to transform and renew the life of the world is now at work among you. God has not even waited for mass repentance and adherence to the Law, as the Pharisees said he would. Rather out of his boundless love for men and through no merit of their own he has offered them a fresh start and inaugurated a New Age. This was why they should repent, or in other words change their hearts and minds, not to hasten the coming of the Kingdom but in thankfulness to God for his goodness in making a new world possible here and now.

The whole of Jesus' ministry turned on this central theme: the Rule of God on earth has begun. God cares for men and women as they are and because of that he has made it possible for them to begin to live in the Golden Age, which, as Jesus made plain, means living in the right relationship to God and to one another. If men would only turn to God in humility and trust, with the simple confidence of a little child instead of with their normal pride and self-sufficiency, they would find themselves living in a new dimension where evil would have no final hold over them and where the power of God would be available to help them. Being born again, putting their lives under the Rule of God, committing themselves without reservation to the service of God – this, said Jesus (for these all mean the same thing), is the pathway to life as it was meant to be.

This message of Jesus, so much more hopeful and reassuring than the threatening warnings of John the Baptist, so much more vital and encouraging than the dreary compliance with rules and regulations which the orthodox rabbis demanded, was indeed good news to the ordinary people of Galilee. In keeping with his emphasis on the love and compassion of God, rather than on his stern requirements, Jesus spoke of the New Age as a time for rejoicing. He spurned the ascetic habits of the professional 'holy man' and likened himself and his followers to a wedding-party. These followers of Jesus who had been attracted to him from the beginning and who had responded to his invitation to become his disciples, were mostly working-men from the same background as himself. The first recruits were four fishermen headed by Simon, later to be re-named Peter. They were to be the nucleus of a community of men, and later of women also, who accepted the Rule of God for their own lives and whose job it would be to bring others into the same service.

Mark in his gospel gives us an example of a day in the life of Jesus at this time, which must have been typical of many. It was, as it happens, a sabbath day in Capernaum. In the morning Jesus preached in the synagogue, where the congregation was at once impressed by the note of 'authority' in his preaching. What the people were used to from the pulpit were dreary expositions of the Law with painstaking quotations of what the great Rabbi so-and-so and the great Rabbi so-and-so else had said about the topic in question. When Jesus spoke to the congregation, however, they felt that here was someone who like the Old Testament prophets gave a message which came straight from God. In the synagogue there was a man whose mind was deranged. The effect on him when Jesus addressed him directly was that his insane babbling stopped and his mind became clear. Once again the congregation were startled into awareness of someone with 'authority' who not only declared the word of God but exercised the healing power of God.

A homely incident took place after the synagogue service in Peter's house, so trivial that most likely the story came to Mark from Peter himself. When Jesus and his four disciples arrived at Peter's house expecting a meal, they found Peter's mother-in-law, who was apparently in charge of the household, sick in bed with a high fever. When Jesus took her by the hand and helped her up the fever left her and she was able to carry on with her chores. In the evening, when the sabbath was officially over and the strict laws for sabbath observance made it permissible, people brought many of their friends or family circle who were sick in mind or body to the house and Jesus healed them. The end of this exhausting twenty-four hours explains the source of Jesus' power to carry out such an exacting ministry. He got up the next morning before daybreak and went off by himself, perhaps to the quietness of the hillside above the town, to renew his strength in prayer.

We may picture Jesus' mission in Galilee as a succession of days like this. It became clear to all that this strange prophet with the gift of healing would let nothing stand in the way of what he believed to be God's will for men, that they should be whole in mind and body. The most loathsome diseases are cured by his laying his hands upon the sufferer, the outcasts of society are befriended, human need, whether it be hunger or sickness, is paramount and no religious taboos, such as observance of the sabbath, are allowed to stand in the way. So, as Jesus' fame spreads and the crowds who flock to hear him and to be healed by him become too great for synagogues and private houses, he has to resort to a little boat offshore on the Lake of Galilee, which he uses as a kind of floating pulpit to address the clamouring throng. Old-fashioned picture books showing an attentive flock grouped round a benign teacher listening to his gracious words against a gentle background of hills and trees must be far from the truth. It is more likely to have been a typically noisy, sweaty oriental crowd, pushing and jostling to hear and to be healed, imposing a well-nigh intolerable strain on Jesus' mind and body.

But there was not only the constant drain on his energy, there was also the mounting tension of opposition. It was not merely that Jesus found that his appeal to the men and women of Galilee to put God and their neighbours' needs at the centre of their lives fell all too often on deaf ears, or that the first flush of enthusiastic response soon faded away, or that many preferred to carry on in their own selfish ways. There was also much head-shaking and open disapproval at the presumption of this village joiner from Nazareth setting himself up as a public figure and claiming to preach and heal in the name of

God. Jesus' own family had doubts about his sanity and tried to persuade him to return home.

More serious opposition came from the professional ecclesiastics. They probably disliked open-air preaching on principle, but they certainly took grave exception to a man who claimed to be speaking and acting in the service of God, yet who mixed with the riff-raff of society – prostitutes, unscrupulous tax collectors, and other unsavoury characters whom any responsible person would not wish to know. Jesus' social life also came under fire. He did not behave in the proper way for a 'holy man', as John the Baptist with his ascetic habits had done. Instead of that, Jesus enjoyed life, eating and drinking like anyone else, so the Pharisees dismissed him as 'a drunkard and a glutton'. His high-handed attitude to the sacred Law of Moses, in such matters as disregarding strict observance of the sabbath, was, they said, unpardonable. Most outrageous of all was his claim to be able to forgive men's sins, which as everyone knew only God could do. So righteous indignation turned into open hostility. Local religious leaders were up in arms and the Jerusalem hierarchy sent agents down to Galilee to report on Jesus' activities. King Herod, who had already got rid of John the Baptist as a troublemaker, indicated that he viewed this new prophet as equally dangerous and undesirable. An unholy alliance of Church and State was forged to eliminate the Nazarene.

At this point Jesus suddenly left Galilee. There may have been a variety of reasons for this. Partly, perhaps, he was not prepared to have his activities cut short by some trumped-up charge by Herod's government. Partly, perhaps, he wanted to escape from his supporters. There was still plenty of enthusiasm for his mission, despite the lapse of many who found his demands too heavy, or who felt that a more militant leader would be more to their liking. But it seems as if Jesus recognised that much of his popularity was based on his healing power alone, and much of it was built on a misguided hope that he had it in mind to choose his time and lead a rebellion against the Romans.

Throughout his Galilean ministry, Jesus had been at pains

to avoid using the word Messiah about himself and to prevent anyone else from calling him by that name. The reason is obvious. The political situation was explosive. A spark would have set off wholesale insurrection. There were enough fanatical patriots in Palestine, and far more eager young Jews throughout the Roman Empire, who were living for the day when the Messiah would appear and strike a greater blow for Jewish freedom than Judas Maccabaeus had done two centuries before. We are told that there was indeed at this point in Jesus' ministry a move to make him king against his will. But this was one of the possible courses of action that Jesus had ruled out in his solitary 'temptation in the wilderness', after his baptismal experience had convinced him that he was indeed the Messiah. The gospels suggest that it may well have been a recurring temptation.

It was thus partly for such reasons that the Galilean ministry came to an end after possibly about two years. In one sense it had ended in disillusionment and disappointment for Jesus. There was no sign of the general change of heart and mind that he had hoped for among the crowds who flocked to hear his teaching or to be led by him. And so it would seem that he decided on a new policy. He had, as we have seen, attracted a group of followers, and from these he had selected twelve men in particular to form as it were an inner circle of disciples. Clearly the number was no accident. It was not eleven or thirteen, but twelve, because Jesus was founding the new Israel. Israel's twelve tribes had been the traditional embodiment of the People of God. In Jesus' view, Israel, or more properly its present representatives in the person of Pharisees and Sadducees, had failed to keep Israel constantly in mind of its God-given mission to lead the whole world by precept and example to the knowledge of the truth about God, about life, about the meaning of man's existence.

Accordingly, with the conviction that he himself was God's agent on earth to bring about a new order, a new set of values, a new outlook and a new beginning, Jesus deliberately created the basis of a new community to do what old Israel had been meant to do but had dismally failed to accomplish. Out of these twelve ordinary men, symbolic of the historic twelve tribes, he would build the new community of God's people, the new Israel. They at least, unlike the clamouring crowds on the Galilean lakeside, had glimpsed something of what Jesus meant by the Rule of God, and had grasped enough to be sent out on a teaching and healing mission on their own. So he would take them apart, away from the crowds, and teach them more intensively what he believed about God and man, about the purpose of a man's own life and about God's purpose for the world.

So Jesus led them out of Galilee into the territory that lies beyond it to the north, and it was then on a country road that Jesus put a searching question to his twelve disciples and got an answer which may be looked on as the turning point of his mission. We are not told exactly how the question arose, but what we do know is that it was the first time that Jesus had asked it. 'Who do people say that I am?' he said. The reply was that some said he was John the Baptist or Elijah come back to life. Then Jesus put the question directly: 'But what about you? Who do *you* say that I am?' In the name of all the Twelve, but with his own intuitive understanding, Peter replied: 'You are the Messiah.' It had meant little to Jesus when from time to time he had been called Messiah in an emotionally charged moment of gratitude, or adulation. But here was a man who had been with him from the beginning, who had known him in public life and private life, and who had reached this conclusion which Jesus himself had long since known to be true. Obviously deeply moved, Jesus re-named Simon, his chief disciple, Peter, meaning the Rock, and declared that on this Rock he would build his Church, promising that the powers of death would never prevail against it.

34. The Thoughts of Jesus

JUST as the gospels give us for the most part only a series of scenes from the ministry of Jesus rather than a systematic record of what he did, so they give us no exhaustive transcript of what he said. One of the writers of the gospels, overwhelmed by the story he has had to tell, closes his narrative with the comment that if the whole tale were told the world itself might not be big enough to hold all the books that would have to be written. We can understand what he meant. Even allowing for the gospel writer's sense of his own inadequacy to deal with so vast a subject, it is clear that all the teaching of Jesus that we are given in the gospels cannot be more than a fraction of what he said throughout his mission.

But like the short anecdotes which cover the whole range of his activities, the selection of the sayings of Jesus which the gospels provide is enough to give us a clear picture of the essence of his message. His main theme, as we have seen, was that a new age had begun: God was no longer to be regarded as a remote and rather terrifying Being beyond the skies who demanded compliance with the Law he had given to Moses – as the orthodox teaching of the time insisted – but as a living Presence in men's lives, understanding and forgiving their failures and offering them the power of new life, showing them indeed how splendid ordinary life could be.

When Jesus was talking to the crowds who gathered round him, his favourite method of instruction seems to have been that of telling them little stories, or 'parables' as they were called. These were homely illustrations, taken from daily life, suggesting in a way that anyone could understand the point that he wanted to make. There are many of these parables recorded in the gospels but we may take two of them as bringing out in a vivid way the theme of Jesus' message. They are, as it happens, perhaps the two best known of all – the Prodigal Son and the

Good Samaritan. Indeed they are so well known that we may well miss the point.

In the story of the Prodigal Son the spotlight is not meant to fall on the boy who goes off in search of a good time, ends up destitute and, when he comes to his senses, returns home sadder and wiser, nor on his elder brother who takes a dim view of the fuss that is made over his homecoming, but on the boy's father. The old man is so delighted to get his son back again that he runs out to meet him, with words of welcome and not of reproach. Jesus' point is that this very human story suggests something of the love of God for even the most undeserving black sheep of his family.

Samaritans were traditionally detested by orthodox Jews. Yet in the story of the Good Samaritan Jesus underlines that it was one of these despised people, and not the pious Jew who passed by on the other side of the road, who helped the injured traveller lying in the ditch. The Samaritan had least reason of all to come to the rescue of the wounded Jew, but he was the one who understood best that human need comes before questions of race or creed.

These two stories illustrate the two commandments that Jesus picked out of the great burdensome mass of obligations contained in the Law which the Pharisees wanted to hang round the neck of every citizen. Jesus maintained that the Law could be summed up in the two commandments: 'You must love the Lord your God with all your heart, with all your soul, with all your mind and with all your strength', and 'You must love your neighbour as yourself.' In loving God, we are to think of someone who is like the father in the story of the Prodigal Son, and in loving our neighbour (which does not necessarily mean liking our neighbour) we are to follow the example of the Good Samaritan who understood that by 'neighbour' was meant anyone at all who needed help.

Most of Jesus' teaching as it appears in the gospels was, however, not directed to the crowds but to his disciples, to men who had committed their lives to God and who wanted to learn more of what that involved. If we keep this fact in mind, it will save us from the foolish mistake that many people make who simply dismiss Jesus' teaching as quite impracticable and unrealistic. We must not take sayings like 'Turn the other cheek', 'Resist not evil', 'Take no thought for tomorrow' and 'Love your enemies' out of their context. Jesus is not addressing governments charged with the task of keeping law and order and protecting their citizens, and he is certainly not advocating peace at any price or national irresponsibility.

When Jesus says: 'turn the other cheek' and 'resist not evil' he is not telling us what we should do when faced with a maniac brandishing a crowbar. (The Christian answer to that might be to look around for a bigger crowbar or preferably to have learned judo or karate.) Jesus is talking about our attitude to someone who has done us a personal wrong and is challenging our instinctive reaction to 'give as good as we get'. His point is that we should rather make every effort to effect a reconciliation even if it involves swallowing our pride. 'Take no thought for tomorrow' certainly does not mean 'make no plans for the future', but rather, 'don't worry about the future', and 'Love your enemies' does not mean 'like your enemies', but rather, 'try to see the other man's point of view'.

In what we call the Sermon on the Mount, which is really a collection of the best-remembered and therefore probably most often repeated sayings of Jesus, we are not given a programme of action which can be put into effect by any political party. Indeed it can hardly be called a programme of action at all, even for individuals. Jesus is not outlining a blueprint for Utopia or a code of social reform. No one apart from Jesus himself has ever loved God with all his heart and mind and soul and strength, to say nothing of loving his neighbour as much as he loves himself. But Jesus presented his followers with the challenge to try to do so.

His whole emphasis is not on rules of behaviour with which we must comply but on the general attitude to life that we must adopt if we want to live in the right relationship to God and to one another. In a sense in the Sermon on the Mount Jesus is painting a picture of himself. He never calls it that, of course, but as we look back over his life and compare it with the lives of the most saintly men of whom we have records in any religion it is clear that no one apart from Jesus has ever measured up to the selfless concern for others and the total commitment to God which he demanded of his followers.

In his teaching, Jesus is concerned to show what happens in a man's life when he gives himself to God and becomes a follower of Christ, and he claims that it is this kind of man who knows what true happiness is. Most of us, if we were asked, would say that a man is happy when he has good health, a tidy bank balance, a worth-while job and a comfortable home. Jesus does not mention any of these but says, in what are called the Beatitudes, that a man is happy when he lives his life in dependence on God, when he knows what sorrow means, when he is passionately concerned about justice, when he is merciful, utterly sincere and bent on promoting the well-being of the community at all levels.

It has been fashionable for some time to contrast Jesus' attitude to life with that of the Old Testament. Jesus, we have been told, stressed the positive approach – what we *should* do, rather than what we should *not* do. To some extent this is true. The overall impression we get from the Law of Moses is a list of the things we must avoid doing. The Ten Commandments emphasise: thou shalt *not* . . . We should be quite wrong, however, if we thought that Jesus substituted for the Ten Commandments some vague instruction to love God and our neighbour and then left it to us to decide how that works out in practice.

It is true that Jesus did not prescribe a code of daily conduct to which we should conform. That was exactly what he criticised the Pharisees for doing. He saw only too well the danger that lay in that kind of attitude to life, of taking credit for being more pious and more virtuous than the man next door. As he put it trenchantly: 'When you have done everything that you are told to do, you can say, we have done no more than our duty.' But he did specify certain things as being wrong at any time and in any circumstances: 'evil thoughts, lust, theft, murder, adultery, greed and malice; fraud, indecency, envy, slander, arrogance and folly'.

He approved of the Ten Commandments as a working rule,

but he insisted that any man who was wholly committed to the service of God should not be satisfied with himself if he had merely avoided breaking them. The sin of murder is not simply a matter of ending another man's life. It is the hate that leads to murder that is culpable. Similarly it is not only the act of adultery in itself that constitutes the offence but the intention that precedes it. In other words, what Jesus is concerned with is the inward disposition to commit a wrong against one's neighbour. This, of course, does not mean the temptation to do it, which is no crime if it is resisted.

There are many other aspects of the teaching of Jesus on which it is impossible to linger: his condemnation of spurious religiosity, his insistence on our welcoming acceptance of God's good gifts of the material things of life, together with his warning against letting them become the be-all and end-all of our existence; his demand that we must be self-critical, his overriding concern for the under-privileged, and his constant stressing of the sheer love of God.

Perhaps we come closest to the heart of Jesus' thinking in the words of the Lord's Prayer. Familiarity and frequent repetition can blunt the cutting edges of these apparently simple sentences which in a masterly way point us to the truth about God and ourselves as Jesus saw it. He begins by inviting us to speak and think of God as Our Father, and we know from elsewhere in the gospels that the word he used and encouraged his followers to use was *Abba*. This was the affectionate name that a Jewish child normally used in the family circle when he addressed his father. What Jesus is suggesting is that in approaching God we are not to think of him primarily as the sovereign Creator of the universe and the Lord of all men and nations. He is of course that, but he is also, more than any human father, one who loves each of his children and who is always ready to understand our difficulties and forgive our follies.

It is this kind of God who holds the reins, and we are told to pray that his will may be done. And what we are told to pray for we are meant to work for. It is a summons to each of us in his own home, or shop, or factory, or office, or in the wider sphere of public life to put service before self, to give of his best and to make his tiny corner of the human stage a better place for his having been here. This is God's world, but just because he is the loving Father of us all he lets us make our own mistakes, for only in this way can we truly learn. When we can say to God, 'Our wills are ours to make them thine,' we have seen the point of 'Thy will be done'.

It is not always easy to know what is the will of God when we are faced with a particular decision. We have sometimes simply to take our courage in both hands and do what we think is best. But much more often we know only too well what is the will of God. Our real difficulty is to do it. Jesus knew all about this when he said that it is a narrow gate and a hard road that leads to the kind of life that God would have us live. But he also implied in the Lord's Prayer that God will give us the guidance and strength that we need if we ask him. So he urges us to make the minimum demand for ourselves: give us our daily bread. We are not encouraged to badger God with self-seeking pleas for our private ambitions – prestige, promotion, affluence or suchlike. These may come our way or they may not. Jesus teaches us to ask for no more for ourselves than that we should be kept fit to do our job.

As part of his realistic view of life, Jesus knew that however hard we try to live up to his standards and follow his example we constantly fail. So in his pattern prayer he teaches that we must constantly ask God's forgiveness for the things we have done that we ought not to have done, and for all the things we have left undone. When we are told to ask God daily to forgive us our sins, it means that a basic element in the Christian life as Jesus understands it is a recognition that everything we do is tainted with self-interest. We never are the kind of men and women that we ought to be, or might be, or could have been. And beyond our personal failure there is our implication through indifference or prejudice or stupidity in the collective guilt of mankind in all its blood-stained story.

So in the final petition of the Lord's Prayer we are urged by Jesus to ask for God's help to avoid temptation and to be delivered from the power of evil. Jesus had no doubt that there is a mighty force of evil at work in the world which militates against every attempt of men of goodwill to bring about a better state of society. Modern psychology would not call it Satan, as the Bible does, but it comes to the same thing. We are all, as Jesus knew, up against something irrational and demonic, however we explain it; something that affects us all and which we cannot overcome by our own efforts. Only by enlisting the stronger power of God can it be defeated, and it was the conviction of Jesus that the ultimate victory lies beyond this present world as we know it.

Meantime, in the thought of Jesus, we must battle on – stumbling, falling, picking ourselves up and fighting again in the knowledge that if we commit our lives to God we are on the winning side. His own life of apparent failure, of repeated disappointment, of suffering and of ultimate rejection is, as we shall see, the paradox that points to the truth about life and the key to the understanding of the mystery of our human existence. If we ask whether his teaching is so far above our heads as to be quite beyond our reach we may single out one of his great sayings as being none too easy to practise but nevertheless superbly reasonable and eminently worth trying: 'Treat other people exactly as you would like to be treated by them – this is the essence of all true religion.'

35. The Mighty Works of Jesus

THE picturesquely phrased 'mighty works' which the gospel writers attribute to Jesus are more commonly known today as 'miracles'. This is a word which to many people suggests some kind of black magic and indeed some of the gospel stories told about Jesus look on the surface very much like just that. When we are asked to believe that someone changed water into wine, walked across the surface of a lake, fed a large crowd with a negligible amount of provisions, transferred evil spirits from a madman into a herd of swine, calmed a storm with a word of command and brought dead people back to life, our first reaction might well be to dismiss these stories as sheer legends.

There was a time when people believed that actions of this kind proved beyond dispute that Jesus was the Son of God. Few of us today would be happy about this attitude. We should point to the fact that stories of a similar kind told in the Old Testament about Moses or Elisha, or in the Middle Ages about St Francis and other saints, or indeed about holy men in non-Christian religions, would now be regarded as nothing more than pious inventions. What we believe about Jesus cannot rest on such dubious evidence as a few incidents which seem to be little different in character from similar tales which are told about other historical personalities for whom no claim has ever been made that they were in any sense divine.

If, however, on other grounds we reach the conclusion that Jesus does not come into the same category as Moses or Elisha or St Francis we should have to look again at these stories of some of his 'mighty works' and ask whether we are entitled to dismiss them simply as legends. First of all, let us see these 'problem' stories in their proper perspective. They form only a tiny part of what the gospel writers call Jesus' 'mighty works'. What the evangelists are referring to are principally acts of healing. According to the record, the ministry of Jesus had two sides to it – preaching or teaching, and healing. We are given detailed descriptions of certain typical examples of cures which Jesus effected in cases of blindness, paralysis, mental illness and the like, but these are claimed to be simply instances of innumerable other acts of healing which he performed in the course of his ministry. These are his main 'mighty works'.

Secondly, the gospels were written by men who were convinced that Jesus was a unique figure in history. As we have seen, his closest followers had reached the conclusion, based on their own experience, that he was the long-awaited Messiah. By the time the gospels were written, however, everything that had happened during his ministry was viewed in the light of what was believed to be the greatest miracle of all time, his Resurrection. We shall later on look at the question of whether this belief was well-founded or not. But obviously to men who believed that Jesus himself had been raised from the dead and that far from being merely the Jews' Messiah, he was in fact the Son of God who had come amongst men for the salvation of the world, such stories as were mentioned at the beginning of this chapter would not seem in any way out of character. Indeed the surprising thing is that the gospels are not studded with the kind of stories of Jesus' supernatural powers which we find in the apocryphal gospels of the second century.

This brings us to the third point, which is that, right from the beginning, our four gospels as we have them in the New Testament were accepted as authoritative because they were reckoned to have been written by men who knew the true facts of the life of Jesus, either because they had been with him during his ministry or because they were in close touch with others who had been his companions. They had been written within a few decades of the Crucifixion, when memories were still fresh and when there were still plenty of people around who had heard at first hand, from people who had been on the spot, the record of what had happened in the few momentous years of Jesus' preaching and healing mission. Later 'gospels' which appeared in the second century and contain a wealth of pious legends were dismissed as spurious or apocryphal and were never accepted by the Church as true.

It is in the light of all this that we should look at the record of the 'mighty works' of Jesus. If the evidence for the Resurrection is sound, we ought not to ask whether Jesus *could* do any of the things mentioned at the beginning of this chapter. The answer is obviously that if Jesus was what the early Christians claimed he was, and what the Church has affirmed about him right down the centuries, we should expect him to do things that no other man has ever done and to say things such as no other man has ever said. If indeed God became man in Jesus and for a space lived our common life, we should be surprised if on occasion the latent power of God did not break through and enable Jesus to act in accordance with higher laws than the normal laws of nature that we know about.

This does not mean, however, that we must necessarily accept every 'mighty work' of Jesus as having taken place exactly as it is recorded in the gospels. The evangelists were all concerned to draw out the significance of the events in the life of Jesus and it is often difficult to say how much is fact and how much is interpretation. We must also allow for occasional misunderstandings, pious embellishments, and the fallibility of human memories. Jesus consistently refused to perform spectacular displays of his power to startle people into belief and in some of his 'miracles' which we find it hard to account for in the light of his attitude we can detect a theological purpose behind the story which explains much of the difficulty.

The story of Jesus changing water into wine, involving the creation of 120 gallons of wine at a wedding party where the guests had already had enough to drink, is much more likely to be a parable of the replacement of the thin water of Judaism by the rich wine of the gospel. The feeding of a vast crowd with a few loaves and fishes when they could without great difficulty have gone home for a meal makes sense if we think of it as a sacramental occasion, an open-air Lord's Supper. The notorious Gadarene swine probably stampeded into the Lake of Galilee, terrified by the clamour of the madman whom Jesus healed. The stories of Jesus walking on the storm-tossed water of the lake and stilling the storm with a word may be meant to illustrate the same power of the Messiah over the winds and waves as had been claimed for God in Old Testament times. We cannot tell precisely what happened in these cases. We can only surmise that these may have been the reasons why such stories are recorded about Jesus at all.

When we are told in one gospel that Jesus put a curse on a fruitless fig-tree which immediately withered, and when we find in another gospel a similar story about a fruitless fig-tree told as a parable about Israel's unfruitfulness as the People of God, we may well suspect that something Jesus said has mistakenly been turned into something Jesus did. The apparently miraculous great haul of fish which Jesus made possible for some of his disciples who had fished in the lake all night in vain may be intended to be an object lesson of the power of Christ to make his followers fishers of men, and another story where Peter is told by Jesus to go down to the lake and cast his line, with the promise that the first fish he hooks will have a coin in its mouth to pay the tax-collector, was possibly said as a joke. There is no record that the coin was found.

It has been worth looking at these few gospel stories in some detail because they do tend to overshadow in people's minds the far greater number of Jesus' 'mighty works' which were concerned with the relief of suffering. If we are to believe the gospel record at all, they were as important a part of Jesus' ministry as his teaching. We must not be put off by the fact that in the time of Jesus all illnesses of the body or of the mind were attributed to demon-possession. People who have lived among primitive tribal communities know that the fear of evil spirits is still very real in some parts of the world today. A sick man can be cured if he believes that the demon has been exorcised or driven out by magic potions, and conversely a healthy man can sicken and die if he thinks that a spell has been put upon him and that evil spirits are working for his destruction.

Modern medical science, however, would not accept that blindness, deafness, and epilepsy are caused by demons, although to the layman a homicidal maniac comes pretty close to being 'possessed by a devil'. In Jesus' day all the ills that flesh is heir to, whether it was disease of body or disease of mind and including death itself, as well as natural disasters such as earthquakes, famines and storms at sea, were laid at the door of Satan, the Prince of Darkness, and his myrmidons of demons. God reigned in heaven, Satan ruled on earth. There was constant conflict between God and his angels, who as his messengers from heaven were responsible for all the good things that happened in the world, and Satan and his ungodly host who were bent on making man's existence a veritable hell on earth.

The only hope for poor afflicted mortals was in Jewish eyes

the coming of the Messiah. When Messiah came, they believed, the power of Satan would crumble. The evil spirits at his command would be defeated by the stronger power of God's agent; Satan and his minions would be sent to everlasting punishment. According to Jesus, this had now begun to happen. With the coming of the new age, the Rule of God on earth, Satan was being forced to loosen his grip on the lives of men by the stronger power of God, working through his Messiah. By healing men's minds and bodies, Jesus was showing that God was now acting in a decisive way to bring to an end the tyranny of evil. Disease and death, and the demons who caused them, were being vanquished. The will of God was being done on earth as it already was done in heaven.

This explains Jesus' attitude towards his healing ministry. He is fighting to free men's bodies as well as their minds from the baleful rule of Satan, so that they may live their lives to the full under the beneficent rule of God. By 'casting out devils' from the insane and the epileptic, he is not only restoring them to health, he is demonstrating that this is God's world and not the Devil's. What is abundantly clear from the record is that the cures Jesus effected were real cures. If he had lived at a time when demon-possession was not the current explanation of disease, the result would have been the same. Blind men had their sight restored, lame men walked again, deranged minds were made whole.

So far as we can make out from the gospels, Jesus had no stereotyped technique for effecting his cures. Sometimes it was by exorcism, sometimes it was by laying hands on the patient, or by a touch, sometimes it involved merely a healing word, sometimes it seems to have been enough if the friends or relatives of the patient had faith that Jesus could heal. In all cases, however, it is clear that it was an encounter with Jesus which enabled his healing power to operate. There is therefore no parallel with modern medical healing techniques, involving diagnosis, prescription of remedies and a period of convalescence. What impressed the people of his time was the instantaneous effect of Jesus upon human suffering.

Nothing could be further from the truth than to think of Jesus' healing ministry as some kind of automatic release of healing power. It was for him a demanding and exhausting business. The ingredients are always, on the part of the patients or their friends, faith that Jesus can make them whole, and on his part compassion for the plight of men and women who are being prevented by physical ailments from living the full life that is meant to be lived by sons and daughters of God. This does not imply by any means that only the physique of an Olympic Games competitor enables a man or woman to establish the right relationship with God or his neighbour. It does mean, however, that every effort on our part, following the example of Jesus, to reduce the sum of human pain and disability is in accordance with the will of God for his human family.

On this whole question of the 'miraculous' element in the life of Jesus we are perhaps less arrogant than our Victorian forefathers in the first flush of scientific dogmatism, when it was believed that nature was a closed system and that we knew all that there was to be known about the laws that govern the universe. We are more prepared now to recognise that the universe is much more mysterious than we thought it was. So many things have happened in our time that a century ago would have been thought 'miraculous', in medical science as much as in the fields of nuclear physics, electronics and the exploration of outer space. We are more conscious through psychosomatic medicine of the interaction between mind and body and therefore perhaps more ready to believe that miraculous cures at such centres of prayer as Lourdes do indeed happen, and that divine healing channelled through a praying group can bring about a patient's recovery.

The impression we get from the gospels is that the compassionate power of God flowed through Jesus in boundless measure because no one before or since his day has ever been so much at one with God, or felt himself to be in such an intimate relationship with him. It is in the light of this that we can perhaps begin to understand his 'mighty works', even on those rare occasions when he turned death into life. We may note

that in all three cases recorded in the gospels the circumstances were peculiarly poignant – the deaths of a small child, a widow's only son, and a dearly loved personal friend. Of course all three whom Jesus restored to life would die again in the normal way when their time came. These few cases where Jesus exercised a power he seldom used would suggest not only that there were no limits to his compassionate concern for others. They would also point forward to the truth which Jesus' Resurrection demonstrated that through him death is merely a sleep and an awakening.

36.   Towards Holy Week

LET us go back to the point in the story when Peter the leader among the closest followers of Jesus had with intuitive insight put his finger on the truth about their beloved but always rather mysterious Master. Jesus had said and done so many things that his disciples had only dimly understood but they all pointed in one direction. The reason why Jesus' most intimate associates had been so slow to recognise him as the Messiah is not hard to seek. He was neither a heaven-sent visitant from the skies nor had he shown any sign of being a politically minded saviour of his people from the Roman oppressors. For men brought up to expect Messiah to be one or other of these things it took time to recognise him in the former village joiner from Nazareth.

It had been the cumulative effect of Jesus' ministry upon his disciples that had led Peter in the name of the rest to this startling conclusion. Their Master was no mere rabbi or even a prophet like John the Baptist. His claim to have the right to criticise the sacred Law of Moses, his scathing indictment of the official representatives of the established religion, his power over disease and death, and above all the sense he gave them that when they were with him they were somehow brought close to God – all this to serious-minded Jews brought up on the Old Testament could on reflection only mean one thing: Jesus must be the Messiah, God's unique representative on earth.

Jesus had reached this conviction himself at his baptism. But in his time of solitary wrestling in the 'wilderness' with the problem of how this should work out in practice he had decided, before ever his public ministry began, that his role as Messiah must be that of Isaiah's Servant of the Lord who would by a life of service and inevitable suffering bring men to the true knowledge of God. Nothing less than this would lead them to the truth about God and themselves, namely that God suffers for his children's folly more than any human father suffers, and that in the service of others we come to see the truth about our own lives. In Jesus' words, we have to lose our lives to find them, that is to say that by giving ourselves for others we reach the fulfilment of our being. This was the role that Jesus had chosen for himself and which he invited his followers to share.

For obvious reasons, because of its political associations in men's minds, Jesus had discouraged the use of the word 'Messiah' about himself. Nor indeed did he call himself the 'Servant of the Lord' in so many words, although his whole ministry was based upon service. What seems to have been fundamental in Jesus' thinking was his sense of Sonship to God, a unique and intimate relationship which is reflected in his frequent reference to God as 'my Father'. But the words that he most often used to describe himself were 'Son of Man'. This takes us back to the book of Daniel in the Old Testament where in one of his visions Daniel sees the empires of the world, pictured as monsters, being replaced by a new kind of community, the 'saints of the Most High', with the Son of Man as their ruler. It would seem then that Jesus in calling himself Son of Man thinks of himself as leader and representative of the new Israel, with his twelve disciples as its nucleus, fulfilling the mission that old Israel had failed to accomplish and ultimately embracing the whole world. The prelude to this future success must be, however, to tread the path of Isaiah's Servant, which meant suffering, self-sacrifice and death.

It is noticeable from the record of the gospels that from the point where Peter made his great confession of faith that Jesus was indeed God's Messiah, there is a new note of urgency and crisis in Jesus' ministry. He had to teach his disciples the hard facts about what Messiahship involved. They could not rid themselves of the idea that it must somehow involve earthly triumph and sovereignty. Jesus had to convince them that the triumph of his cause could only come through rejection, humiliation and death. They were helped to see something of what that ultimate triumph would mean in the dramatic experience of the Transfiguration, when they had a vision of the glorified Christ as he was to be, and saw Jesus as the sole Saviour of men.

Meantime, however, the goal was Jerusalem, the centre of the religious life of the nation. Jesus as God's Messiah was determined to throw down the gauntlet there to the custodians of Israel's faith who had perverted the purpose of God as enshrined in the Law and the prophets. He set out to make a stand for the God of Moses, Amos, Jeremiah and Isaiah against the travesty of religion that both Sadducees and Pharisees were offering to the people. The People of God were like sheep without a shepherd. Satan reigned even in God's holy Temple. The rich faith of the psalms had been replaced by meaningless ritual sacrifices and pettifogging rules for daily behaviour. Self-righteousness and bigotry were enthroned in place of compassion and simple piety.

So in the name of God Jesus set his face towards Jerusalem to do battle with evil as he had always done, but now it was not with Satan's power over men's minds and bodies but with his power over the state religion itself. The sense of crisis and urgency shines through the record. However long the journey to Jerusalem may have taken, we are constantly aware of the fixed purpose of Jesus. There is a revealing scene of the Master striding ahead with the disciples following behind dazed and apprehensive. They had never been more conscious of the gulf that lay between them for all their constant companionship, and of the mystery that lay at the heart of their relationship.

They reached Jerusalem at the time of Passover. This was

the annual commemoration of God's deliverance of his people from slavery in Egypt more than a thousand years before. It would seem that Jesus had deliberately chosen this festival, which attracted Jewish pilgrims from all over the world, to challenge the power of evil which dominated the holy city, and to deliver God's people from a greater bondage than that of any human oppressor. It is thus in the spring of the year, most likely AD 29, that what we now call Holy Week begins. The gospel account of it is more detailed than in any other part of the story of Jesus, suggesting that it was regarded as the most important part of the record and also perhaps that it had been written down earlier than the rest of the narrative.

Between what we know as Palm Sunday and Good Friday, Jesus performed three significant and symbolic actions, apart from engaging in controversy with the ecclesiastical authorities, teaching in public and instructing his disciples in private. The first symbolic act was his entry into Jerusalem, where he deliberately carried out to the letter an Old Testament prophecy that when Messiah came to the holy city he would come not as a panoplied conqueror on a charger but 'humble and riding on a donkey' as a Prince of Peace. As the enthusiastic crowds waved palm branches and laid their cloaks in the path of the prophet and healer from Galilee, it is perhaps unlikely that they knew the scriptures well enough to realise the significance of Jesus' act. The authorities, however, knew only too well that Jesus was now openly identifying himself with the Messiah. His popularity with the crowd compelled them to be cautious, but clearly this dangerous impostor who had now put himself within their power must be got rid of.

Jesus' second symbolic act confirmed their resolution. The Temple in Jerusalem was constructed in a series of open courts, each of increasing 'holiness' until at the centre there was reached the Tabernacle, containing the Holy of Holies, the symbol of the presence of God in the midst of his people. The outermost court was called the court of the Gentiles. What lay behind this was the excellent idea that there was a place for non-Jews within the House of God. By accepting the Law of Moses, a Gentile was entitled to pass the barrier leading to the court of Israel, and thus become incorporated in the People of God.

The priestly Sadducees, however, who controlled the Temple had allowed the court of the Gentiles to become little more than a fairground. It was cluttered up with the stalls of vendors who sold birds and animals officially certified free from blemish and therefore suitable for sacrifice. In addition the annual Temple tax payable by all Jews had to be paid in ritually approved coinage. Booths for changing any other kind of money into 'clean' money were also located in the Gentiles' court. The result was that the Gentiles were literally being pushed out of the House of God by this blatant commercialism which brought considerable revenue to the priesthood.

This was the unholy scene which confronted Jesus as he entered the Temple. Snatching up some rope, he made a rough and ready whip and indignantly drove the traders with their sheep and cattle out of the Temple, overturning the tables of the money-changers and scattering their coins on the ground. It was not a humanitarian protest against the practice of animal sacrifice, although elsewhere in the gospels we are told that Jesus thought this senseless. It was a protest in the name of God by his Messiah against the travesty of religion that was being encouraged in the historic shrine of the People of God. The Temple was meant to be a house of prayer for all nations. The priesthood had turned it into an open market and a veritable den of thieves. The Gentiles were not only being squeezed out of their legitimate place within the symbolic area of God's concern and denied access to him. Worse than that, they were being discouraged from ever wanting to know more about the true God by this caricature of what the faith of Israel was really all about.

In the mind of Jesus he has struck a blow for God against Satan in the very place where Satan ought never to have been allowed entrance. In the mind of the authorities this was the last straw. The only question was how they could arrest him without causing an uproar among the people. Jesus was spending each night of Holy Week with friends in a village outside the city. During the day he was surrounded by his supporters and the Jerusalem crowds had as little love for the Sadducees and their minions the Temple police as had Jesus himself. Unexpected help came the way of the authorities when one of Jesus' own disciples offered to lead the police to a spot where they could apprehend him quietly under cover of darkness.

No one has ever understood the motives of Judas Iscariot. It seems hardly likely that he was moved by greed, for the reward was trifling. Was he a disappointed patriot who had at last come to the conclusion that he had backed the wrong kind of Messiah, or did he think that by forcing Jesus' hand to resist arrest he might yet drive him to exert his supernatural powers and turn the tables on his enemies? We shall never know. At all events, it was with the knowledge that one of his own closest friends had betrayed him that Jesus arranged to hold his last supper with his disciples.

It was a secret rendezvous and it was at this Last Supper that Jesus enacted his third piece of symbolism. It came at the end of a meal which had for all present a sense of finality, heightened by Jesus' words that one of the little group had turned traitor. He then took bread and wine and enacted his death before them. He broke the bread, blessed it and gave it to them saying: 'This is my body which is given for you: do this in remembrance of me.' Then he took the cup of wine, and having similarly blessed it, he gave it to them with the words: 'This cup is the new covenant in my blood which is shed for you.'

These solemn words and actions, as St Paul tells us, were among the earliest traditions to be handed on to converts in the first years of the Church's mission, and they are still at the heart of the chief sacrament in the Church's worship. But what did Jesus mean by them? He knows he is going to his death, not merely because of the vindictiveness of the Jewish religious leaders or because one of his disciples has betrayed him. He is giving his life for his friends as the ultimate act of the service which has been the keynote of his whole ministry. One of the gospels includes at this Last Supper the impressive object lesson in service where Jesus washes his disciples' feet. It is in the same spirit that he now speaks of his death.

As Son of Man, conscious of his unique relationship to God and of his unique vocation, Jesus is about to fulfil the last and greatest act in the role of the Servant of whom Isaiah had spoken. He will give his life in the belief that only through his death will God's purpose for the world be realised. Only through his death will the Rule of God come, as he said, 'with power'. When he speaks of the new relationship or covenant between God and man that his death will bring about, he is speaking of the life of the new Israel which was at that moment represented by eleven timid ordinary men. But such was Jesus' faith that he believed that out of this sorry handful God would create the new community, the Church, which would be his instrument for the salvation and enlightenment of the world.

37.   From Death to Life

FROM the house where the Last Supper had been held, Jesus led his disciples to the Garden of Gethsemane, a small plantation at the foot of the Mount of Olives. There is to this day a copse of ancient gnarled olive trees on the same spot and no place in or around Jerusalem so vividly recalls the events of those last few days of Jesus' earthly ministry.

This was the scene of his Agony, more terrible, it would seem, than even the physical torture of Crucifixion. The darkness of the night intensified the darkness of his soul. It was not merely horror at the frightful death that faced him but the revulsion of perfect goodness at the diabolical evil that could possess otherwise decent men – the malice of the Pharisees, the vindictiveness of the Sadducees, the fickleness of the crowd, the cowardice of his own disciples, the treachery of one who had been his friend.

Here indeed was Satan enthroned over human life, using honest men in his service and turning them into devils like himself. Jesus falls on the ground and passionately prays to God that he may be spared this ordeal. Yet almost on top of this instinctive cry comes his supreme affirmation of total obedience: 'Father, not my will but thy will be done.' After this inward turmoil, Jesus is at peace and his composure, except for a brief moment as he hangs on the Cross, does not desert him from now until the end. Soon into the silence of the garden comes the sound of voices and hurrying footsteps. The Temple police, led by Judas, make their way through the trees and in the light of the flickering torches the traitor's kiss identifies his Master. Jesus is arrested and led off for trial while his eleven remaining disciples run for their lives.

Before his Crucifixion on Good Friday, Jesus appeared before four different judges. Two of them were ecclesiastics, Annas, formerly high priest and still a power in the land, and Caiaphas, his son-in-law, the reigning high priest and Jewish head of state under the Roman procurator. There was an informal hearing before Annas, late on the Thursday night and just after Jesus' arrest, which seems to have been inconclusive. The second great betrayal by one of Jesus' disciples, however, came now in the courtyard of the high priest's house when Peter, who had summoned up enough courage to come back to the scene, was challenged with being a follower of the prisoner and swore to high heaven that he had never even heard of him.

On the Friday morning, the Sanhedrin, the supreme Jewish court of law, presided over by the high priest, had been hurriedly convened and met just after daybreak. The reason for haste was that the ecclesiastics were anxious to get the trial and execution over before the Passover, which began on Friday evening. Their difficulty was to get their witnesses to agree and they were not assisted by Jesus' refusal to answer the charges. There came a moment, however, when Caiaphas asked Jesus point-blank whether he claimed to be the Messiah, at which stage Jesus for the first time openly acknowledged that he did. No more evidence was needed. The Sanhedrin had no option but to condemn Jesus to death. Unless they had admitted his claim, they were bound to pass sentence on a man who was a self-confirmed fraud, a blasphemous wonder-worker and a danger to the stability of the community.

The power of life or death, however, was not in Jewish hands. Roman justice must be satisfied and so Jesus was taken to the Praetorium, the headquarters of Pilate, the Roman procurator, who was resident in Jerusalem for the duration of the Passover to stamp out any possible trouble among politically minded pilgrims at a time when they were commemorating their liberation from a foreign yoke. As a conscientious Roman official, Pilate would be unwilling to interfere in local religious disputes, especially when it involved the death sentence. On the other hand, he was out of favour with his own government in Rome and dared not risk antagonising the leading Jews.

The charges brought against Jesus by the Jewish prosecution were three in number: firstly, that he was an agitator; secondly, that he had discouraged people from paying their lawful taxes to Rome; and, thirdly, that he called himself King of the Jews. Pilate had no love for the Jews. He distrusted their leaders and patently did not believe they had a case against Jesus. But it was as much as his own life was worth to risk a charge of failing in his loyalty to the emperor by condoning even the possibility of treason against Rome on the part of Jesus, and he knew that the Jewish lawyers were prepared to implicate him in just such a charge. He sought a loophole by sending Jesus to Herod, the nominal ruler of Galilee, whose subject Jesus was and who was in Jerusalem for the festival. This fourth 'trial' was a farce. Herod made no pretence of holding a judicial investigation and when Jesus refused to gratify his demands for a 'miracle', Herod handed him over to the soldiery who staged a burlesque coronation of the so-called 'King of the Jews'.

Pilate's last effort to evade the responsibility of sentencing an innocent man to death likewise failed. It was the custom at Passover that Roman clemency should be shown to some notable criminal under sentence of death. Pilate proposed that Jesus should be given this free pardon. There was, however, a more popular candidate. Barabbas, a rebel against Rome, presently due for execution, provided the ecclesiastics with their excuse. By encouraging the supporters of Barabbas to demand the death of Jesus, they persuaded them that they would thus secure the release of their hero. So the mob obligingly surrounded the Praetorium with cries of: 'Release Barabbas; crucify Jesus' and Pilate had no choice. He sentenced Jesus to be scourged and then crucified.

There are many terrible ways of dying. Crucifixion under the Roman Empire was certainly one of them. The victim was first beaten almost lifeless and was then compelled to carry the cross-bar of his cross to the place of execution. There his hands and feet were nailed to the cross which was then hoisted into position. Jesus was so exhausted by the ill-treatment he had received that he was unable to bear the weight of the cross, and a bystander, a pilgrim from North Africa, was forced to carry it for him. The route of men condemned to death lay along what is now known as the Via Dolorosa and ended on a rocky knoll outside the city walls, known as Golgotha, for which the Vulgate name is Calvary. The site is believed to be inside the present Church of the Holy Sepulchre.

At nine o'clock on the morning of Good Friday, Jesus was crucified between two bandits. The customary placard nailed above his head and which normally described the nature of the crime, bore the words: 'The King of the Jews'. This was on Pilate's instructions and was his final jibe at the people he hated. It was the practice of some of the wealthy women of Jerusalem to attend public executions of this kind and to offer drugged wine to the victims to deaden the pain. Jesus refused to accept it. The cross was a low erection with the head of the condemned man not much above the heads of the bystanders. Jesus had therefore to bear the scathing and abusive taunts that were hurled at him, and by the same token some of his women followers who were also there with his Mother, were able to hear his prayer for forgiveness for his enemies, his momentary cry that God had forsaken him, and his final commitment of his soul to his heavenly Father.

At three o'clock in the afternoon Jesus died. This was much sooner than in the case of most victims, some of whom lingered for days. When the soldiers came to hasten the prisoners' deaths so that their bodies might be taken down before the beginning of Passover, which on this occasion coincided with the Jewish sabbath, one of them stuck his spear into Jesus' side to make certain that he was really dead. Permission was given by Pilate to a well-to-do member of the Sanhedrin, a secret sympathiser with Jesus, to remove the body from the Cross, wrap it in a linen shroud and lay it in one of the neighbouring cave-tombs, rolling the normal cart-wheel stone along its grooves to close the entrance.

If we try to assess the state of mind in which the disciples of Jesus found themselves on the evening of Good Friday, we should have to guess that it was sheer despair and total bewilderment. They had spent three years of their lives in the service of a leader who had won their allegiance by giving them a new understanding of the power and purpose of God, who had shown them a new meaning in life, whose words and actions had made such an impact upon them that they had been forced to the conclusion that he must indeed be the Messiah. He was not the kind of Messiah that they had been expecting but no other category seemed adequate. If there was any sense in life at all, the one thing they were sure of was that God had been speaking to them in the words that Jesus had spoken, and that God had been working through him to make men whole in mind and body and to help them to become the sons and daughters of God that they were meant to be.

But now their faith and hopes had crashed in meaningless disarray. They had seen the Messiah humiliated, beaten and crucified. Despite Jesus' repeated warning that death awaited him in Jerusalem, they had refused to believe it. Nowhere in the scriptures had it ever been suggested that Messiah would be executed like a common criminal. Never in their own thoughts had they entertained the possibility that the enterprise could have ended like this. Satan had proved to be stronger than God. There was no sense in anything. No fact of history is more certain than that on that Good Friday evening the disciples of Jesus were at their wits' end.

What is equally certain, however, is that a few days later these same disciples were changed men, jubilant and full of hope for the future, and that a few weeks later they had embarked on the first stage of the gigantic task of converting the world to the faith that Jesus is Lord. The incredible had happened. The Master was not dead but alive. God had raised him from the tomb. Jesus had appeared to them, had spoken to them. They knew now that God and not Satan had had the last word. He had proved stronger than evil, stronger than death.

It is impossible to account for the lives of Christian saints and martyrs, for the work of Christian poets, painters and musicians, for Dante, Milton, Michelangelo and Bach, for the splendour of cathedrals, and the nameless devout Christian craftsmen in wood and stone whose legacy has enriched the whole of mankind, unless that tiny handful of the disciples of Jesus had come to believe in the Resurrection. Without that belief there would have been no New Testament, no Church, no Christendom. Without it the Church's sponsorship of the first schools, universities and hospitals would never have happened, and the long story of social reform which has had behind it the inspiration of dedicated Christian men and women would never have been written. Much of all this might have come about under different auspices but if we stick to the facts of history these things have all taken place because the first followers of Jesus believed that he had risen from the dead.

But of course it can be argued that it is one thing to say that the disciples believed in the Resurrection of Jesus and quite another to say that their belief was founded on fact. Let us at once recognise that we cannot *prove* that Jesus rose from the dead, any more than we can *prove* that there is a God at all, or that life is anything more than a meaningless jungle or that the universe did not come into existence by anything more than a series of flukes. In all such matters which cannot be mathematically proved or disproved, we have to think in terms of reasonable probability. In this light the Resurrection of Jesus would seem to be both eminently reasonable and highly probable.

There are minor discrepancies in the gospel evidence as to exactly what happened on Easter Day – which is not surprising in view of the fact that it was a unique event in history, startling and unexpected – but the unanimous witness is that the tomb in which the body of Jesus had been laid on Good Friday was empty on Easter Sunday, and that on that day and for a short

time thereafter on a number of occasions Jesus appeared to and was recognised by his closest followers, either individually or in groups. It is a surprisingly unexciting and almost prosaic record. A good film director could have made much more of it. The impression left on our minds is that it was a deliberately unspectacular design on the part of Jesus to convince a sufficient number of his followers that he was indeed alive and present with them in a more intimate way than even during the time of his ministry before the Crucifixion.

If this is not what happened, how did the belief in the Resurrection arise, a belief which is universally attested by every New Testament writer? Some have thought the disciples were suffering from hallucinations. But they were hardheaded fishermen, mostly, who show no signs elsewhere of being subject to this kind of brain-storm. Was it then wishfulfilment? It cannot have been that, for they were certainly not expecting the Resurrection. When they were first told of the empty tomb they dismissed the story as nonsense. Nor did they believe it because the scriptures suggested it, for they were hard put to it to find anything in the Old Testament to back up their conviction that Jesus had risen.

Perhaps then Jesus did not really die on the Cross but recovered in the tomb and rejoined his followers. This is of course possible, but what is not possible is that a half-dead, mutilated Master could be transformed into the unanimous picture of a triumphant Christ victorious over death. Or perhaps the disciples stole the body of Jesus and invented the whole story of the Resurrection, in which case we should have to believe not only that they were completely dishonest but that they were also prepared to suffer torture and death for a faith which they knew was a fraud. Perhaps again there had been some mistake about the exact place where Jesus had been buried, or the Jewish authorities themselves removed the body to forestall future veneration. In this case, whenever the disciples began to talk about the resurrected Lord, which was the last thing the Jewish authorities wanted, all that would have been necessary would have been for the opposition to produce the body.

In short, whatever explanations of the Resurrection have been suggested, other than that which the New Testament gives, raise more problems than they solve. This does not mean that the gospel evidence answers all our questions. We do not know for example what happened within the tomb between Good Friday and Easter Day or who it was who rolled away the stone from the mouth of the sepulchre. Nor can we explain the nature of the risen body of Christ, which according to the evidence was recognisable as Jesus but in some way different, and which was not subject to the same laws which govern the normal type of human body that we know. St Paul speaks of the body after death as a transformed, 'spiritual' or 'glorified' body and that is about as far as we can get.

Christianity was not founded on the teaching of Jesus but on the belief that Jesus had risen from the dead. Without that faith, the Church would never have been born. What could have happened without the Resurrection-faith is that the followers of Jesus might have constituted themselves as a sect of the Jewish community, flourishing for a time and then disappearing among the hotch-potch of religious movements in the ancient world. This did not happen because the followers of Jesus believed that the greatest miracle of all time had demonstrated once and for all that this is God's world and that he had not allowed the most perfect life of which we have any record to be snuffed out by malice, envy, ignorance and stupidity. But of course in the last resort the greatest proof that the Resurrection happened is not any historical evidence of the event itself but the lives of countless men and women within the Christian Church over the past two thousand years who have testified to the power of the risen Christ in their own lives.

38. The Birth of the Church

FOR those who like to think of the Bible as a great drama unfolding the story of what God has done to save us from the consequences of persistently making wrong choices and trying to run the world in our own way instead of in God's way, we are now at the beginning of the third act. After the Prologue in the early chapters of Genesis, which sketched with stark realism the plight in which men have always found themselves when left to their own devices, governed by the law of the jungle and the policy of every man for himself, came Act I, occupying the rest of the Old Testament. This described God's choice of a particular community, Israel, beginning with Abraham. Through its experiences and the guidance it was given by the inspired leadership of men who were prepared to listen to the prompting of God: the prophets, poets and sages whose message is recorded in the Bible, Israel was to become an example to the rest of the world of what it meant to be a People of God and to bring others to the knowledge of the truth about God and themselves.

Act I is the longest of the three acts of the drama and necessarily so. Life has to be lived and worked out in the storm and turmoil of political and social history. The people of Israel had to learn, and the rest of the world had to learn from Israel's tragic failure to become such a People of God, that, even with the best intentions, the downward pull of human pride and self-interest is stronger than all the good counsel which can be given by men with deeper insight than the rest of us into the truth about life. Something had to happen to human nature itself to straighten out the perverse twist which always defeats men's best-laid plans and their noblest aspirations. The world had to be shown through Israel's example that the chief obstacle that prevents men from living in the right relationship to God and to one another is basically selfishness, whether it shows itself in ruthless ambition, contempt for weakness, exploitation of others, oppression, dishonesty, greed or prejudice.

Mankind needed a new and visible pattern of goodness and a new power to re-make human nature. Act II of the divine drama – the story of the life, death and Resurrection of Jesus – has described the supreme intervention of God in the life of the world to do for man what man could not do for himself. The claim of the Bible in this central act of the drama is that God came down to our level to lift us up to his own. In Jesus he not only said the last word on how life should be lived but through the Risen Christ he gives to all who are prepared to commit themselves to him in loyalty and service the power to defeat the evil in themselves and in the world around them. The message of Act II is that the twist in human nature has been straightened out by a new type of man, no longer self-centred but God-centred, and that, through allegiance to Christ and in fellow-ship with him, the new community of the People of God, the Church, is given the supernatural power which is needed to renew the life of the world.

This is the theme of Act III of the divine drama which is still far from finished. The beginning of the story is told in the rest of the New Testament, following the gospels. It presents a picture of very ordinary men and women, obviously far from perfect, setting their hands to the task of transforming society to bring it more into harmony with the will and purpose of God, starting with themselves. But it is only a beginning. The New Testament takes us no further than the first steps in the re-creation of the life of the world by the new Israel, the Christian Church. The story of the Church in the last two thousand years, with its astonishing achievements as well as its ghastly failures, is still the tale of the Church's infancy, and no one can tell how long it will be before its task is accomplished. So Act III is still being played out wherever men and women in the power of Christ try to make our common life reflect more adequately the pattern which Jesus demonstrated to be the will of God for his world.

It takes a strong effort of the imagination to relate the setting of the gospels to the world as we know it today. Apart altogether from the revolutionary changes of the past fifty years which have ushered us into the age of technology, nuclear energy, electronics and the investigation of outer space, modern life has for most of us to be lived in cities where conditions are vastly different from the pastoral setting of the gospels. Hills and lakes, country roads, farms and villages are associated in our minds with holidays rather than with the way we have to earn our living and the place where we spend most of our time. Admittedly townsmen and countrymen alike have the same basic problems when it comes down to brass tacks – building a home, rearing a family, coping with the cost of living, facing old age and the prospect of death.

But life as it was lived by Galilean peasants and fishermen is not the life that most of us know. On the other hand, when we pass from the gospels to the rest of the New Testament we are in a world that is essentially familiar, where life is not governed by ecclesiastical law but by secular law, a world of great cities, international trade, commercial enterprise, competing philosophies and religions, class-structure, racial problems, higher education and professional sport. There is a further contrast between the final picture that the gospels leave in our minds and the background of the rest of the New Testament. The gospels end with the transformation of the despair of the followers of Jesus after the Crucifixion into the new hope that was awakened on Easter Day, as with growing conviction one after another came to believe that their Master was not dead but gloriously alive and present with them wherever they might be.

But the scene is still set on the same tiny stage on which the events of Jesus' life and death had been enacted, and the players are still the small circle of Jesus' closest disciples and their associates. The rest of the New Testament is, however, played out on a stage which reaches to the boundaries of the civilised world. The little group has developed into a world-wide mission, thrusting spearheads into the four corners of the empire. Christian communities are to be found in Italy, Greece, and Asia Minor. The Church is taking shape as an international movement recruiting its members from all races and social classes, challenging the religions and philosophies of the pagan world, battling against idolatry and superstition, forcing its way against heavy odds into the capital of the empire, Rome itself.

The story of how this came about and of the chief architect of this astonishing development, Paul of Tarsus, a converted Jewish rabbi, is told in the brilliantly graphic narrative called the Acts of the Apostles. This was written by Luke, a companion of Paul on some of his missionary journeys, who combined his own professional skill as a doctor with a quite remarkable gift as a narrator. He wrote the book of Acts as a sequel to his version of the gospel, to show how the ministry of Jesus was continued by the work of his followers. In it he tells the gripping story of the first thirty years of Church history from about A D 30 to A D 60, showing how, in that short space of time, a faith that was born in Palestine spread like wildfire throughout the Mediterranean lands. His purpose was to tell how the Church began, how much its early success was due to Paul, and to persuade educated pagans that Christianity was no hole-in-corner Jewish sect but a significant world movement worthy of attention by all thoughtful men.

Luke takes up the story at the beginning of the book of Acts more or less where he left off at the end of his gospel. He first shows us the disciples of Jesus, now recovered from the shattering blow which the Crucifixion had dealt to their faith and loyalty, and finally persuaded that the Resurrection meant that what they had thought was the end of the venture was in fact only the beginning. Much that Jesus had said about the necessity of his death and his hope of what lay beyond it which they had not understood at the time now became clear. It was a period of reflection and of further instruction by the Risen Lord during which the Old Testament scriptures came alive with new meaning.

Above all, the disciples came to understand that Jesus had to die in order that they might truly live, that he could now be with each one of them wherever the purpose of God should take them. They saw his life, death and Resurrection as a mighty act of God for the renewal of the life of the world. The powers of evil had done their worst and had nevertheless been defeated by the stronger power of God. The way to the new age of which prophets and psalmists had spoken was now open. God had offered men a fresh start and enabled them through Jesus to come into the right relationship with himself and with each other, with forgiveness for past failure and the promise of his power to help them.

When the Risen Christ was satisfied that his closest followers were convinced of the truth of the Resurrection, and of his continuing presence with them, his appearances to his disciples ceased. This is pictorially described in the story of his Ascension, a few weeks after the Resurrection, which is the biblical way of saying that in the minds of the disciples Jesus was now exalted and enthroned as Lord. So as they await the gift of the Holy Spirit, which Christ has promised them, his disciples meet for prayer in Jerusalem in the upper room which had been the scene of the Last Supper. It was during this time of waiting that the little community of Jesus' followers, now numbering over a hundred, decided at the instigation of Peter to fill the vacant place in the apostolate caused by the death of Judas Iscariot. There are different versions of how the traitor had met his end. Luke says he died of dropsy, elsewhere we are told that he hanged himself. In either case his fate would seem to match his treachery.

It is clear that from the beginning Peter is the acknowledged leader of the community and that great importance is attached to the significance of the number of the apostles. There had to be twelve to preserve the continuity with the Old Testament tradition that there were twelve tribes of Israel. For this was the new Israel, deliberately founded by Jesus on the nucleus of twelve disciples, to fulfil the task of evangelising the world, which the old Israel had failed to do. So a twelfth man was chosen from among those who had been with Jesus from the beginning of his ministry, who could testify at first hand to what he had himself seen and heard in Galilee and Jerusalem and who had himself met the Risen Lord. Thus right from the start Christianity claimed to be a faith that is grounded in historical events that could be vouched for by those who had been on the spot.

The period of reflection and prayerful expectancy came to an

end on the day of Pentecost, or Whitsunday as we know it, seven weeks after Easter Day. This was the real birth of the Church. Pentecost was even more popular than Passover with Jewish pilgrims from overseas. Crowds flocked to Jerusalem for the occasion. It had originally been a festival to mark the ingathering of the first-fruits of the harvest but it had come to be a commemoration of the giving of the Law to Moses on Mount Sinai. It was on this day that the followers of Jesus, gathered together presumably somewhere in the precincts of the Temple, were caught up in a communal religious experience which they had no doubt was the promised gift of the Holy Spirit.

They became ecstatic like the early prophets in the Old Testament, their inward sense of the powerful presence of God issuing in unintelligible language, as has also happened in religious revivals through the centuries ever since, and as is common among the so-called pentecostal Christian sects today. It was something they could only explain in terms of a rushing wind and fiery flames, ancient symbols of the presence of God, inspiring and cleansing them, and filling them with super-natural power. Those of the bystanders who were sympathetic were equally moved; those who were sceptical concluded that the apostles were drunk.

In telling the story, Luke sees in this experience of the apostles a variety of meanings. For the Jews Pentecost signified the giving of the Law, for Christians it signified the replacement of the Law by the Spirit. And as for Jews it also marked the offering of the first-fruits of the harvest, so for Christians it signalised the first-fruits of the Spirit. Throughout the story that he tells of the spread of the gospel throughout the world, Luke sees the Spirit of God at work, breaking down the barriers that had divided men from one another. From ancient times language had been one of these barriers. In the old story of the Tower of Babel it had been regarded as a punishment for men's pride in trying to make themselves equal with God that they were no longer able to understand each other, but were kept apart by the differences in their tongues.

So Luke sees as the first-fruits of the God-given power of the

Spirit that men can now begin to understand each other in the common language of Christian love. He pictures the various racial groups who were gathered in Jerusalem for Pentecost as being amazed that they could hear these Galileans speak in their own tongues. By the time Luke came to write his story, the gospel was indeed being preached and understood by men of all these nations. It was not a miracle of language, however, for all those present in Jerusalem could understand Aramaic or Greek, but a pointer to the barrier-breaking power of the Spirit of Christ at work in the world, bringing men of all types and races into one great Christian brotherhood.

It was as a sequel to Pentecost that the Church began its mission. The time for reflection was over, the time for action had come. The Twelve and their associates went out into the streets of Jerusalem to proclaim the gospel, inviting men to turn their backs upon their old lives, and to be baptised into the fellowship of the followers of Jesus, acknowledging him as Christ and Lord and sharing in this new power of his Spirit. A new chapter in the story of the People of God had begun.

39. The Conversion of Paul

No one can fail to marvel at the consummate skill with which Luke tells the story of the first thirty momentous years of the Church's expansion in fewer than thirty short chapters. When we think of all that must have happened in this crucial time, of the problems the missionaries must have had to face, above all that of transposing an essentially Jewish faith into a message which would make sense to pagans who knew nothing of Palestine and had no particular love for Jews, Luke's masterly compression of the story into one small book seems all the more astonishing.

He does it by telling his story in terms of people, for this of course is how the Spirit of God works in the world. So Luke does not give us long descriptions of the superstitions that infested the pagan world, or a dry-as-dust chronicle of the progress and setbacks of the young Church. Instead he selects incidents in the lives of Peter and Paul and their associates, and in a series of deft thumb-nail character-studies brings to life the various people who helped or hindered them. He leaves us with a vivid impression of the jostling, bustling workaday world of the Mediterranean seaboard, its trade and traffic, busy city streets, unruly mobs, Jewish synagogues, pagan temples, philosophers, magicians, imperial officials, wealth and poverty – and moving through it all a small band of dedicated Christian missionaries, bent on winning the world for Christ, undaunted by every obstacle, indifferent to every threat, courageous almost beyond belief.

But let us follow Luke's story from the beginning. The mission which began in Jerusalem on the day of Pentecost was at first successful. This was partly due to the apostles' gift of healing, which as in the case of Jesus went hand in hand with their preaching. They disclaimed any personal credit for their cures, attributing them to the power of Christ working through his followers. But much of the success of the mission was due to the impression made by the apostles themselves. They were splendid advertisements for the faith they invited their country-men to share. Loyal to their Jewish tradition, they fulfilled their religious obligations in the Temple, but in addition they met in each other's homes for prayers and eucharistic celebra-tions. The authority of the Twelve was supreme in matters of doctrine and in the earliest stage the little community pooled its resources in a common fund.

The fact that even in these first days of the Church's story there were black sheep within the fold is not disguised. Two unsavoury characters tried to defraud the common fund and met an untimely end, which was regarded as no more than they deserved. Outside opposition came first from the Sadducees, the powerful priestly party, whose leader Caiaphas, the high priest, had engineered the Crucifixion of Jesus. From their point of view, it was intolerable that a movement which they had hoped to crush by executing its leader now showed every sign of becoming a threat to the established religion. They were dissuaded from dealing with the apostles as they had dealt with Jesus by the moderate counsel of Gamaliel, a highly respected Pharisee who, as we learn later, had been the teacher of St Paul, and the apostles escaped with a flogging. Yet despite all threats from the authorities and an official ban on their public preaching, the apostles continued with their mission in Jerusalem, backed by strong popular support and drawing an increasing number of believers.

So far Luke has painted an idyllic picture but one that certainly rings true. The Church was a relatively small community and despite the occasional backslider among its members, the enthusiasm and obvious sincerity of the apostles, their indifference to official opposition, their ministry of healing and their message of new life in fellowship with the Risen Christ, had an appeal for ordinary men and women who found little satisfaction in the rigmarole of the Temple or the arid worship of the synagogues. What the apostles offered was a faith that was alive, and membership of a closely-knit community that cared for all its people.

But growing numbers provided their own problems. Common ownership of property proved to be no longer practicable. The Twelve found the combined burden of evangelistic work and administration too much for them and they decided to appoint an additional group of seven men to handle the practical side of the organisation, particularly in the matter of poor relief. Since the seven men all have Greek names, it looks as if this was also a move to give Greek-speaking Jewish Christians from overseas, now resident in Jerusalem, some share in the government of the Church, side by side with the native-born Aramaic-speaking Jerusalem Christians. Two of the seven, Stephen and Philip, now emerge as advocates of a more radical missionary approach, and it would seem that it was through these more liberal overseas Jewish Christians that the Church began to break away from its exclusively Jewish background.

Stephen was the first spokesman of the Church to make a clear distinction between the old faith and the new. He marks a halfway stage between the conservatism of the Twelve and the radicalism of St Paul. A brilliant debater, he argued in the synagogues in defence of the Christian interpretation of the Old Testament scriptures and brought down the wrath of the Jewish hierarchy upon his head. Haled before the Sanhedrin, he boldly questioned the authority of the Law and the value of the Temple, denouced the Jews for killing the Messiah and proclaimed his faith in Christ as Lord of all nations. This was as much as saying that the Jews were no longer the People of God and that this role had now been given to the followers of the Crucified. The disciples of Jesus had so far seemed to the authorities to belong to the lunatic fringe. Stephen's revolutionary attitude, however, appeared to them as both blasphemous and pernicious. He was rushed out of the city and stoned to death by an infuriated mob, thus becoming the first martyr for the Christian faith.

He died as his Master had done, praying for his murderers, and Luke tells us that among those who witnessed his death with approval was a young rabbi from Tarsus called Paul. St Augustine dated the beginning of the conversion of Paul to Christianity as the moment when he saw Stephen battered to his knees by the stones yet praying for forgiveness for his persecutors. The death of Stephen also marked the beginning of the persecution of the Church. The more radical elements who shared Stephen's views had to flee from Jerusalem; only the more conservative Twelve and their associates were allowed to remain. However, instead of exterminating the Christian heresy the persecution encouraged it, for wherever the fugitives went they proclaimed their faith and the gospel spread throughout Palestine.

Notable among these evangelists was Philip, one of the Seven, who broke through the ancient barrier of enmity between the Jews and the Samaritans by preaching the faith of Christ with marked success among the people of Samaria. Another step forward was taken by Philip through an apparently chance encounter with a high-ranking African official who was on his way home after attending the Jewish festival of Pentecost. This implies that the man was an adherent of the Jewish faith, like many other thinking people in the pagan world, who

were attracted by the Old Testament teaching about God and Judaism's high moral standards, but who were not prepared to become full members of the Jewish community, which involved total obedience to the Mosaic Law, including circumcision and rigid observance of dietary regulations.

The African must have heard something in Jerusalem about the new faith, for as he rode in his carriage on the highway between Palestine and Egypt he was reading aloud, as the custom then was, from the passage in Isaiah which speaks of the Servant of the Lord. Overhearing him, Philip seized the opportunity to explain the meaning of the words in terms of Christ. The encounter ended with the baptism of the African into Christianity, and the new faith thus demolished another barrier, and moved still further from its purely Jewish background.

Luke now turns the spotlight on Paul, the man who is the real hero of his story. His conversion to Christianity is without doubt the most significant event in the whole history of the Church. Paul, or to give him his Jewish name, Saul, had been born in the city of Tarsus in Asia Minor, the son of a rigid Jewish Pharisee, who had seen to it that his brilliant and scholarly son had been brought up according to the strictest Jewish practice. Paul's father, perhaps by purchase, had acquired Roman citizenship, to which his son was also therefore entitled, and so Paul, brought up as a Jew in a Greek city with Roman status, combined in himself the three influences that dominated the early story of the Church.

As part of his training to be a rabbi Paul had studied in Jerusalem under Gamaliel, one of the greatest of the Pharisees, but he had also learnt a trade, as was the wise practice with scholarly boys destined to be teachers of religion. In Paul's case it was tent-making, which was one of the staple industries of Tarsus. We can be pretty sure that Paul was not in Palestine during the ministry of Jesus. Being the kind of man he was, he could not have sat on the fence. We should have heard of him either as a violent opponent or a disciple.

His first appearance in Luke's narrative, was, as we have seen, at the stoning of Stephen. We may surmise that he had returned to Jerusalem from Tarsus sometime after Pentecost to find the capital buzzing with talk of the Nazarenes, crazy followers of a man who had believed he was the Messiah and who had been properly put to death for his blasphemy. They now claimed that he had risen from the dead; there was talk of miraculous healings being performed by his disciples, and a kind of mass hysteria seemed to have seized hold of them. This was probably how Paul looked on the new Christian movement, as a staunch Pharisee who knew that Messiah would come one day in God's good time but that certainly he could not have been a carpenter from Nazareth who had died a felon's death. Following the moderate counsel of his teacher Gamaliel, Paul no doubt took the view that the whole thing was a nine days' wonder.

But as a year or two went by, the Nazarene heresy instead of dying out gained ground, and took a new and dangerous turn under the leadership of men like Stephen. It was now beginning to challenge the divine right of the Jews to be the People of God and the claim of the Law to be God's infallible revelation of his will and purpose for the world. It seems as if Paul and Stephen, from opposite sides, were the first to see that Judaism and the new faith were like oil and water. Since arguments had failed to convince, violence might have more effect, and Luke implies that Paul not only approved of Stephen's murder but engineered it.

When the persecution of the Nazarenes broke out after Stephen's death, the most venomous scourge of the heretics was Rabbi Paul of Tarsus. With all the bigotry and cruelty of a Torquemada he hounded men and women from their homes for beatings, imprisonment and death in a frenzied effort to make them recant. Not content with cleaning up Jerusalem, he got authority from the high priest to pursue these heretics wherever they might be found. It was reported that Nazarenes were stirring up trouble in the synagogues in Damascus, and Paul set out for that Syrian city with murder in his heart.

It was on the road to Damascus that the incredible happened. Paul became a Christian. He left Jerusalem a bigoted, intolerant Pharisee. He arrived in Damascus shattered, humiliated and in an agony of remorse for what he had done. Nothing less than what Paul says himself can explain this. He came face to face with the Risen Christ. In this blinding vision of Jesus of Nazareth, not as a self-deluded claimant to the title of Messiah, but as indeed the Christ of God foretold by prophet and psalmist, Paul's whole world came tumbling about his ears. It was not the Nazarenes who were crazy, it was he himself who in his madness had been guilty of the unspeakable crime of trying to stamp out the very memory of the heaven-sent Holy One of God.

We may guess with St Augustine that Paul's conversion was not altogether a bolt from the blue. His own account of what happened suggests that for some time he had been fighting against growing uneasiness. Could a man like Stephen who died praying for his assassins be an enemy of God? Could it be God's will that helpless men and women should be harried to death in the name of religion? Had Paul himself found peace with God in his meticulous obedience to the Law? And when Isaiah had spoken of the suffering and death that awaited the Servant of the Lord, may he not have meant the Messiah? Paul's redoubled fury against the Christians sounds like the work of a man who was trying to kill his conscience. At all events, what is certain is that from that moment on the Damascus road he became a man in Christ, ready to face torture, imprisonment and death for the crucified carpenter of Nazareth.

40. Jews and Gentiles

THE story of the Church from the conversion of Paul, probably in AD 32, until his death in AD 64 is largely the story of Paul himself. There were of course countless other Christians, named and unnamed, who played their part in spreading the faith from Palestine through the whole civilised world during these three crucial decades, but the master-mind behind the strategy which had by the end of that time established a network

of tiny groups of Christians from Jerusalem to Rome and held them together as members of one Church was undoubtedly Paul's.

It meant endless travelling by sea and on land, visiting and revisiting congregations, settling disputes, giving encouragement and advice and enduring unbelievable hardships. Yet amid all this he found time to write a remarkable series of letters to the various communities and to a variety of people. Some of them have been lost, but some of them have found their place in the New Testament side by side with the gospels as foundation documents of the Christian faith. In telling the story of Paul we have therefore not only Luke's narrative in the book of Acts but supplementary information from Paul's own letters, which reveal a man's mind as nothing else can.

When Paul reached Damascus after his conversion, physically stricken and in turmoil of spirit, with no reason to expect anything but hostility and distrust from the Christians he had set out to crush, he was put on his feet by two simple words spoken by an obscure believer in that city who called him 'Brother Saul'. This acceptance of the 'scourge of the saints' as one of themselves led to his baptism as a full member of the Christian community. But for a proud man whose life had been turned upside down there was need for some hard thinking. Like Jesus after the crisis of his baptism, Paul went into retreat in the solitude of the neighbouring desert to clear his mind and plan the road ahead.

Returning to Damascus with his mind made up he proclaimed his new faith in the local synagogues with such effect that, having enraged the Jews by what seemed to them his unforgivable treachery, he had to flee from their fury and was ignominiously lowered over the city walls by night in a basket. Some time later, having met with similar opposition from the Jews in Jerusalem, he was sent back to his native city of Tarsus for his own safety. There and in other parts of Asia Minor and Syria he spent several years in apparently unspectacular missionary work, until the call came which put him right in the centre of the stage, where he remained until the end.

Meantime, with the dispersal of the more radical Christians

from Jerusalem and the conversion of their arch-enemy Paul, the Palestinian churches had a spell of peaceful development. Peter emerges from the record as the most active evangelist among the apostles, and indeed as the foremost advocate next to Paul of a wider view of the Church's mission, for which he was taken to task by the more traditional Jewish Christians in Jerusalem. It was at his instigation, and as a result of what he could only believe to be the direct prompting of the Spirit, that for the first time not merely Samaritans, or an African adherent of the Jewish faith, but a Roman army officer and his family were admitted by baptism into the Christian community.

It is difficult at this distance of time and with our very different background to realise the intensity of feeling which was aroused among orthodox Jewish Christians at the prospect of Gentiles becoming part of the fellowship. They saw themselves as the new Israel, the new People of God, and two thousand years of history behind them had identified Israel and the People of God with the Jewish race. Traditionally Gentiles were people who lived in pagan darkness and who could only come to the true knowledge of God by conforming to the divinely given Law of Moses and becoming incorporated into the People of God by circumcision and acceptance of the other regulations of Jewish life. The fact that some Jews had become Christians, believing that Jesus was the Messiah, did not mean that they were prepared to throw overboard lightly the heritage of centuries. This problem of how far Christians should conform to Jewish practice was one that bedevilled the Church throughout its early years.

In Luke's view, and he was himself a Gentile, it was only the incessant prodding of the Holy Spirit, which ultimately became irresistible, which persuaded the conservative Jerusalem Christians reluctantly to accept the fact that in the sight of God Gentiles were as eligible to become members of the People of God as were Jews. Paul was the chief protagonist of this revolutionary doctrine. He carried it to its logical conclusion by maintaining that all that was necessary for membership of the Christian Church was commitment to Christ and admission by baptism, and that circumcision and other hallowed Jewish traditions were irrelevant for Gentiles who sought to become members of the new Israel. Luke's view was that it was not only Paul's radical thinking on the matter that was guided by the Holy Spirit but that God was also speaking to more ordinary minds and directing them in the same way.

Thus, as it would seem almost by accident, some of the Jewish Christians who had shared the liberal views of Stephen and had been driven from their homes in Jerusalem and forced to seek refuge in some less bigoted centre, found themselves in Antioch, the Syrian capital. There they had talked about their new faith to all and sundry, as a result of which a strong body of Gentiles had turned from paganism to Christianity. Cautious as always, and suspicious of any untoward developments, the leaders of the orthodox Jerusalem church sent a delegate to investigate. This was Barnabas, an open-minded man of splendid character, who at once saw that here was a situation of great promise which could only properly be handled by one man. So he went off to Tarsus to find him.

Thus Paul was summoned out of his obscurity to become head of the mission at Antioch. Together he and Barnabas worked for a year there and built it into the first great centre of Gentile Christianity. It was in this city that for the first time the followers of Jesus, who were previously known as Nazarenes, or followers of the 'Way', were given the name of 'Christians', a nickname which like that of 'Methodists' and 'Quakers' in later times came to be proudly borne as an honourable title. The irony of the situation cannot have been lost on Paul! He was now leader of a church which his persecuting zeal had been responsible for starting.

Persecution of the Christians had again broken out in Jerusalem, this time instigated by the civil power. One of the Twelve was martyred, Peter was thrown into prison and the remainder were scattered. Sympathisers among the prison guard enabled Peter to escape and before he left the city he nominated James, the brother of Jesus, as head of the Jerusalem church. Thus at the end of the first stage of the Church's story, about fifteen years after the Crucifixion, we find two main centres of Christianity: the mother church at Jerusalem, pre-

sided over by the ultra-orthodox James, whose sympathies
with Judaism made him more acceptable to the Jewish religious
authorities than the Twelve, and the progressive young
Gentile church at Antioch, presided over by Paul, which was
becoming the real power-house of the faith and the headquarters of the next stage of its missionary expansion.

Agreement had been reached between the Twelve and Paul,
before persecution dispersed them, that Paul would make the
Gentile world his parish, and accordingly in AD 46 he set out
from Antioch on the first of his adventurous missionary
journeys. His companions were Barnabas and John Mark, later
to become the author of the earliest of the gospels. They took
ship via Cyprus and landed in the south of Asia Minor. Paul
seems to have suffered from recurrent bouts of malaria, one of
which may have been the cause of their leaving the swampy
coastal area and heading north into the mountains. For some
unknown reason, John Mark deserted the party and returned
to his home in Jerusalem, while Paul and Barnabas went on
into Galatia.

For all his conviction that his vocation was to be the apostle
to the Gentiles, Paul was equally convinced that it was his first
duty to preach the gospel to the Jews. They were after all the
people of God's choice, it was to them that God had spoken
through the Law and the prophets, and it was to them that the
Messiah had been sent as the fulfilment of God's promise that
through Israel the world would come to the knowledge of the
truth. Accordingly Paul's normal missionary practice on
arriving in a new area was to make contact with the local Jews
through the synagogue and, wherever opportunity offered, to
proclaim salvation and forgiveness of sins through faith in the
Risen Christ and not through the Law.

In the synagogues he found not only Jews, but Gentiles who
had become full converts to the Jewish religion, and an even
greater number of Gentiles who had discovered in Judaism a
meaningful combination of faith and moral principles which
they had sought in vain elsewhere. In the temples and shrines
of pagan gods and goddesses they found religion without
morals. In pagan philosophy they found morals without religion.

In Judaism they found both, but they were not prepared to become full converts because of the Jewish requirement that they must submit to circumcision and accept the multifarious restrictive practices which Judaism imposed. It was on this class of devout and thoughtful pagans that Paul made the greatest impression. They found in the gospel he preached all that they valued in Judaism, without the unacceptable demands of full conversion. It was as much Paul's success in weaning these Gentile adherents away from the synagogues, as anything he said about the inadequacy of the Law, that brought down the wrath of orthodox Jews upon his head throughout his missionary campaigns.

This was the technique Paul adopted on this first missionary venture into hitherto unfamiliar territory. When he was rebuffed by the Jews he turned to the Gentiles, but Jewish animosity pursued him from one town to another. At one point in his travels, he found himself among superstitious rustics who took the two apostles to be gods come down to earth disguised as men, but with Jewish prompting they were soon equally ready to regard them as devils, and Paul was stoned and left for dead. Yet the results of this turbulent campaign, which may have lasted up to two years, was that Christian communities were established in several centres in Galatia and Paul could reckon that his efforts had not been in vain.

On his return to his headquarters at Antioch, Paul had to face a new problem, this time within the Church itself. Some of the right-wing conservative Jewish Christians from Jerusalem had come to Antioch in his absence and had upset the largely Gentile membership of the church there by maintaining that in order to become proper Christians Gentiles should first become full Jews. That meant not only circumcision and adherence to Jewish food laws, but also avoidance of all social contact with their former Gentile friends.

It was perfectly clear to Paul that unless this matter was settled it would mean the death of the Church. There could be no second-class Christians. Gentiles and Jews must somehow learn to live together on equal terms. If the Jerusalem church persisted in its narrow policy it would mean either two separate churches, one for Gentile Christians and one for Jewish Christians, or else the end of the Gentile mission altogether. Some kind of compromise must be reached. Accordingly a delegation, headed by Paul and Barnabas, went to the mother church at Jerusalem to thrash the matter out. This meeting of the two sides in AD 49 at the first General Council of the Christian Church ended in victory for Paul and the liberal point of view. It was agreed by the Jerusalem Christians that subject to minor reservations Gentiles were to be admitted into the Church by profession of faith and baptism, without having to comply with the demands of Jewish Law. Paul's chief supporter among the Jerusalem Christians was Peter, but even the ultra-Jewish James, now head of the mother church, spoke in his favour.

The upshot was a written decree embodying the Council's decision, armed with which Paul and Barnabas went back to Antioch triumphant. For Paul it was a double victory. Not only had he won his case, but he now had the backing of the Jerusalem church authorities. For one who, however he regarded his own commission as having come directly from Christ himself on the Damascus road, was still treated with some suspicion as not having been one of the original twelve apostles, this was indeed an achievement.

It was while he was on his way to this Council of Jerusalem that Paul wrote the earliest of his letters which have been pre-served in the New Testament to the little Galatian communities which he had founded on his first missionary tour. Apparently they had been upset by the same type of trouble-makers who had questioned Paul's authority at Antioch, and who had insisted on Gentiles accepting Jewish ritual obligations before they could become proper Christians. Paul's letter to them is a massive declaration of Christian freedom and of the equality of Jews and Gentiles in the sight of God.

41. In the Heart of the Empire

EQUIPPED with the important written decree of the Council of Jerusalem, Paul soon set out from Antioch again, partly to set at rest the anxiety of the small Galatian churches which he had founded on his first tour, and partly with his mind on further expansion of the Church. He invited Barnabas to share in this second foreign mission enterprise. Barnabas agreed, providing his young relative John Mark could also be one of the party. This proposal Paul flatly turned down. Mark had deserted them before and Paul would not have him. The two older men had sharp words on the subject, the upshot of which was that Barnabas and Mark went off on their own to Cyprus while Paul with a new associate, Silvanus, set out to break new ground.

Having revisited the young churches in Galatia, where Paul picked up a new recruit, Timothy, to take the place of John Mark, they headed westward. But for one reason or another they were prevented from working in every promising area into which they tried to penetrate and they found themselves eventually at an apparent dead-end in Troas on the Aegean Sea, the site of ancient Troy. Yet, looking back later on this unsuccessful tour, they were able to see the hand of God in the very frustration of their plans. For it was at Troas that they were moved to cross the sea from Asia Minor into Macedonia, thus taking the Good News officially for the first time into what we now know as Europe.

An important fourth member joined the team at Troas. This was Dr Luke, later the author of the third gospel and the book of Acts, which becomes from this point in the story Luke's personal version of what happened. If he was a Christian doctor practising in Troas, he may have been called in to attend Paul during one of his bouts of illness, and it may have been at Luke's suggestion, reinforced by a vivid dream of a Macedonian, perhaps Luke himself, saying: 'Come over to Macedonia and help us!' that Paul decided that this was what God was calling him to do next. It is noticeable that at this point Luke introduces 'we' into his narrative. He is now telling the story from the inside.

So they took the first available ship across the Aegean in the autumn of AD 49, and at Philippi, a few miles inland, the scene of the famous battle between Brutus and Antony a century before, they founded the first Christian congregation in Macedonia, with a successful business woman, a fortune-teller and a jailor as the first Gentile members. The mission ended with a beating and imprisonment for Paul and Silvanus, but the little church grew in numbers and became Paul's favourite among all the communities he founded, the only one he allowed to help him with money, and the church to which he later wrote the most affectionate of all his New Testament letters.

It would seem that Luke stayed on in Philippi to consolidate the mission. The narrative changes back from 'we' to 'they' and loses much of its vividness. But the other three went on to Thessalonica and Beroea, where the mission resulted in the formation of two more Christian congregations. The campaign in Thessalonica lasted long enough for Paul to take a job at his own trade as a tent-maker. The ancient world was full of religious charlatans who sponged on gullible audiences and it was Paul's proud boast that he supported himself – and often his companions – with the sweat of his own brow. Jewish opposition to Paul eventually drove him out of Macedonia. Silvanus and Timothy, being less notorious and in Jewish eyes relatively harmless, could be safely left behind to build up the young churches.

Paul had another attack of his illness at this time but despite it he went on by ship to Athens, the home of poets and philosophers and the most lovely city in the ancient world. But Paul had no eyes for the glories of its architecture, or, if he had, he saw its temples and statuary as monuments to ignorance. Athens was to him a hotbed of idolatry and trivial philosophising. It was not the Parthenon that moved him, but the sight of an altar dedicated 'To God the Unknown'. Word of this strange

little Jew with a new message, accosting passers-by in the
market place, came to the ears of the philosophers of the city
and Paul was invited to state his case before them. Although he
went out of his way to meet them on their own ground, his
claim that God had raised Jesus from the dead was too much
for them. He left Athens with the laughter of the philosophers
still ringing in his ears. Apart from making a few converts he
had to reckon that his mission to Athens had been a failure.

It was as a despondent and discouraged man that Paul went
on to Corinth, a large commercial seaport with a population of
half a million and a reputation for profligacy which was prover-
bial in the ancient world. He found work at his trade, but his
depression did not leave him until the arrival of Silvanus and
Timothy from Macedonia with the news that the little churches
there were growing by leaps and bounds and that Christianity
had become a talking-point throughout the whole area. This
was the tonic that Paul needed. Until then he had not known
whether his message and his missionary technique which had
been successful in the east would be equally successful farther
west among people of different races and backgrounds. His
experience at Athens had led him to think not.

Now, however, he could plunge into missionary work in
Corinth with confidence and new vigour. From Corinth he also
wrote letters of encouragement and helpful advice to the
Thessalonian church. Paul stayed in Corinth for eighteen
months, building up a congregation drawn largely from the
poorer class of the city with a fair sprinkling rescued from the
gutter. The whole of this second tour had lasted about three
years and by the spring of AD 52 Paul was back in Antioch.

Next year he was off again on his travels, revisiting the young
Asian churches he had founded and eventually making Ephesus
in the far west of Asia Minor his headquarters for a campaign
lasting three years, during which time the whole province
became his parish. Luke gives us a lively picture of Paul's
battle against the practitioners of black magic who preyed on the
superstition and credulity of the people. We can see him working at his trade, holding meetings whenever possible, keeping
in touch with the churches everywhere. The church at Corinth

was causing him particular anxiety at this time, and from his letters to them we can glimpse both the magnitude of the problems he had to cope with and the difficulties of a young church struggling to hold on to Christian faith and standards in the midst of paganism.

Before he left Ephesus, he almost paid the price of his success as a missionary with his life. The city was renowned for its temple of Diana, which was one of the seven wonders of the world, and a popular centre for pilgrimages. The craftsmen of Ephesus, silversmiths and coppersmiths, did a roaring trade in souvenir images of the goddess which they sold to pilgrims. Now as a result of Paul's mission sales had slumped. A mass meeting of the craftsmen was held which ended in a riot, and it was with difficulty that Paul was dissuaded from trying to quell it. He would certainly have been torn to pieces.

From Ephesus he went back to visit the young churches in Macedonia and also stayed for a while in Corinth. Again rest- less, he was now planning to visit Rome and even Spain, and his great letter to the Romans, which has been called 'the gospel according to St Paul' was written at this time to tell them of his intentions. It gives us some idea of the fantastic range of the apostle's mind to read this powerful exposition of the Christian faith, in which he unfolds God's plan for the salvation of the world, and then to contrast it with the detailed practical concern for the daily life and welfare of a single congregation illustrated in his letters to the church at Corinth.

One of Paul's great anxieties was the safeguarding of the unity of the Church. It can readily be understood how difficult this was with small scattered congregations, some largely of Jewish background, some mainly Gentile, with differing native tongues and diverse cultural and racial backgrounds. Apart from his own personal influence, exerted through visits and letters, he laid great store by a money-raising scheme he had devised whereby the young churches throughout the Mediter- ranean world were encouraged to contribute to a fund for the relief of the poverty-stricken mother church in Jerusalem. This was not only to further a sense of unity but also to bind more closely together the Jewish and Gentile traditions within the Christian Church.

His intention after his third missionary campaign was to head a delegation of representatives of the younger churches to Jerusalem, which would take the contributions of their various communities to the mother church in the holy city. So he made his way eastwards, picking up the delegates on the way, including Luke from Philippi, at which point the 'we' of Luke's travel-diary replaces the impersonal 'they' of his narrative, and once more the story gains in vividness which is now maintained right to the end. In one of his letters Paul speaks of the various ordeals he has had to face in the course of his missionary activities: imprisonment, floggings, shipwrecks, cold and hunger, danger from floods, bandits and angry mobs. Luke mentions some of them, but when we see how his story comes alive when he was actually present, it makes us realise what a tale he could have told if he had been with Paul all the time.

There is a sense of foreboding in the narrative at this point, almost like the account of Jesus' final journey to Jerusalem. Paul knows that Jewish fanaticism is building up against him and he seems to have recognised that this would be his last visit to the holy city. On arrival there he was given a cautious welcome by the Jerusalem church leaders, but despite his readiness to go to almost any lengths to show his respect for Jewish traditions, he was set upon by an infuriated mob in the Temple, because of a wholly false report that he had taken a Gentile into the enclosure forbidden to non-Jews. He was saved from certain death only by the prompt action of the commander of the Roman garrison which was quartered in the Temple precincts to deal with emergencies of this kind.

This was in AD 56 and from now until the end of Luke's story Paul is in Roman custody. It was only his Roman citizenship that stood between him and the blood-lust of Jewish fanatics determined by hook or by crook to be revenged on the arch-traitor. The anxiety of the succession of Roman officials who dealt with Paul's case to protect him from the murderous designs of his Jewish compatriots is a tribute to the power of Roman law. If Paul had not been a Roman citizen he would never have survived his last visit to Jerusalem.

Instead of that he was taken for trial under escort to Caesarea, seat of the Roman government in Palestine, where he spent two

years in prison, mainly due to delay in appointing a new governor. The only person who would seem to have profited from
this prolonged stay in Caesarea was Luke, who no doubt used
his time to advantage to gather information about the ministry
of Jesus and the early days of Christianity, which he later
incorporated in his two books. Whether Paul was tired of his
protracted confinement, or whether he was alarmed that a new
charge of treason was being brought against him by the Jews,
he brought matters to a head by formally declaring: 'I appeal
to Caesar.' This meant a demand for trial in Rome by the
supreme court.

Thus Paul achieved his wish to visit Rome but under far
different circumstances from those he had intended. Luke's
dramatic story of the voyage to Rome including shipwreck on
Malta is a masterpiece of descriptive writing, and he ends his
account of the first thirty years of Church history with a picture
of Paul in the capital waiting for his appeal to be heard. On the
surface it would appear to be an unsatisfactory ending. What
happened to Paul? Was he tried and acquitted, and did he then
set out on further adventures? There is a possibility that he
did, but, whatever happened, early tradition is unanimous that
he was martyred at the same time as Peter in AD 64 during the
persecution of the Christians under the mad emperor Nero,
who laid at their door the blame for the great fire of Rome which
destroyed half the city.

But in finishing his book where he does, Luke had achieved
his aim of showing how the gospel had been brought from
Jerusalem to Rome through the guidance of the Holy Spirit
and mainly through the work of Paul. Luke's last words in the
book of Acts show that he meant the story to end there with
Paul in Rome, in his own rented house, free to receive visitors –
and, as we know, also able to write letters to the churches – and
free to proclaim the gospel in the heart of the empire without
hindrance from anyone. The Church had reached the end of its
childhood and was now ready to advance to the conquest of the
world for Christ.

42. The Faith of the First Christians

IT has been said that properly speaking the only character in the Old Testament is God. In this sense the only character in the New Testament is Christ. It was not that some Jews who had been brought up to believe in the God of the prophets and psalmists substituted for this a belief in Christ when they became Christians. Much more it meant that through their encounter with Christ their ideas about God came alive. All that they had been taught about God was now crystallised and focused in Jesus. In the things he had done and said they believed that they had seen God at work and had heard his voice, and when they thought about God in worship, in prayer and sacrament, as well as in the daily affairs of life it was in terms of Jesus.

It was only in a later stage than the period covered by the New Testament that attempts were made to express in formal creeds what the Church believed about God and ourselves, and what the coming of Christ had meant for mankind. Creeds became necessary when the Church had to make it clear to the world at large and to itself what all Christians believed and what they did not believe. In the early days, however, within New Testament times, that is roughly within the first century AD, the Church was still finding its feet and tentatively working out its faith.

Many minds grappled with the problem of expressing in words what it meant to be a Christian. This is the main theme of the letters of Paul and the other writers of the letters which are to be found in the Bible between the book of Acts and the book of Revelation. Paul of course dominates the scene, partly because he was the ablest among the early Christians, and partly because of the sheer volume of his writing, which makes up more than a quarter of the whole of the New Testament.

But although Paul's thought has had a more far-reaching influence on Christian theology over the past twenty centuries than that of any other of the New Testament letter-writers, it would be wrong to regard him as the sole or even as the chief artificer of the Christian faith as it came to be later expressed in the creeds. It is not certain, for example, how many of the letters that were once credited to Paul were actually written by him, and there are certainly a number of other letters in the New Testament which have never been attributed to him. We should therefore think of the second half of the New Testament as being a variety of attempts by quite a wide range of rich and creative minds within the first Christian century to express one or other aspect of the faith that they had come to believe.

But when we are talking about first-century Christian theologians, we have to include the writers of the gospels as well. As we have seen, they were not simply biographers of Jesus, content to record a factual narrative of what happened in Palestine around the year AD 30, but men who were convinced, before a single word of their gospels was written, that they were not telling the story of a wise teacher or a great prophet or a courageous martyr, but a story such as had never before been written, about a man who was in some respects unlike anyone else who had ever lived. When they write about Jesus of Nazareth they are writing about someone who, as they had come to believe, was no less than the Saviour of the world.

Since so many different minds are represented in the pages of the New Testament, so many writers with differing personalities and points of view, we should not be surprised at the variety of ways they adopt to express their faith, their convictions about who Jesus was, and what he meant for mankind. Moreover, if they were Palestinian Jews addressing their fellow countrymen, they would obviously express their faith in the Old Testament terms with which they were all familiar. If on the other hand they were trying to communicate with people whose background was the Gentile world, they would obviously try to couch their message in language with which their readers or listeners were more at home.

We should therefore not expect to find in the New Testament cut-and-dried answers expressed in uniform language to all the questions we should like to ask about what Christianity meant to the first Christians. They were still thinking things out, and their ideas about Christian belief and practice were still to some extend fluid. They were, as much as we are ourselves, conditioned by their upbringing, by the age they lived in, and limited by the same inability to say what tomorrow had in store. They had the same sense of being at the mercy of events over which they had no control, of the massive power of evil in the world, of their own vulnerability and mortality. They too had moments of despair when nothing made sense.

Yet they knew at the bottom of their hearts, if not in the forefront of their minds at some moment of catastrophe, that things were not the same in the world as they had been before the coming of Christ, and it was this conviction that later on came to be expressed more formally in the Church's creeds. The creeds were constructed by the Church under the guidance of the Holy Spirit in an attempt to put into summary form the impact of Christ upon the world as it has been recorded in a variety of ways in the pages of the New Testament. Just as the Old Testament points forward to Christ, and the gospels record the fact of Christ, so the rest of the New Testament describes the effect of Christ on the life of the world as seen through the eyes of those of his followers who were closest to him in time.

But amid all the variety of expression and the different ways in which New Testament writers convey their message, there are certain convictions common to them all which taken together formed the faith with which they challenged the world in their day. First of all, they believed that the world made sense. They were sure that the universe, which was no less mysterious for them than it is for us, had not come into existence by accident. There was a mighty purpose behind its creation, and although many things about life were difficult to understand, they had no doubt that a wise and benevolent Providence was in control.

They were equally convinced of the reality of evil, partly in the hearts of men – pride, self-seeking, envy and greed – and partly as a demonic power in the world itself which was constantly at war with God's good purposes and which frustrated the best intentions of men of goodwill. This was what as Christians they were called to fight against – the evil in themselves and in society at large. But they were not fighting a lonely battle, because God had entered the lists in a new way in Christ and was fighting with them and in them.

However they express it, whether they speak of being in Christ, or of the Spirit of Christ being in them, the New Testament men with one accord affirm their belief that since the coming of Christ the power of God has been working in them and through them to change their own lives and the whole face of society. By his Resurrection Christ had shown that he was stronger than the evil that had nailed him to a cross, stronger than death itself, and through allegiance to him his followers could share in that victory.

Thus as they looked out on a world that was just as frightening and bewildering as it is today, the first Christians could face the future with confidence and courage. They knew that in the end the power of evil would not prevail, and however long the war lasted the decisive battle had been fought and won. They knew that they would not live to see God's final victory over the forces that opposed him. It was enough that they should play their part by trying to do his will in the knowledge that they were on the winning side.

To be a Christian meant commitment to Christ, accepting him as Lord and Saviour, and coming through him into the right relationship to God, a relationship of trust and obedience, which involved coming into the right relationship with one another, in charity and mutual service. This was when life really began, for they knew that their bodies were subject to all the changes and chances that flesh is heir to, including death. Yet the death of the body was not the end of life, but the beginning of a new and fuller experience of the life they had begun to know through Christ.

They believed that through Christ they had been saved from a life of futility, of self-centredness, of emptiness and despair, so they called him Saviour. They knew that he had the key to the mystery of their existence, that in him they had come to know the mind and purpose of God, so they called him Lord. They were certain that he had come when the time was ripe as the climax of the long story of God's dealings with Israel, that he was the Messiah of whom prophets and psalmists had spoken, so they called him Christ. They knew that they had seen in him a man who could make men what men were meant to be, so they called him the second Adam. In him they had seen God, so they called him Son of God.

The New Testament writers in using words like these produce an impressionist picture of Jesus rather than a systematic doctrine expressing their belief as to who he was, how exactly he was related to God, and how he fitted into the divine government of the universe. All of that came later when the Church had to state its faith in terms that could be defended against rival philosophies and religions. In the first century, when the Church was still struggling to gain a hearing, the writers of the New Testament gospels and letters were more concerned to tell the story of what had happened in Galilee and Jerusalem, or to deal with the practical problems that faced the young congregations, than to write text-books of theology.

Yet when these later attempts were made to present the Christian faith to the world in more intellectual terms, there was nothing in the presentation that was not already implicit in the New Testament. The creeds of the Church are grounded in the Bible. But of course the thought-forms of later centuries were as much the product of the age in which they were constructed as the terminology of the New Testament itself. Every age, including our own, has to re-interpret Christianity in its own language. Some of the thought-forms that lie behind the historic creeds of the Church are as meaningless to us today as would have been the thought-forms of the first Jewish Christians if they had attempted to formulate their faith systematically in their own day.

The supreme value of the New Testament, and its perennial power to speak to every century, is that it springs from real life as it has been since the world began. Here were men and women like ourselves for whom life had become different. They had been brought up, either as Jews or Gentiles, in a world where fatalism, apathy, or sheer perplexity over the apparent meaninglessness of life had been mildly corrected by some kind of lip-service to gods or a God who might make some sense of it all. In place of that when they were confronted by Jesus, what he had said and what he had done, the world became a different place. Life now had meaning and purpose. They were exhilarated, dedicated and confident.

God had become a reality, they had stretched out their hands and there was Someone there to grasp them. They knew that they were weak and shiftless mortals, failures in everything that really mattered, but God had come to them in Jesus, with forgiveness for the past and hope for the future. They had been called into his service, to put their own lives in order with his help and guidance, and then to try to bring their families, their friends, their communities, to see that what the power of God had done for them he could do for everyone.

This was certainly the motive behind St Paul's missionary enterprises. He knew that he had been an intolerant, bigoted, prejudiced man. But Christ had laid hold of him and he had been changed. If he could do this for Paul, he could do it for everybody. Not only Paul, however, but all the New Testament writers say the same thing. They do not for a moment claim to have become saints. They are still, as they know very well, subject to temptation and liable to failure, but they have seen the vision of what they might become and what the world might become, and in that conviction they face the future undaunted.

43.   The End of the Story

IF we think of the birth of the Church, and its struggle in the first Christian century to gain a foothold and make some impact on the life of the world, as the beginning of Act III of the divine drama which the Bible unfolds, we can take heart as we look at the life of the Church today. Almost twenty centuries have gone by since these epic days of the Church's infancy, and for all we know it may still not be past its teething stage. The New Testament gives us no reason for thinking either that the mission of the Church to renew the life of the world would be a short one or that it would be a triumphal progress all the way.

The first Christians had no illusions about the power of evil both in human nature and in human institutions. The Church, the new People of God, inheriting the role of Israel as God's agent to bring the world to the knowledge of the truth, had been founded by Jesus on twelve ordinary men, one of whom had betrayed him, one who for fear of his own skin denied that he had ever known him, and ten more who in the moment of crisis deserted him. The picture that we get from Luke and the writers of the New Testament letters is of small Christian congregations of men and women who have seen the vision of what life could be, but who are constantly under pressure from their own weakness and from outside opposition to lower their standards and to be content with something less than the best.

They had committed their lives to Christ, and in their hearts they knew that his way was the only way for themselves and for the world. They found in their faith an anchor which held them steady in adversity, and they were strengthened by their fellowship with others and by the grace of God which was given to them in common worship, in the ministry of word and sacrament, through the scriptures and through prayer. But they were still sinners, fallible mortals subject to temptation and prone to stumble and fall. This was acknowledged by all of them, whether they had experienced a sudden transforming conversion like St Paul or whether they had become Christians in less spectacular ways.

It is in this light that we should view the record of the Church since New Testament times and the spectacle that it presents today. Jesus did not build his Church upon saints and his summons to his disciples was not to cultivate holiness in seclusion, but to go out into the world and do his work there, with all the conflicts and compromises that that necessarily involved. As we know only too well his cause has constantly suffered through the ignorance, prejudice, stupidity and sheer perverseness of his followers, and if the Church had not been divinely ordained it must have perished long ago.

If it was difficult for the early Christians, living within the aura of the ministry of Jesus at a time when the Resurrection faith and the sense of the inbreaking of the supernatural power of God into daily life was at its most intense, to sustain their high calling and live consistently in accordance with the pattern Jesus had set – and which indeed most of them desperately wanted to follow – it is not surprising that the record of the Church in later centuries contains so many dismal chapters. Some would say that the Church lost its claim to be in any sense a unique society when Christianity became the official state religion of the Roman Empire in the fourth century A D, and when from then on it became enmeshed in the political ambiguities which are inevitable in any power structure.

Yet if Christianity was to fulfil its role as the salt that would give savour to society, or the leaven that would work its way into the life of the world, it could not avoid becoming involved up to the hilt in the machinery that makes up the political, social and economic life of the world. It has of course been tarnished in the process. The great issues that concern mankind never work out in terms of black and white. Manoeuvre and compromise are essential in any attempts to make possible a more just and equitable and wholesome life for all men. But when we reflect on the intractable material of human nature, the remarkable thing is that since New Testament times the Church has achieved so much. Millions of men and women of all races and classes have found new meaning and purpose in life through being confronted by the saving power of the gospel. The dignity of human life has been defended even amid the folly and cruelty of war. In education, care of the sick, the aged and the under-privileged, the Church has throughout the centuries itself led the way and has encouraged the civil powers to further its pioneering efforts. Social reform and furtherance of human rights, often campaigned for by solitary Christians with little enough encouragement from less sensitive ecclesiastical authorities, have still owed undoubted progress to the inspiration of the Church's faith.

Yet many people now feel that the Church has had its day and is no longer necessary. Empty pews and dwindling congregations would seem to support their view. But this has happened more than once even in the short space of twenty centuries, and unless the story that the Bible tells is nonsense from beginning to end there is no ground for despondency. It is the purpose of God that there should be in the world a community of men and women, dedicated to his service, bound together in dependence on the Spirit of Christ to seek to live themselves in the right relationship to God and to each other, and to work in the name and in the power of Christ to rid the world of all that prevents men and women everywhere from having the full life of sons and daughters of God that they were meant to have.

It may well be that the organised Church in its present form will have to go much farther downhill before it recovers. Machinery that gets rusty has to be overhauled or scrapped. While it is certain that Jesus founded the Church, it is far from certain that he intended it to take the outward shape of any one of its present branches. Yet amid much that is irrelevant in the Church's present activities, it is still the custodian of God's revelation and that is imperishable. It is still the channel of supernatural power and whatever changes in its structure are made, men and women will always find, in its worship, in its sacraments and in its scriptures, the renewal of their own lives and the strength and incentive to move society so far as they can to conform more and more to the mind and spirit of Christ.

We are living at a time when not only the present form and methods of the Church are questioned but apparently also the traditional Christian faith itself is widely suspect. This would be nothing new if the attack on the faith came from outside the Church. From New Testament times onward Christianity has always been under fire from one quarter or another. The difference in our own day is that the assault seems to come from within the Church itself, and is concerned not merely with questioning this or that dogma, or one or other aspect of traditional views on the Bible. Again this would be nothing new.

What seems to be happening is much more radical. People read in the newspapers that Christian theologians now speak of the 'Death of God', claim that we can know little or nothing about the historical figure of Jesus, advocate some kind of secularism, and talk about 'religionless Christianity'. Many of these catchwords do not, of course, mean what they appear to mean and ordinary citizens have neither the time nor the inclination to read for themselves the various books in which Christian thinkers make plain what they mean or do not mean when they use phrases of this kind. Nor is the ordinary citizen generally aware that there are fashions in theology as in everything else, and that the theological pendulum tends to swing backwards and forwards from conservatism to radicalism and vice versa.

But there is undoubtedly a present ferment in Christian thinking and it would be surprising if this were not so. We have after all in our generation lived through – and are still living through – a gigantic revolution in which the apparently solid foundations of the nineteenth-century world have been shaken. The Victorians did not believe in the possibility of man's conquest of outer space or of nuclear war and genocide. They did not think in terms of automation, electronics and computers. Their understanding of human psychology was elementary and the recent advances in medical science were in their day still a closed book. Christian thinking has to come to terms with all these revolutionary changes and take a new look at traditional expressions of its faith. We should not be alarmed if in their attempt to grapple with the problem of what Christianity has to say in this time of revolution some Christian thinkers express themselves in revolutionary language.

So we find ourselves at a somewhat confusing but intensely exciting point in Act III of the divine drama and we literally do not know what will happen next. But then neither did the early Christians when Act III began. It was no doubt an intimidating prospect for these small groups of men and women, surrounded by pagan hostility, with the threat of persecution, imprisonment or sudden death never very far away. Yet they found strength in each other, and in their allegiance to Christ. In a world where everything was uncertain, they found their only certainty in him. It was because of this that they could go about their business in quiet confidence, leaving the future in the hands of God.

It was because of this faith that they were moved to carry on Christ's work in the world, in care and compassion for all sorts and conditions of men, since these were all brothers for whom Christ had died. They remembered Jesus' words about what it meant to be a true follower of his: not to cry 'Lord, Lord,' but to feed the hungry, welcome the lonely, nurse the sick and care for the misfits. It is this same faith that still moves Christian men and women today, on all levels of society and in all corners of the globe, to break through prejudice and suspicion, to rise above questions of race and colour, and to show in practical ways their belief that this is God's world and that all men and women are equally his children, needing help and friendship and love.

But while the divine drama is still being played out and we are all invited to take our part in it by trying to do God's will, the Bible does not leave us in any doubt about the final outcome. We may, if we like, call the book of Revelation, the last of the New Testament writings, the Epilogue to the drama, for it tells us how the story of the Bible will end. Whether we as individuals choose to co-operate with God in his great purpose of re-creating the life of the world in the spirit of Christ, the ultimate issue is not in man's hands but in God's. The power of evil has been broken once and for all by Christ and, however long the war between the forces of goodness and the forces of darkness may last, the victory of Christ is assured.

The book of Revelation is a strange and cryptic work, full of imagery and symbolism. It was written towards the end of the first century at a time when the Church was facing persecution so violent that it seemed to many that it could not survive. The inspired writer of Revelation dares to draw aside the veil that shrouds the mystery that lies beyond sense and sight and beyond space and time. In his visions he sees the final downfall of evil and the triumph of God, the end of suffering and sin and death, and the perfect fellowship of the People of God with their Lord in the heavenly New Jerusalem. He brings us back full circle to the point at which the story of the Bible began when he shows us man at last re-entering Paradise from which since Adam's Fall he has been estranged.